LOVE, EROTICISM AND FEMALE SEXUALITY IN CLASSICAL SANSKRIT LETERATURE

Love, Eroticism and Female Sexuality in Classical Sanskrit Literature: Seventh–Thirteenth Centuries

SHALINI SHAH

MANOHAR
2026

First published 2009
Reprinted 2026

ISBN 978-81-7304-831-9

Published by
Ajay Kumar Jain *for*
Manohar Publishers & Distributors
4753/23 Ansari Road, Daryaganj
New Delhi 110 002

Printed at
Replika Press Pvt. Ltd.

For

Nanaji (M.L. Shrimali) and Mama (K.M. Shrimali)
who first taught me to look at Sankrit literature
with a sociological and historical perspective.

Contents

Acknowledgements

This book has taken shape from my Ph.D. thesis submitted to the University of Delhi in 2001. In writing it I have received help from numerous quarters. I would like to thank my supervisor Prof. D.N. Jha for his guidance and Prof. K.M. Shrimali for his critical comments all through. Prof. Monica Juneja helped me with the readings on 'theories of looking'. Dr. Vandita Arora always came to the rescue with the Sanskrit translations. I have also benefited from the critical comments of Professors Suvira Jaiswal, Sukumari Bhattacharji and Kumkum Roy. A wide circle of relations and friends here and abroad willingly checked references or procured articles for me—I can't thank them enough.

This book owes its genesis to the faith which my teachers in St. Stephen's College, Dwivedi Sahib, Amin Sahib, and the late Hala Sahib reposed in me. I hope it lives up to their expectations. My family was an invaluable support system. Sunil always chipped in with typing assistance, and the empathy he had for a researcher was very welcome too. I thank my young son Susheem who was often at the receiving end of a pre-occupied mother, but still managed to blossom into a contented child. Above all, I acknowledge a deep sense of gratitude to my parents for being there for me, and sharing many of my household responsibilities, without which this work could never have been completed.

SHALINI SHAH

Roman Equivalents of Nāgarī Letters

Vowels

a	अ	ā	आ	i	इ	ī	ई		
u	उ	ū	ऊ	ṛ	ऋ	e	ए		
ai	ऐ	o	ओ	au	औ	ṁ	अं	ḥ	अ:

Consonants

k	क्	kh	ख्	g	ग्	gh	घ्	ṅ	ङ्
c	च	ch	छ्	j	ज्	jh	झ्	ñ	ञ्
ṭ	ट	ṭh	ठ	ḍ	ड्	ḍh	ढ्	ṇ	ण्
t	त्	th	थ्	d	द्	dh	ध्	n	न्
p	प्	ph	फ्	b	ब्	bh	भ्	m	म्
y	य्	r	र्	l	ल्	v	व्	ś	श्
ṣ	ष्	s	स्	h	ह्				

Conjunct consonants

kṣa	क्ष	tra	त्र	jña	ज्ञ	śra	श्र

Abbreviations

AS	*Aṣṭāṅgasaṁgraha*
CII	*Corpus Inscriptionum Indicarum*
CS	*Carakasaṁhitā*
EI	*Epigraphia Indica*
JAOS	*Journal of the American Oriental Society*
KSS	*Kathāsaritsāgara*
MN	*Mādhavanidāna*
SM	*Sūktimuktāvalī*
SRK	*Subhāṣitaratnakoṣa*
SS	*Suśrutasaṁhitā*, with the commentary of Ḍalhaṇa

Introduction

This work sets out to discuss what has been described in the ancient Indian tradition as *kāma* or sexual desire. *Kāma* was one of the four[1] goals of human life—*dharma*, *artha* and *mokṣa* being the other three. What prompted me to undertake an analysis of the texts dealing with *kāma*, is my concern with women in general, and the social relations between men and women in particular. In rewriting a new women's history, the psycho-dynamics of the private sphere (which after all is the designated place of women in patriarchy) will need to be subjected to careful analysis. The patriarchal tradition completely subordinated women's goals in the spiritual and material spheres to the dictates of men. A woman who followed the *pativrata dharma*, the duty of an ideal chaste wife, was said to achieve both *artha* and *mokṣa*. In the *kāma* tradition, on the other hand, women have a far more visible (even though not always as a subject) role to play. Perhaps this was because in the Indian tradition, unlike the Greek tradition for instance, *kāma* was conceived predominantly in heterosexual terms.[2]

HISTORIOGRAPHY

The extant literature can be analysed under different rubrics. There are monographs on erotic/sexual life in ancient India in general. Then there are works that focus on women in the early medieval context. Significant for our purpose are various studies that deal specifically with Sanskrit literature, many of which also touch on the classical texts of the seventh to thirteenth centuries. Furthermore, historians of the early medieval period have used the erotic texts as sources, or have commented on the concerns that are the focus of this work.

One of the earliest writings on Indian erotic literature was R. Schmidt's *Beitraege Zur Indischen Erotik* published in 1911. It was an account of the contents of published and unpublished *Kāmaśāstra* texts, arranged under different heads with copious quotations and translations. J.J. Meyer published his *Sexual Life in Ancient India* in 1930 but dealt chiefly with the two epics, the *Rāmāyaṇa* and the *Mahābhārata*, with compilations from the *Smṛti* texts in the footnotes, so that his study has no direct bearing on my problem. In fact, in spite of the suggestive title, Meyer's book avoids discussion of even the *Kāmasūtra*, the text *par excellence* on the science of erotics. S.K. De's significant monograph *Ancient Indian Erotics and Erotic Literature*, published in 1959, deals with love and erotic sentiments in both Sanskrit and non-Sanskrit texts of the pre-classical period such as the *Ṛgveda*, *Atharvaveda*, Buddhist *Therīgāthā*, and Hāla's remarkable collection of verses, *Gāthāsattasaī*. Referring to the classical period of Sanskrit literature, he observed that we find erotic poetry blooming in its fullness; poetry which vindicated the claims of women as 'objects' of divinely inspired passion. De noted, quite perceptively,[3] that in classical Sanskrit erotic poetry 'the physical charms of men are seldom directly described; but those of women are profusely and frequently depicted with a passionate intensity of detail.... It is remarkable that in describing feminine charms only such details are selected as have frank sexual appeal.' However, De failed to develop this insight in any paradigmatic manner in his monograph. He also fell short of commenting on the gendered nature of the sources that gave rise to dissimilar treatments of men and women and their bodies in the erotic *kāvya*. If there was grossness in the depiction of the female form, De tried to explain it by stating that 'love was being conceived in its concrete richness'; that the 'essential realism of his (the poet's) passion makes him put a larger emphasis on the body; and love appears more as self-fulfilment than as self-abnegation'.[4] De gently chides those who condemn Sanskrit love poetry as sensual: 'the standards and limits of propriety as well as prudery are different for different people', he says. That the standards of propriety were also different for men and for women was something De did not grasp. Chandra Chakravarty, in his short monograph *Sex Life in Ancient India* (1963), is ambitious in terms of the themes covered: primitive tribes, health, marriage, tantric worship and even some exemplary narratives in ancient India which deal with sex. The last chapter of this monograph, which gives the book its title, is merely a description of a few coital positions from Vātsyāyana's *Kāmasūtra*, which are then copiously explained in the footnotes with details from modern medical treatises that refer to matters such as frigidity. Chakravarty supplements the medical tracts with desultory sociological data to explain everything from sexual congress to sexual hospitality mentioned in the ancient texts. Chakravarty's work is too convoluted to make any academic sense. There is no context and no perspective to the mish-mash of data that he has collected. Like De, N.N. Bhattacharyya in *History of Indian Erotic Literature* (1975), is of the view that in the literary sources the erotic is presented as a sensation with 'direct appeal to the female body'. He too eschews analysis of the relevant texts from either the historical or the sociological perspectives. His study is a compendium on erotic literature intended for the general reader.

Several works deal specifically with women in the early medieval context. Saroj Gulati's *Women and Society: Northern India in the Eleventh and Twelfth Centuries* A.D. (1985) lacks analytical rigour, often taking for granted what actually needs to be explained. Moreover, she has barely consulted the sources that are central to my study. Two monographs on women, both published in 1987, Tripat Sharma's *Women of Ancient India from 320* A.D. *to circa 1200* A.D. and U.P. Mishra's *Prachin Bharata mein Nari 600-1200 Isvi*, do cover the period of study, but lack conceptual or historical application regarding the lives of women. Like Gulati's work they too do not focus in any substantive manner on the relevant sources. A more nuanced understanding of the issue of control over female sexuality in the ancient Indian historical context was furnished by feminist scholar Uma Chakravarty in her important article 'Conceptualising Brahmanical Patriarchy in Early India: Gender, Caste, Class and State', published in 1993. Chakravarty pointed out that for the brahmanical system, based as it was on status by birth, purity was contingent on the control of female sexuality. She commented on the role of the state in regulating women's sexuality in the private sphere. Gender and caste were, thus, the organizing principles of the 'brahmanical' social order, and were intimately interconnected. What was being safeguarded through the control of female sexuality was not only caste purity, but also the purity of the paternal bloodline. Without total control of female sexuality the system of patrilineal inheritance could not be passed on with any certainty. The gender perspective also informs the work of R.P. Sharma whose *Women in Hindu Literature* was published in 1995. Sharma stated that a 'large part of Sanskrit erotic literature is openly voyeuristic'.[5] Sharma also seems to be acutely aware of the asymmetrical male and female sexual relations. While referring to Vātsyāyana's *Kāmasūtra*, he refers to the daily life of the male as depicted in this text as a 'round of pleasures', but that of his wife as a 'round of duties'.[6] Sharma goes on to observe[7] pithily that 'no acquisitive system, whether Aryan Hindu or any other, recognizes the autonomy of the female, and it cannot therefore allow the semantics of love to emphasize an unqualified sharing of certain feelings and experiences between equal heterosexual partners'. Thus, says Sharma, the *Kāmasūtra* formulated an ethics of male sexuality from the male point of view and assigned to the female the 'status of a sex object'.[8] Kumkum Roy's interpretation of Vātsyāyana's *Kāmasūtra* in 'Unravelling the Kāmasūtra' (1996), lead to similar conclusions. Roy commented on the way female sexuality was circumscribed within the confines of patriarchy. A gendered attitude is reflected not only in the text but even in modern writings on, and editions of, this ancient text.

Gender analysis is noticeable in two important works which make a specific aspect of eroticism, homosexuality, the focus of research: Giti Thadani's *Sakhiyani* (1996), a path-breaking work on lesbian desire within Indian culture, and Ruth Vanita and Salim Kidwai's *magnum opus Same-Sex Love in India* (2001). The importance of these two studies stems from the fact that they bring to centre-stage[9] an aspect of eroticism that has been completely marginalized within a pervasively heterosexual Indian cultural complex.

In Rahul Peter Das' *The Origin of the Life of a Human Being: Conception and the Female According to Ancient Indian Medical and Sexological Literature* (2003) women, empirically speaking, occupied centre-stage, though the same cannot be said of their analytical visibility. Das' analysis of the role of women in conception, and in the physical act of sexual intercourse that brings about conception, lacks critical insight. He fails to notice that female desire is either marginalized (as in sexological texts) or treated as a disorder (as in the Indian medical tradition).[10]

D.D. Kosambi in his brilliant introduction to the edited volume of Vidyākara's *Subhāṣitaratnakoṣa* gave a Marxist critique of this anthology, compiled around CE 1100. Kosambi called this 'class literature', 'circumscribed literature'.[11] He noted that *śṛṅgāra* pervaded the poetry of this anthology. A 'woman may be a household animal to him [the poet/*rasika*] but she is also the one luxury of the rich that he can savour at first hand with the highly developed technique of the *Kāmaśāstra*'.[12] While the androcentrism that attributes the subject status to males and the object status to females of this class literature caught Kosambi's attention, he was puritanical and made certain simplistic statements. He talked about a certain 'healthiness' in the sexual depiction where 'we hear little of prostitution, and nothing of homosexuality or other abnormalities'.[13]

Sukumari Bhattacharji in her *History of Sanskrit Literature: Classical Age* pointed out that what passes for love in Sanskrit literature is in most cases mere love.[14] Desire almost always begins and ends with the body (the female one). Bhartṛhari, Bilhaṇa and Jayadeva all glorify the body and the lust it provokes, which no love poetry can afford to ignore but which all true love poetry has to transcend in order to attain beauty and richness. Bhattacharji[15] also commented on the gendered difference in the presentation of *nāyaka* and *nāyikā* in this literature. While the poetical texts defined the *nāyaka* according to his character, the *nāyikā* was characterized in relation to the manner in which she was treated by men. A.K. Warder in his monumental five-volume *Indian Kāvya Literature* (1972–88) did not have anything to say on the gendered nature of poetry, but his work is rich in empirical detail and deals with most of the sources, particularly the verses of female poets that I shall be using in this work. A refreshingly original perspective on the literature of love is that of K.S. Srinivasan. In his *The Ethos of Indian Literature: A Study of its Romantic Tradition* (1985), he grappled with the vexed problem of Indianness in Indian literature. His proposition was that the roots of Indian literature lie in the people's poetry—the bardic songs which celebrate love among the common folk. He saw Hāla's *Gāthāsattasaī* of the first century CE as the earliest available specimen of such literature. Srinivasan was of the view[16] that trading caravans and Prakrit-speaking Jaina monks moving along the *dakṣiṇāpatha* between Madurai and Ujjain via Pratiṣṭhāna, disseminated these love songs (spicy love songs being ideal for weary travellers to recite). Following the logic of his proposition, Srinivasan suggested a linkage between the Prakrit tradition and the early Tamil tradition,[17] citing parallels in the *gāthā* and the *saṅgam* poetry, the latter being the offshoot of the former. This relation, he said, was not just in the theme of love but in language as well. In fact, he looked upon[18] early Tamil as Dravidi Prakrit, a term first used by R.L. Mitra and agreed upon by T.V. Mahalingam. Srinivasan[19] stressed the female authorship of these Prakrit songs. In the *Gāthāsattasaī* there are about 262 poets of whom seven are women. He further pointed out that of the eight Eṭṭuṭokai anthologies in the *saṅgam* literature, six comprised love songs (*aham*). Of the 473 poets, 30 were women. Srinivasan considered the Prakrit love songs the main inspiration behind the classical Sanskrit lyrical love poetry as well, particularly visible in Govardhanācārya's highly erotic *Āryāsaptaśatī*. Govardhanācārya in fact described Prakrit as the abode of Sarasvatī, adding that the muse was forcibly harnessed to Sanskrit (*balena nītā*).[20] Ānandavardhana in his seminal treatise on poetics *Dhvanyāloka* quoted copiously from the Prakrit tradition of love poetry. Srinivasan thus identified the original love tradition in Indian literature as being both non-Sanskritic and feminine.

One of the most significant works to emerge on the Sanskrit language and literature in recent times has been Sheldon Pollock's *The Language of the Gods in the World of Men* (2006). Pollock pointed out that when the language of the gods, the Vedic Sanskrit used exclusively for liturgical purposes, entered the world of men in the early centuries of the first millennium CE, the cosmopolitan era of the Sanskrit language began. The Sanskrit literature now produced was this-worldly (*laukika*) in its themes. Pollock is, however, silent on the gendered dynamics of this *laukika* world in spite of the use of the phrase 'world of men' in the title of his book. He argued that through the medium of *kāvya* (which includes the *praśasti* inscriptions) Sankrit came to define a global cultural formation or 'cosmopolis' that transcended political boundaries and religious affiliations, uniting intellectuals and their masters in a common aesthetic culture that stretched across a wide geographic expanse. Sanskrit thus expressed, according to Pollock, a transcendent aesthetic power. But what was the nature of this aesthetic power?

Who determined the contours and substance of this aesthetic power, and to what end? These are questions that Pollock does not answer.

B.P. Mazumdar's monograph on the socio-economic history of northern India covered a short period of just over a century (CE 1030–1194). However, his discussion of the social history lacks any analysis and is nothing more than a recounting of empirical data under such sub-headings as caste, profession, education, and the position of women. Although Vasudeva Upadhyaya's *The Socio-economic Condition of North India: 700–1200 AD* (1964) covers almost the entire early-medieval period, he based his work essentially on archaeological sources. Romila Thapar dealt with this period in a more general manner while writing her book *A History of India* (1966) that covers more than two millennia of history. She refers[21] to the 'cult of erotics' which had come into its own not only in *kāvya* literature but also in temple sculpture and tantric rituals in the latter part of the first millennium CE. Thapar disagrees that this pervasive eroticism had anything to do with the 'decline of culture' or 'depravity of tastes'; she sees it as a 'celebration of sensuousness' in an 'age of abandon'[22] when the puritan impress of Buddhism (that associated guilt with pleasure) was lifted. Here Thapar recapitulates the views of Dasgupta and De[23] who had talked in terms of the 'pessimism of the Buddhist ideal gradually disappearing and being replaced by more accommodating views on the values of pleasures'. It needs to be examined, however, whether it would be correct to characterize the early medieval period as an 'age of abandon'. After all, the brahmanical normative texts of this period tend to project women in a way not much different from that of the Buddhist texts. They all adopt the typical misogynist view which objectifies woman and holds her responsible for man's digression from virtuous behaviour. Within the non-prescriptive texts too, a woman only served as the object of the male gaze. So if there was an 'age of abandon' and new 'values of pleasures', they were entirely for male consumption. Examining the social context of the erotic cult, Thapar said that the 'seclusion of women' introduced by feudal chivalry in upper-class society was responsible for making a mystery of the simplest of man-woman relationships. While this led to the sublimation of desires[24] in the European context, in India it led to the uninhibited expression which was a way of registering a protest against unnatural social conventions. It is difficult to agree with Thapar. After all, the patriarchal household which restricted female mobility to the domestic unit and circumscribed the wife's sexuality within marriage did not spring up and abruptly end in this period. The *pativrata* ideology, which with its obsession for women's chastity had resulted in severe conditions of seclusion, had been an important element of the ancient period (particularly brahmanical *varṇa* society) for many centuries, and continued to be important thereafter. It has to be asked, therefore, what was new about women's seclusion that led to this response.

B.N.S. Yadava[25] in his micro-study of the feudal society in twelfth-century northern India talked of the deeply erotic tendencies in art, literature and certain forms of temple worship which indicate a preoccupation with the life of *kāma*. As a Marxist he linked this feature of the superstructure to its economic base. Yadava[26] saw these as reflective of the luxurious culture of the courts and the aristocracy of the times who had the leisure and the resources to patronize that literature and art which satisfied their craving for sensual gratification. R.S. Sharma's *Early Medieval Indian Society: A Study in Feudalisation* (2001) dealt with many aspects of economic and social development in the early-medieval period. Although he has focused on neither gender nor the sources that I have examined, his broad analysis of the historical forces operating at this point of time informs this work. Daud Ali's recent significant work, *Courtly Culture and Political Life in Early-Medieval India* (2004), deals with the important institution of the early-medieval court and utilizes both inscriptions and a variety of Sanskrit literary sources of the period to illumine the aesthetics of courtly life. While Ali shows an awareness[27] of the gender asymmetry in courtly relations and in cultural practice, he does not elaborate on this insight.

Art historian Devangana Desai,[28] commenting on the socio-cultural setting of the erotic sculptures produced in the early-medieval period, referred to the *sāmanta*-dominated feudal society as one that suffered the obsessions of 'sex and war'. Desai's work being on erotic sculpture, whatever she says about literature is only incidental—to provide the setting for her analysis. Two other art historians Vidya and Harsha Dehejia have also dealt with the representation of love and eroticism in Indian art. Vidya Dehejia's edited volume *Representing the Body: Gender Issues in Indian Art*

(1997), contains a collection of stimulating essays on the issue of whether the representations of women and men in Indian art has been a gendered one. The essays also grapple with the issues of patronage and the nature of spectatorship. Considering that art, like text, is a cultural production, the discussion in this work has served as a useful interpretative model for my study. Harsha V. Dehejia's more recent edited volume, *A Celebration of Love: The Romantic Heroine in the Indian Arts* (2004), celebrates the idea of love, and the *nāyikā* in love across India and across different genres of literature and different art forms, particularly miniature paintings.[29]

THE HISTORICAL SETTING

The period considered in this book, covering a span of nearly 600 years (the seventh to the thirteenth century) saw the making of early medieval India. These were the centuries which saw the crystallization of a feudal society in much of South Asia. Although since the publication of R.S. Sharma's classic work on Indian feudalism (first published 1965), there has been much debate[30] on the nature of this feudalism, it is still valid to argue, as Daud Ali does,[31] in favour of a feudal courtly culture for the entire period from the fourth century onwards up to CE 1200. In fact, in his elaboration of an aristocratic courtly culture Ali talks of a hierarchized notion where even the bearing and speech were graded.[32]

Concerning the transition to early medieval India B.D. Chattopadhyaya[33] has considered the emergence of regions. He points out that the emergence of local states was the crucial agency behind regionalization. However, even in the period of region formation there was a trans-regionality of aesthetic culture, as both Pollock and Ali[34] have pointed out, and it was this culture that shaped much of the classical Sanskrit literary discourse. Another crucial debate in the context of the early-medieval period has been about the nature and extent of urban decay. While there is now a growing realization that the six centuries 600–1200 need not be seen as unchanging, a case has been made for 'revival' of the metal economy, trade and urbanization (third phase) from the mid-ninth century. Yet the validity of arguing in favour of the decline of an essentially urban cultural ethos still remains valid.[35] Unlike Vātsyāyana's *Kāmasūtra* (third century) which has a cultured, urbane *nāgaraka* as its *nāyaka*, Kokkokā's *Ratirahasya* (tenth century) is addressed to a king who patronized this text.[36] Further, a perusal of Dāmodaragupta's *Kuṭṭanīmatam* (late eighth century) shows that the author had a village-bred pseudo-*nāgaraka* in view while delineating the character of Cintāmaṇi who frequented the quarters of the prostitutes and could not quite carry off the persona of a cultured man. In fact, in place of the *nāgaraka* it is the *bhaṭṭaputra* (perhaps brahmin donee's son) *rājasuta* (feudal princes) or religious *ācārya* who figures as paramour of courtesans in the *Kuṭṭanīmatam*.[37] It is significant that in Vātsyāyana's *Kāmasūtra* it is said for the *nāgaraka* that he should be a man of learning (*grahītavidyā*), have wealth and should be a householder.[38] Also, such an urbane man is advised in the *Kāmasūtra* to live in a *nagara*, *paṭṭaṇa* or *kharvaṭa*, or in a place which is the resort of many persons. Commenting on this statement, Yaśodhara[39] is not so insistent on the cities as a must for *nāgaraka*; he says one can stay in any place where one can live well. The loss of urban ethos left its particular impact on the *veśavāsa* (the culture of the *gaṇikā*). Motichandra[40] makes an important observation that a survey of prostitution in Kashmir from 700 to 1100 shows that there is a greater emphasis on the sex aspect of the profession and its perfidies, and that the dignity attained by courtesans of the earlier period was now lost. Even the *viṭa* who were generally accomplished men had lost their former zest. Kṣemendra's caricature of *viṭa* in *Samayamātṛkā* is a case in point. *Viṭas* now acted as mere pimps and hangers-on. As a matter of fact, the *veśa* culture suffered a definite decline in early medieval Kashmir. I submit that this degradation was directly linked to the eclipse of the urban centres and urban prosperity that had been the mainstay of this social group.

Many literary as well as inscriptional sources[41] seem to confirm the precariousness (of both their prosperity and clout) of the urban mercantile classes. Buddha Prakash gives instances testifying to the weakened position of the *nāgaraka* class. The Faridpur copper-plate inscription of the sixth century, for instance, which refers to *viṣayapati* but not to any others of the urban bourgeoisie. He points out that instead of the board of *nagaraśreṣṭhin*, *sārthavāha* and *prathamakulika*, some other persons, possibly from the landholding class, were nominated to assist the *viṣayapati* in his administrative work.[42] B.P. Mazumdar[43] too points out that when the merchants did come into wealth, instead of using it as commercial capital they used it to buy land as security, and thus acquired vassaldoms. Needless to add, their cultural aspirations were perhaps no different from the other feudal elite.[44] Even when the trade, urban centres, and monetary economy revived after 1000, what is important for our purpose is to ask whether and how this impacted the cultural and literary output. The answer seems to be in the negative, as most of the literary works examined below seem to have been patronized either by kings or their *sāmantas*. It was this shrinking socio-economic base which provided the setting for what D.D. Kosambi in his introduction to Vidyākara's *Subhāṣitaratnakoṣa* calls a class literature. Writing on the historical background of the classical literature Lienhard[45] opines that the urban milieu was of the utmost importance in fostering and sustaining such literature. Only in the city was an exchange of ideas and criticism made possible by personal contacts among poets, artists, and scholars. Although Lienhard shows no awareness of urban decay from the sixth to ninth centuries in most parts of the Indian subcontinent, and how that may have affected the quality of literature, he goes on to elaborate on why the literature was bound to be a city phenomenon. He points out[46] that while in principle all levels of educated society had access to poetry, in practice the chief difficulty for educated people in the countryside would be to obtain manuscripts, and geographical isolation would have entailed little opportunity to people to listen to recitations, which was an important way of dissemination. The setting of a metropolis or provincial capital was thus important for sustenance of this literature. Rājaśekhara in *Kāvyamīmāṁsā*[47] relates that when the king wished to put new *kāvyas* to the test he summoned an eclectic assembly of intellectuals, arranged festivals in their honour and called extra meetings of those scholars who were neither citizens of that town nor courtiers but had come from foreign parts (*deśāntara*). It is obvious that in times of urban decay such an elaborate way of convening a *kāvyagoṣṭhī* may not have been easy, and literary production and its recognition would have surely suffered. In fact, it is quite likely that in the absence of a nurturing urban milieu, literary production lost its vitality and tended to become repetitive in terms of theme and content.

While we witness a decline of the commercial classes in this period, there was on the other hand the rise of several grades of landed intermediaries. A medieval text, *Aparājitapṛccha*[48] (from Cālukyan Gujarat), has classified feudatories in descending order on the basis of the number of villages held by them. These were the *mahāmaṇḍaleśvara*, *māṇḍalika*, *mahāsāmanta*, *sāmanta*, *laghusāmanta*, and so on. Bāṇa also refers to them in his *Harṣacarita*.[49] Thus, a pyramidal structure was created with the king at the top. The '*sāmanta*-feudatory' system[50] was, in fact, the distinguishing feature of early medieval polity. The fragmentation of sovereignty had left a major impact on the institution of kingship. B.N.S. Yadava[51] points out that the king was now less the head of a state as compared with more ancient times like the Mauryan period. Yadava contrasts the daily activity of the king as narrated in *Arthaśāstra*, and even Kālidāsa's *Abhijñānaśākuntalam*, with the description of the king's activities in early medieval literature like *Naiṣadhacarita*. The *Mānasollāsa*[52] too is dominated by descriptions of the *vinoda*, *bhoga* and *krīḍā*[53] of the king rather than with those activities that deal with the matters of state. The *Harṣacarita*, the biography of a king, scarcely touches on the political functions of the king. When Bāṇa is not narrating the dramatic personal fortunes of the king, he gives an excellent word picture of a feudal court. The lack of vigorous political activity is also evident in the play *Ratnāvalī*, which, ironically, is considered to have been authored by Emperor Harṣa of Kannauj. In the first act of the play, Udayana says 'my kingdom is free from enemies, the entire burden of government is entrusted to an able minister, and my subjects are free from all troubles'. So Harṣa, the king-dramatist, makes Udayana, and in his person his own self, free of the affairs of the state because there are able ministers. Udayana is virtually free to do other things, the most important being yielding to amorous delights. And he pursues it with a vengeance.[54] Yadava therefore concludes[55] that the hold of religiosity and the pursuit of pleasure and pastimes appear to have grown at the expense of the essential duties of kingly office. And what the king did, the feudatories only copied with equal if not greater vigour.[56]

The gross sensuality of this aristocratic courtly culture and the pursuit of a pleasurable life are some of the hallmarks of the age.[57] Kosambi, in his introduction to the *Subhāṣitaratnakoṣa*,[58] talks of increasing erotica in classical Sanskrit literature under courtly influence: 'every portion of the anthology is permeated by the theme of sex. Even in dealing with the gods it is their night life which is most often treated with ... complete lack of reticence'. He notes[59] that the average Sanskrit poet wrote for the patrician and mainly within the limits of the latter's common experience, which was precisely sex and religion.[60] Desai has also commented[61] on the fact that the two central interests of the feudal aristocracy were sex and war. These were the twin themes on which the emotions of medieval high society were concentrated. As Dasgupta and De[62] have argued, 'works of literature are not mere plays of imagination, or of solitary caprices of the brain, but they may be said to be transcripts of contemporary manners or as representing certain kinds of mind'. In fact, this is precisely how the ancients understood the functioning of the literature. Mammaṭa in *Kāvyaprakāśa*[63] underlines that 'one can know from the *kāvya* the manners and customs of the age' (*kāvyaṁvyavahāravide*). The eroticism of the secular literature was thus a reflection of the luxurious culture of the courts and aristocracy, in other words the leisurely class of the time. If the poets and writers were falling in line by catering to the increasing demand for erotica by the feudal classes, it was because they were inextricably linked to the latter through the ties of patronage. As Kosambi notes, the professional writer was a member of the leisure class,[64] which in turn was appended to the ruling class. Poet Maṅkha in his *Śrīkaṇṭha-carita* tells us how he presented his epic at the *goṣṭhī* organized by his brother who was a minister in the court of King Jayasiṁha of Kashmir. Pollock[65] is of the view that the venue of the recitation of Maṅkha's *kāvya* amounts to a sort of inchoate literary public sphere consisting of scholars, literati, and men of affairs from home and abroad, but 'no king'. Yet this kind of gathering could not have been easy to sustain. As Maṅkha himself is told by an ambassador in the audience, 'All poets, yourself excepted, have served only to teach men how to beg.'[66] In *Kāvyamīmāṁsā*[67] Rājaśekhara commenting on the creative process of the litterateur says: he must ask himself questions like 'what is my inborn talent?', 'what does society favour', 'what does my patron favour?', and 'what kind of poetic assemblies does the patron occupy himself with?'. The literature thus became a private literature, neither accessible to the common people nor reflective of their taste. Barbara S. Miller[68] and Richard Eaton have shown that patronage affected both the form and content of the work of art.[69] De too notes[70] that 'court influence undoubtedly went a long way, not only in fostering a certain languor and luxuriance of style,[71] but also in encouraging a taste which preferred the fantastic and the elaborate[72] to the fervid and the spontaneous'. Kosambi[73] has commented on the 'florid Sanskrit poet' and his 'hedonist patron'. However, it was not the poetic genius but the social sensibility that was at fault here.

The writer–patron link was a very significant one. Almost all famous writers of our period, Bāṇa, Mayūra (at Harṣavardhana's court), Bhavabhūti (Yaśovarman of Kannauj), Rājaśekhara (Pratihāras), Bilhaṇa (Chalukyas of Kalyāṇa), Jayadeva,[74] and Govardhanācārya (Lakṣamaṇasena of Bengal) were court-poets. Lienhard[75] points out that even texts dealing with the theories of *kāvya,* like e.g. Mammaṭa's *Kāvyaprakāśa* and Viśvanātha's *Sāhityadarpaṇa,* constantly stress this link. One of the most important aims (*prayojana*) of the court-poet is to gain undying fame in which he allows his lord and master to share by adding lustre to the court by his very presence, or, more directly, with praise[76] through the composition of *carita* and *praśasti.* Bāṇa's *Harṣacarita* and Bilhaṇa's *Vikramāṅkadevacarita* are cases in point. For their effort the poets earned wealth from their royal patrons. Mammaṭa[77] specifically refers to the poet Dhāvaka being so indebted to king Harṣa. The limitation of the socio-economic base which led to the litterateur's dependence on feudal sustenance explains on the one hand verses of outrageous court flattery[78] and on the other the moods of black depression caused by acute insecurity[79] and even rebelliousness. In one verse from Jalhaṇa's anthology, dependence on the king for livelihood is described as a bad dream without sleep and a living death.[80] Some like Bhartṛhari[81] rebelled against this state of affairs—he declares,

> You are a king of opulence; I am a master of infinite words.
> You are a warrior; I hold a skill in eloquence which subdues the fever of pride.
> Men blinded by riches serve you; but they desire to hear me that their minds may be pure.
> Since you have no regard for me, the less have I for you.
> O king! I am gone.

Economic insecurity and competition for royal attention led more and more litterateurs to a preference for what De[82] calls 'what catches the eyes over what touches the heart'.

An interesting fact about court patronage in the early medieval period is, that there was mobility of the litterateur class from one court to another, even while artisans and peasants suffered from increasing immobility. Poet Bilhaṇa travelled from Kashmir to the Deccan. Rājaśekhara, hailing from Maharashtra, served the Pratihāra court of Mahendrapāla and Mahīpāla in Kannauj. Daṇḍin, a brahmin from Gujarat, was patronized by the Pallavas of Kāñcī. A.K. Warder[83] finds that this mobility gave writers intellectual autonomy. Since writers could choose their patrons they could not be subjected to any given paradigm. However, if the tastes of these aristocratic patrons and the mechanisms of patronage (dependence on the fancy of the king forcing them to write in order to catch his eye) were not very different, then for the writer ultimately the choice was really a false one. Under feudalism, immobility reduced the peasantry to the status of serfs; similarly, the ties of patronage stifled the intellectual creativity of the litterateurs as a class. It would not be an exaggeration to say that many such litterateurs were reduced to the status of intellectual serfs. Pollock,[84] ignoring the class quotient of the literary texts, prefers to talk in terms of a boundary-less cultural formation or 'cosmopolis' uniting intellectuals and their masters in a common aesthetic culture.

It is also crucial for us to reflect on the woman's place in all this. Does she have a subject status, or agency within this social milieu? In this period we notice a clear equation of enjoyment (*bhoga*) of the world with enjoyment of women.[85] A number of inscriptions[86] of feudal kings and their *sāmantas* that are available, invariably refer to their heroic deeds and conquests as also their capacity to make love to women from different places. The acquisition of land, and access to women were a measures and marks of status for these men. One verse of Mayūra,[87] court-poet of Harṣa, while describing the political conquest of his patron actually reads like a conquest of a woman through the clever use of the device of the pun (*śleṣa*). It says, 'we regard you, your Highness alone, indeed as the real husband of the Earth, for having touched her person (*aṅga*) and caressed her hair (*kuntala*) and thrown aside her long robe (*cola*) and taken possession of the central region (*madhyadeśa*), your hand is now laid on her girdle (*kāñcī*).' However, there was no such coterminality of political and sexual conquest in case of women. The inscription[88] of the Anantavāsudeva temple erected by Candrādevī in 1278 mentions her husband who had practised with her 'diverse kinds of pleasures in which delight was attendant upon amorous pleasures'. For women, pleasure was conjugal, and political prestige accrued from the husband. This was bound to be so since women had a subsidiary status both politically and socially. In a verse of *Nāradasmṛti* (*prakīrṇaka*) the relations between the ruler and his subjects have been linked to that between husband and wife, implying the subjection and dependence of the latter. In another verse of the same text, quoted with approval by Lakṣmīdhara in *Kṛtyākalpataru*, the dependent people are regarded as subjected to the will of the ruler.[89] It is thus clear that when one played the role of a subordinate partner in the political sphere, one could not be truly autonomous in the game of pleasure relations either.

I have elaborated on both the inscriptional and textual references which highlight the predominant erotic sentiments with its gendered implications in the early-medieval context. Yet the notion of self-discipline and mastery over the senses was not entirely absent from the courtly concerns.[90] The flip side of unbridled *bhoga*/enjoyment was the danger of losing control. Somadeva in *Yaśastilaka*[91] states, 'Kings who enjoy pleasures at will (*svairvihārasārah*) leaving the charge of the kingdom in the hands of the officials are foolish indeed. They might as well sleep leaving the cats in charge of the milk.' A number of *praśastis* also tend to emphasize the self-restraint[92] on the part of the kings who behaved like Kārttikeya[93] (in not keeping the company of women) and avoided being Indra[94] (who committed debauchery with others' wives) and were satisfied with the company of their own wives.[95] Just as in sexual enjoyment, so also in sexual restraint, men/kings alone had the subject status. The pleasures were theirs and the glory of being a *jitendrīya*/*vītarāga*[96] was also theirs. In the literature *dhīra* (as *dhīrodātta*, *dhīrodhata*, *dhīralalita*, and *dhīrapraśānta*) is an important category of *nāyaka* among both the *uttama* and *madhyama* types,[97] and he is someone who has control over his senses. On the other hand, in poetics[98] while we do get a classification of *nāyikā* into *dhīrā*, *adhīrā*, and *dhīrādhīrā*, this sub-classification has nothing to do with the *nāyikā*'s control over her senses; rather it has to do with the manner (more or less anger) of her conduct *vis-à-vis* the straying *nāyaka*.

SOURCES

From a purely literary point of view the significance of the period under survey is that it marks the end of the classicism (represented by Kālidāsa) on the one hand, and the beginning of Jayadeva's *Gītagovinda* which in Sanskrit poetry stands by itself—a form *sui generis*. The literature produced in this period was heavily dominated by erotic themes. As we have seen, erotica was high in demand as far as the aristocratic feudal classes were concerned. Virtually all genres of Sanskrit literature, be it *nāṭya*,[99] *kāvya*,[100] *kathā*[101] or *ākhyāyikā*,[102] have *śṛṅgāra* as a major sentiment or *rasa*. Apart from this, there was *kāmaśāstra*[103] literature, which dealt specifically with the science of erotics. In at least two works on poetics—Rudrabhaṭṭa's *Śṛṅgāratilaka* and Bhoja's *Śṛṅgāraprakāśa*—the erotic sentiment is the chief feature. My study utilizes, for its analysis, literature from all these genres.

Critic Rudraṭa says in his *Kāvyālaṁkāra*[104] about the *kathā* that the conclusion of a *kathā* may be obtaining a girl, thus the aesthetic experience will frequently be *śṛṅgāra rasa*. *Mahākāvya* are also particularly rich in erotic poetry partly because the subject matter of the *mahākāvya* provide ample opportunity for such descriptions. According to Daṇḍin's *Kāvyādarśa*,[105] among the themes that are mandatory for *mahākāvya* are seasons, gardens, sporting in the water, drinking parties, love sports, love in separation (*vipralambha*) and love in union (*saṁbhoga*). Even in the classical literature known as *khaṇḍakāvya* or *muktaka* (where every stanza is complete in itself), there is a preponderance of *śṛṅgāra rasa*. The style favoured for *śṛṅgāra rasa* poetry had been (since the eighth century) essentially Vaidarbhī (as against Gauḍī) due to its lucidity and flowing manner. Also, in these lyrics a large number of metres had been employed and a majority of them had the epithets for 'fair maidens'[106] such as Tanvī, Cañcalākṣī, Vidyunnmālā, and so on. Not only does this point to the original connection of these metres with erotic themes, it also indirectly confirms the male authorship of this poetry. As for the content of the *muktaka* genre of *kāvya*, while love is the favoured theme it treats woman as an erotic object for the enchantment of men.[107]

Śṛṅgāra rasa is the heart of the erotic *kāvya* literature and is looked upon by the theoreticians of the science of poetics as the foremost[108] (*aṅgīrasa*) of the sentiments, easily within the experience of one and all.[109] We therefore need to look at this *rasa* in some detail. The *śṛṅgāra rasa* since the time of Bharata's *Nāṭyaśāstra* has been considered bright (*ujjvala*), pure (*śuci*) and beautiful (*darśanīya*). Ānandavardhana considered it to be the sweetest[110] and the most delicate of the emotions of men of cultivated taste. In an unsophisticated rustic (*hīnapātra*) there is *śṛṅgāra* but only in a way, as an example from Hāla's *Gāthāsattasaī*[111] depicts. The term *grāmya* had a pejorative meaning in the Sanskrit lexicon, meaning coarse and vulgar (*aślīla*). What the courtly *kāvyas* encouraged was a cultivated and mannered love.[112] Bhoja, in his treatise *Sarasvatīkaṇṭhābharaṇa,*[113] also said that love in birds and bees[114] was not a *rasa*, but only its semblance, that is, *rasābhāsa*. Thus, love as understood by the word *śṛṅgāra* in the theories of Sanskrit poetics was essentially an elite phenomenon firmly belonging to the human world.[115]

I suggest that this making of *śṛṅgāra rasa* as an elite androcentric phenomenon within Sanskrit literary tradition was a deliberate exercise. Srinivasan[116] has shown quite convincingly that original inspiration for all the love songs, Sanskrit as well as Tamil, lay in the Prakrit love songs of which Hāla's *Gāthāsattasaī,* is the earliest extant specimen. He has also tried to show the presence of female authorship in a big way within the Prakrit poetry and the early Tamil tradition. Rājaśekhara, the famous tenth-century writer, makes a significant observation in the prologue of his Prakrit play *Karpūramañjarī*:[117] the Prakrit language itself is smooth (*saumāro*) as a woman (*mahilā*) whereas Sanskrit is harsh, like a man (*puruṣa*). Interestingly the play *Karpūramañjarī* was specifically produced by Rājaśekhara at the request of his wife Avantisundarī, and in this play the poet introduces an elaborate discussion on love.[118] Jayavallabha in his Prakrit anthology *Vajjālaggam*[119] notes that while Prakrit poetry which is charming, full of sweet sounds, loved by young ladies (*juvaiee janavallabha*)[120] and characterized by the sentiment of love is available, then who can possibly bear to read

Sanskrit poetry. As Hāla too asks in his *Gāthāsattasaī,*[121] 'Aren't people ashamed to discuss the philosophy of love when they can neither read nor hear the elixir of Prakrit poetry?' Govardhanācārya in his introduction to *Āryāsaptaśatī*[122] also points out that although the Prakrit language is capable of greater sweetness (*vāṇī prākṛta samucitarasa*) he has forcibly[123] harnessed it to write a Sanskrit *kāvya* (*balanaiva saṁskṛta nītā*). It is a different matter that Govardhana did not quite succeed, and *Āryāsaptaśatī* degenerated into another erotic text for courtly consumption. Perhaps this forcible harnessing of an essentially folk tradition of love poetry (where women had a more realistic presence and also subject status as authors) was done in order to earn a livelihood. As Mammaṭa says in his *Kāvyaprakāśa*[124] *kāvyaṁ yaśase arthakṛte*, that is, literature is for the sake of glory and wealth. For these benefit 'men' took over love poetry and made of it an artificial commodity of conspicuous consumption.

The *śṛṅgāra rasa* as outlined in Sanskrit poetics has two main manifestations, the *saṁbhoga* and the *vipralambha śṛṅgāra*. While dealing with the *saṁbhoga śṛṅgāra* the poetic convention demanded that the writer avoid vulgarity of any sort. Daṇḍin in his *Kāvyādarśa* says that an erotic idea if conveyed indirectly is saved from vulgarity.[125] Ānandavardhana[126] notes that any vulgarity (*grāmyatā*) or impropriety (*anaucitya*)[127] would debase *śṛṅgāra rasa*. Thus words that refer to bodily functions are to be avoided unless they are used metaphorically.[128] It is said, for example, that the poet should never use the word *yabh* (copulation). As one theorist delicately puts it, 'a poet should avoid the use of the word which begins with the letter *ya*'.[129] The conventions demanded that the sentiment of *śṛṅgāra* should be suggestive (*dhvani*). This is the reason why in Ānandavardhana's seminal work on poetics, *Dhvanyāloka,* which deals with suggestion or *dhvani* in poetry, many examples are furnished from *śṛṅgāra rasa* poetry and the greatest number of verses quoted here are from Prakrit poetry. In classical Sanskrit poetry, all verse, whether describing love in separation or in union, is about and on love, but never the verse of a lover. There is no love lyric in this sense in Sanskrit. The attitude and training of the Indian poet was such that the idea of using poetry to express his private feelings hardly ever occurred to him.[130] In Sanskrit, love poems are universals in a type-cast situation and not named characters in a particular circumstance. However, a few verses of poetesses that we find in Sanskrit anthologies such as the *Yaḥ kaumāraharaḥ* of Śīlābhaṭṭārikā which expresses longing for a lost intimacy, has a haunting personal quality to it, and is virtually unique in classical Sanskrit poetry.

It is a truism of history that sources need to be studied within a spatial and chronological context. But there are limitations in analysing literary sources of our kind from this angle given the paucity of relevant data. It is more fruitful to examine these sources from the perspective of their class base—in terms of both authorship and patronage. The close relationship between the literary and social structure of consciousness makes it imperative for a social historian to subject literary texts to this kind of critique. Furthermore, we need to analyse the androcentrism of these sources. Even a cursory glance at some of the relevant texts of our period tends to dispel the notion of female centrality within the *kāma* tradition. The absence of female centrality does not mean that love and eroticism exist without the presence of a *nāyikā* (more so given the heterosexual bias of the Indian erotic texts); but that within the discussion on erotics the *nāyikā* is not the subject but the object. The erotic is presented as a definite feeling of sensation (for men) with direct reference to the female body which is perceived as the inert, fetishized object of the male gaze. While the *nāyaka* is not objectified in the *nāyikā*'s erotic yearnings, in the *nāyaka*'s desire every single part of the female anatomy becomes such an object of longing. Thus, epithets like *pīnastanī* (one with high breasts), *rambhorū* (one who has thighs like the plantain trees), *varārohā* (one with fine hips), *suśroṇi* (having good buttocks and loins) abound for the *nāyikā*. Significantly enough, the word *varāroha* when used in the masculine means an excellent rider.[131] It would appear that a *nāyikā* was no more than the dis-embodied parts which the *nāyaka* could fantasize about. Gender is instituted through the stylization of the female body. The reading of verses in the anthologies gives us a feeling of *déja vu*. Like modern commercial advertising, just about everything is described with reference to (or in association with) erotic female charms. Jalhaṇa's *Sūktimuktāvalī* furnishes many such examples. In one verse the rising sun is conceived as 'shining like a string of emerald around the plump breasts of the goddess of the sky'.[132] In another verse *campaka* fruits are like 'hard rounded breasts of women'.[133] In yet another verse, the rays of the moon are compared to 'the sportive smiles of a charming young lady'.[134] In Śrīdharadāsa's anthology *Sadukti-karṇāmṛta* in one of the verses the droplets of water are likened to the sweat on the cheeks of the mountain girls brought on by the act of love-making.[135] In another verse in this anthology,[136] the rising disc of the moon resembles the breasts of a Hūṇa woman pressed by her lover. We thus see that for all the *upamāna* (objects), the *upameya* (subjects of comparison) are some part of women's physique.[137] It has to be remembered that the lack of female subjectivity and the objectification of women is an important element in the construction of femininity within the patriarchal discourse.

In *Kāvyamīmāṁsā*,[138] Rājaśekhara presents the metaphor of a masculine *kāvyapuruṣa* (literature) being led by feminine *sāhitya-vidyāvadhū* (knowledge of poetics). In spite of the use of this metaphor, the masculine authorship is glaringly obvious. The connoisseurs (*rasika* and *sahṛdaya*) of these texts too were essentially males. Although Vijjikā has one play *Kaumudīmahotsava* attributed to her, this is an ascription which is by no means undisputed.[139] None of the verses from this text figure under Vijjikā's name in the anthologies. In the period of analysis I have not been able to locate any *kāvya* which can be said to have been authored by a woman. There is, therefore, no reason to believe that women poets were exposed to a public audience, which *kāvya* writing would have necessarily entailed.[140] The Sanskrit *kāvya* is described in the Indian tradition[141] as only of two types, *dṛśya* (drama) and *śravya* (recitative). There is no category meant only to be read. The oral performative dimension rendered the Sanskrit *kāvya* a pre-eminently social, almost a congregational, phenomenon. From a gender perspective, this would have created problems for women composing *kāvya*. They could not have had much access to learned gatherings (*goṣṭhī*), and this would have hampered their pursuit of *kāvyaracanā*. What we have of the women's writings are only stray verses, and it is the literary merit of these verses that ensured their preservation in the anthologies and in the texts on poetics. For instance, Śīlābhaṭṭārikā's *Yaḥ kaumāraharaḥ* is admitted by the entire tradition of Indian poetics to be one of the greatest ever written. Mammaṭa[142] cited it as an example of a great poem that contains no figure of speech.

Rājaśekhara (ninth century) complimented a handful of women poets,[143] where he described Śīlābhaṭṭārikā as commanding the *pāñcālī* style along with the great poet Bāṇa. Vijjikā is declared by

Rājaśekhara[144] as the Sarasvatī incarnate of the Karnāṭa *deśa*, who, next to Kālidāsa, was the very abode of the *vaidarbhī* style.[145] Apart from Śīlā and Vijjikā some others like Morikā and Mārulā are mentioned in a verse by poet Dhanadeva,[146] who says that in spite of being women (*strīyo'pi*) these ladies were adept (*vijñā*) in the writing of poetry (*kāvyaṁ kartuṁ santi*), achieving education (*vidyāṁ vetuṁ*), winning a discussion (*vādino nirvijetuṁ*), and attaining proficiency in speaking everything (*viśvaṁ vaktuṁ yaḥ pravīṇasya vandyaḥ*). Jalhaṇa[147] cites some more of Rājaśekhara's laudatory remarks on Sanskrit poetry by women. Prabhudevī is described as a great poet of the Lāṭa region, a woman of taste and the abode of all arts, who went on to live in the hearts of the people after her death. Subhadrā is praised for having taken permanent lodging in the hearts of the lovers of poetry by the sheer beauty of her verses. Rājaśekhara not only tried to preserve for posterity the name and contributions of some of these women, but also gave a rare theoretical justification for their activity. In *Kāvyamīmāṁsā*,[148] he goes to the extent of saying that like men, 'women could also be poets (*puruṣavat yoṣito'pi kavī bhaveyuḥ*)'.

He notes that 'the cultured soul or the genius inheres in the self irrespective of a distinction between man and woman (*saṁskāro hyātmani samvaiti na straiṇaṁ pauruṣaṁ vā vibhāgampekṣate*)'. Nonetheless, Rājaśekhara[149] uses a quaint term, *śāstraprahat-budhayaḥ*, that is, one whose mind is assailed by learning, to describe princesses (*rājaputriyo*), daughters of ministers (*mahāmātraduhitaro*), courtesans (*gaṇikā*), and the wives of jesters (*kautukībhāryā*).

In the early-medieval period, neither do we get a *kāvya* by a woman author nor do female characters (with the occasional exception) as a rule speak in Sanskrit in the male-authored plays. In classical Sanskrit plays women speak only Prakrit, because as a *dṛśya kāvya*, the play was to be enacted before an audience well-versed with the *Nāṭyaśāstra* principle that refined speech (Sanskrit), was to be used only by men[150] of higher *varṇas*, while the colloquial language or Prakrit, was to be assigned to women, children and men of low birth.[151] Only by queens, *apsarās*, courtesans, and female artists could Sanskrit speech be employed, depending on the situation. Yet, in Kālidāsa's plays, neither *apsarā* (celestial nymphs) like Menakā and Urvaśī, nor queens like Dhāriṇī and Mālavikā, nor a *naṭī* (a female performing artist), nor a *parivrājikā* (female mendicant) like Gautamī, ever speak in Sanskrit. Only in Śūdraka's *Mṛcchakaṭika*, does *gaṇikā* Vasantasenā speak Sanskrit. It would not be an exaggeration to state that the classical Sanskrit literature produced in this entire period is essentially a gendered literature written by and for men.

Neither would it be wrong to surmise that the circle of learned women was a very constricted one at all times, even though some exceptional aristocratic women managed to be part of it. Avantisundarī, the royal Cahamāna princess who married the poet Rājaśekhara, was such an exception. Her erudition is praised by her poet-husband Rājaśekhara, who quotes her thrice[152] as holding a different opinion on the principles of aesthetics. The Cālukyan queen Vijjikā was another learned woman who quite self-consciously calls attention to her intellectual attainments. Disdaining Daṇḍin's description of Sarasvatī in the opening verse of his *Kāvyādarśa* as all white (*sarvaśuklā*), Vijjikā declares 'not knowing that I, Vijjikā, am dark like the blue lotus ... Daṇḍin has vainly said that Sarasvatī is all white'.[153] In yet another verse Vijjikā reiterates her genius as a poet. She says, 'one was born of the lotus, another on the beach, and a third of the anthill; these (Brahmā, Vyāsa, Vālmīki) are great poets and to them I pay my homage, but if some later men should try to please us with prose and verse compositions, well, I, the beloved of the king of Karnāṭa, place my left leg on their heads'.[154] Interestingly Vijjikā in her homage to the connoisseurs, does not address them as *rasika* or *sahṛdaya* but with a gender-neutral term *janasya*. They, she says, 'express their keen delight by still contemplation and a body horripilated at the beauty of the poet's idea which lies not in the words themselves, but which vibrates in the words that overflow with emotion'.[155] It is thus obvious that cultured education which was necessary to enable one to take to the vocation of poetry-writing was not unobtainable on account of one's gender; it was instead the social construction of 'correct' gender roles for women that made it difficult for them to acquire such an education. As Bhoja[156] notes in his *magnum opus Śṛṅgāraprakāśa*, there are men who talk incorrect Sanskrit and women who are masters of Sanskrit, and he cites the example of Vijjikā. Bhoja goes on to quote a verse which throws some light on Vikaṭanitambā's private life. Vikaṭanitambā's poetry was extolled by Rājaśekhara[157] as sweeter than the words of the beloved. Yet this scholarly woman poet, it appears, was married (*tasmai dattā*) to an illiterate man who could not pronounce three cerebrals together in a conjunct consonant—he would change a cerebral into a dental, and a dental into a palatal.[158]

The literary texts used as sources for the analysis in this work are all datable between the seventh and the thirteenth centuries. However, the date of one text, Śūdraka's *Mṛcchakaṭika*, is highly controversial. A legion of scholars, Mehendale, Saletore, Manomohan Ghosh, Sten Konow, J. Carpentier, Jacobi, Pischel, Gawronski, A.B. Keith and J. Jolly[159] have discussed the problem of dating from various possible angles. The opinions expressed and the dates ascribed are so divergent that they could easily form an independent treatise.[160] The reason why I have chosen to place *Mṛcchakaṭika* in my period of study is because of the fact that Śūdraka is mentioned in Vāmana's text on poetics, *Kāvyālaṁkārasūtra.*[161] Vāmana has been placed by scholars such as S.K. De[162] and P.V. Kane[163] between CE 750 and 850. This is because while Vāmana quotes from Bhavabhūti's *Uttararāmacarita* and *Mahāvīracaritam*; Rājaśekhara in the early-tenth century quoted from Vāmana. As for Śūdraka's identity, Saletore[164] treats him as a historical figure of southern India. He identifies Śūdraka with one Śivamāra I who ruled the Deccan between 675 and 725. Jolly in his monograph on Hindu Law[165] has shown that the legal procedure outlined in Act V of *Mṛcchakaṭika* is found in the law books of the sixth and seventh centuries. Thus a scholar like Manomohan Ghosh[166] is inclined to place Śūdraka's play in the post-Gupta centuries.

THE PROBLEM

One of the problems about writing on sexuality is that it is often dismissed as a 'natural instinct' of humankind, deeply personal and enacted in private, with no relevance for a social historian as a fruitful academic subject. But as Padgug[167] pertinently notes, 'sexuality is relational. It consists of activity and interactions—active social relations—and not simply "acts", as if sexuality were the enumeration and typology of an individual's orgasms.' Padgug dismisses the notion of sexuality as a mere physical act on the part of individuals. Not only is sexuality defined publicly, most obviously appearing in public customs like marriage, but it is also regulated by public discourse (for instance the normative injunctions). This probably led Maurice Godelier to surmise that it is 'not sexuality that haunts society, but society which haunts the body's sexuality'.[168] As Halperin, Zietlin and Winkler[169] argue, sex is not an independent variable which could be described in a coherent linear narrative with minimal reference to the other areas of human interest. Rather we take the multiple and competing significance of sex at any one time to be intelligible only in relation to the warp and woof of the entire social fabric. Halperin,[170] theorizing about sexuality, says that 'unlike "sex" sexuality is a cultural production; it represents the appropriation of the human body and of its physiological capacities, by an ideological discourse. Sexuality is not a somatic fact; it is a cultural effect. Sexuality, then, does have a history.' If the body had been the determinant of sexuality, there would have been a more uniform kind of sexuality all over the world. But this is not the case. Sexuality differs from one period to another, from one culture to another, and more importantly it differs in terms of gender. The content of sexuality, its experience, and its institutional forms are highly variable.

Thus, sexuality in history can no longer be treated as a 'virgin field'; the new social historians have to challenge the ignorance enveloping this subject.[171] Sexuality for a social historian is a 'subject' in itself; rather, it is a field which can be studied in terms of how society and various groups within that society construct sexual desire. Since human sexuality is deeply embedded in a socio-economic, political and cultural matrix, an analysis of sexuality offers the historian an opportunity to explore possible relationships between social structures and the normative cultural values. It also permits the historian to explore the relation between actual behaviour and the prescribed norm.

A major impetus for writing about sexuality came with the effective rebuttal of an essentialist position of Freud that saw sex as an innate biological drive (a given rather than acquired) which is then moulded, modified or repressed by the operation of social forces. To view sexuality as a repression of an innate drive was to present individuals as passive and society and culture as ahistorical. Also this essentialist approach saw this innate sex drive as basically male and firmly heterosexual.[172]

Against this essentialist position, Gagnon and Simon[173] argued that sexuality is subject to socio-cultural moulding to a degree surpassed by few other forms of human behaviour.[174] As Mary Douglas[175] also noted, 'nothing is more essentially transmitted by a social process of learning than sexual behaviours'. Foucault[176] too rejected sex as an autonomous realm or a natural force, and traced the socio-historical sources of sexual desire. Arguing from a post-structuralist perspective, he talked of sexuality in different discourses. A serious criticism of Foucault's work is that it does not examine the relationship between gender inequality and sexuality, nor does his account of the different discourses on sexuality pay much attention to the fact that men and women often have different orientations to sexuality, even different discourses.

These theoretical formulations owe a great deal to a century of questioning the notion of natural man[177] by Marxists, structural anthropologists, etc. Although Engels[178] took the lead in perceiving sexual relations as social relations he failed in making it a concern central to historical materialism.[179] One reason for this neglect was that sexuality was dismissed by earlier Marxists as superstructure since family and marriage that constructed and managed sexuality were part of superstructure. But given the tenaciousness of these forms (family/marriage) provisionally at least the organization of sexuality[180] requires a separate analysis rather than letting the study of sexual dynamics be subsumed in the study of kinship, reproduction, family, household and the like. Furthermore, as Gayle Rubin[181] asserts, there is a need to 'introduce a distinction between an economic system and a sexual system, and to indicate that sexual systems have a certain autonomy and cannot always be explained in terms of economic forces'. The problem with this view, however, as Padgug[182] pointed out, was that it partially accepted the distinction between a sphere of work and a sphere of sexuality. An important attempt to break out of this impasse came from Joan Kelly Godol in her essay 'Doubled Vision of Feminist Theory'[183] where she indicated that economic and gender systems interact to produce social and historical experiences; that neither system was causal, but both operate simultaneously to reproduce the socio-economic and male-dominant structures of a particular social order. Suggesting that gender systems have an independent existence, she nonetheless argued that the relations of the sexes operate in accordance with, and through, socio-economic structures as well as sex/gender ones. Godol introduced the idea of a 'sexually-based social reality', but she tended to emphasize the social rather than the sexual nature of that reality and, most often, 'social' in her usage was conceived in terms of the relations of production.[184]

Recent theorists have been more perceptive in their formulations that elements of class and sexuality do not contradict each other or exist on different planes but produce and reproduce each other's realities in complex ways.[185] In fact, the feminist comprehension that sexuality, class and politics cannot easily be disengaged from one another must serve as the basis of the materialist view of sexuality in the historical perspective as well.[186] Ste. Croix[187] treated women as a class insofar as their labour, both productive and reproductive, was controlled and dominated by men to serve their own ends. Gerda Lerner[188] too pointed out that while class for man is based on his relationship to the means of production, for women class is mediated through sexual ties to a man. We thus see that for women sexual subordination is virtually a constituted element of their gender status under patriarchy.

Sexuality was the linchpin of gender inequality, Catherine Mackinnon[189] argued in her sharply polemical style. She made the most explicit theoretical attempt to subsume sexuality under feminist thought. She wrote, 'sexuality is to feminism what work is to Marxism; that which is most one's own, yet most taken away.'[190] Under patriarchy the organized expropriation of the sexuality of some for the use of others defined the sex woman. Mackinnon asserted that 'heterosexuality is its (patriarchy) structure, gender and family its congealed forms, sex roles its qualities generalised to social persona, reproduction a consequence and control its issue.'[191] Although sexual relations were defined by Mackinnon as social, there is nothing except the inherent inequality of the sexual relations themselves to explain why the system of power operates as it does. The source of unequal relations between the sexes is, in the end, unequal relations between the sexes. Although the inequality, of which sexuality is the source is said to be embodied in a 'whole system of social relationships', how this system works remains unexplained.[192] What is less agreed upon, then, is the extent to which sexuality can be seen as a site of male power distinct from something that patriarchal power acts upon and influences. Social control of women through sexuality was thus the outcome of gendered power inequalities rather than its purpose.

The critique of heterosexuality (as instrumental in the oppression of women) was also at the centre of Adrienne Rich's[193] influential article wherein she implied that heterosexuality is neither natural nor freely chosen but an institution to which one is socialized, even compelled, because without it other institutions like marriage and the family crucial to women's subordination will be difficult to maintain, and without it men will not be able to count on a guaranteed access to women's sexual and reproductive capacities. A lesbian, according to Rich, is one who refuses a man sexual access and lives outside the traditional structure. Her existence, therefore, has to be marginalized or suppressed for it challenges the order not of nature but of patriarchy. Rich even proposed to bring a 'woman-connected existence' that lacked an explicitly sexual component under the rubric of 'lesbian continuum'.

For the feminists, then, under patriarchy sexuality has to be viewed[194] not merely as a matter of personal fulfilment, but as an arena of struggle in which male dominance and women's subordination can either be most powerfully reinforced and maintained, or fundamentally challenged. The radical feminist sexual ideology can be summed up as follows.[195] In patriarchal societies sexuality becomes a tool of male domination through the sexual objectification of women. This is a social mechanism that operates through the institution of masculine and feminine roles in the patriarchal families. The attendant ideology of sexual objectification is sadomasochism, that is, masculinity as sadistic control over women and femininity as submission to the male will. The feminist should therefore reclaim control over female sexuality by developing a notion of sexuality that is more concerned with intimacy rather than performance. Human sexuality should be a form of expression between people that creates bonds and communicates emotions.

The radical feminist view of sexuality came in for criticism from another group of feminist theoreticians who can be called 'libertarian feminists' for they emphasized the theory of pleasure rather than danger. As Carol Vance[196] pointed out, sexuality is simultaneously a domain of restriction, repression, and danger as well as a domain of exploration, pleasure, and agency. To focus only on pleasure and gratification ignores the patriarchal structure in which women act. Yet to speak only of sexual violence and oppression ignores women's experience with sexual agency and choice. The libertarian feminists viewed human sexuality as primarily an exchange of physical, erotic, and genital sexual pleasure. They also valorized any form of sexual relationship between fully consenting and equal partners. But while consensual sexual activity between equals was the operative phrase, the concept of consent was not rigorous enough. It failed to explore hidden power structures that placed women in unequal and hence coercive positions.[197] This group of women scholars went to the extent of saying that feminism as a theory was incapable of analysing sexuality as successfully as it had analysed gender. For feminism, said Rubin,[198] simply lacked an 'angle of vision' which could encompass the social organization of sexuality. She argued that it was essential to separate gender and sexuality analytically to more accurately reflect their separate social existence, for sexuality is not a derivation of gender. Pat Caplan,[199] however, made a forceful case for a cultural construction of sexuality, where she pointed out that sexuality, like gender, was socially constructive. When historians look for ways in which the concept of gender legitimizes and constructs sexual relationships which are social relationships they develop insight into the reciprocal nature of gender and sexuality. The major weakness of both groups of feminist theoreticians, the radicals and the libertarians, was that they were treating historically-developed gender identities as if they were human universals. This brief survey of different theories on gender and sexuality has, it is hoped, placed the empirical data from my literary sources in a sharper focus.

NOTES

1. These goals first emerged in the post-Vedic *Gṛhyasūtra* texts, the *Hiraṇyakeśī Gṛhyasūtra* being the earliest.
2. This is something that Basham (1981: 173) finds worth applauding in Indian civilization, for he writes, 'In this respect ancient India was far healthier than most other ancient cultures'.
3. S.K. De, 1969: 12, 38.

4. Ibid.: 36–7.
5. R.P. Sharma, 1995: 160.
6. Ibid.: 243.
7. Ibid.: 154.
8. Ibid.: 164.
9. As Thadani (1996: 12–13) notes, 'This study is concerned with articulating, inscribing, narrating and theorizing languages of feminine sexuality, cosmogonies and philosophies that have either been deliberately obscured, appropriated, mutilated or consigned to silence and oblivion'.
10. S. Shah, 2007: 20–1.
11. D.D. Kosambi, 1957: xlvi, l.
12. Ibid.: xlvii.
13. Ibid.: xli.
14. S. Bhattacharji, 1993: 13, 161.
15. Ibid.: 133.
16. K.S. Srinivasan, 1985: 42.
17. George L. Hart, in 1969, had made much the same point. The ancient Tamil and Maharashtrian literature, according to him, had a common metrical system, techniques of rhyme, and many themes and conventions.
18. K.S. Srinivasan, 1985: 60.
19. Ibid.: 25, 37.
20. *Āryāsaptaśatī*, 1.52.
21. Romila Thapar, 1966 (rpt. 1981): 256–7.
22. In the 1955 Indian History Congress presidential address, K.M. Pannikar referred to the marked decadence having overtaken Hindu society between the eighth and twelfth centuries. All spheres of culture proclaimed loudly the decay of taste and attitudes. The decadence was directly linked to the manifestation of sensuousness in the society. Thapar uses the term sensuousness more positively, but, neither Pannikar nor Thapar bring a gender perspective to their analysis. Decadence and obscenity lay not in the notion of sensuousness, but perhaps in a voyeuristic delight in the female form as such.
23. S.N. Dasgupta and S.K. De, 1962: 19.
24. That is, a non-sexual love relation between the knights and their socially superior lady.
25. B.N.S. Yadava, 1973: 323.
26. Ibid.: 329.
27. Daud Ali, 2004: 187, 216–18, 237, 257.
28. Devangana Desai, 1975: 152.
29. S. Shah, 2006(b): 204–6.
30. D.N. Jha (ed.), 1987; D.N. Jha (ed.), 2000; B.D. Chattopadhyaya, 1994.
31. Daud Ali, 2004: 22.
32. Ibid.: 264.

33. B.D. Chattopadhyaya, 1994: 35.
34. Sheldon Pollock, 2006: 15; Daud Ali, 2004: 264.
35. In spite of B.D. Chattopadhyaya (2003: 155–6) arguing that the spatial imagination of the first millennium *kāvya* is dominated by the city, and shows no impact of ruralization that is supposed to have accompanied the urban decline.
36. Daud Ali (2000: 169) notes in the context of early-medieval India that the ruling classes no longer comprised primarily of twice-born urbanity. The category of the *nāgaraka* or urban courtier (in the sense that we find in the *Kāmasūtra*)—seems to have as an important social appellation disappeared by this time. However, he is of the view that this disappearance does not so much reflect the decline of cities or urban culture as the emergence of new social contexts which demanded different categories. In fact, Ali (1998: 166) refutes the existence of any binary opposition between a *nāgaraka* or a king in the court, and talks of the close connection that the world of the city-dweller had to that of the king.
37. A.M. Shastri, 1975: 166–7.
38. *Kāmasūtra*, 1.4.2.
39. *Jayamaṅgalā* 1.4.2.
40. Motichandra, 1973: 192.
41. B.P. Mazumdar, 1997: 142–50.
42. Cited in D. Desai, 1975: 115.
43. B.P. Mazumdar, 1997: 146.
44. In fact, Daud Ali (2004: 254) is of the view that there was an almost universal adoption of courtly aristocratic culture within the expanding penumbra of 'good society'.
45. S. Lienhard, 1984: 15–16.
46. Ibid.: 41.
47. *Kāvyamīmāṁsā*, ch. 10, p. 142.
48. Cited in D. Desai, 1975: 148.
49. V.S. Agrawal, 1964: 221–4.
50. B.D. Chattopadhyaya, 1994: 194.
51. B.N.S. Yadava, 1973: 115–17.
52. S.S. Mishra, 1966.
53. Daud Ali (2004: 98–9) points out that the older metaphor of rule as feeding gradually gave way to a wider language of enjoyment (*bhoga*).
54. I.D. Serebryakov, 1972: 185.
55. Yadava, 1973: 117.
56. B.P. Mazumdar (1960: 358) recounts some interesting evidence in this regard.
57. Yadava, 1973: 323–42.
58. D.D. Kosambi, 1957: xlvii.
59. Ibid.: xlvi.

60. Even something as prosaic and an act of piety as the building of a temple is described in highly erotic terms in a Kalacurī king's inscription (*CII*, vol. IV, pt. II, no. 93, verse 25, p. 490).
61. D. Desai, 1975: 152.
62. Dasgupta and De, 1962: LII.
63. *Kāvyaprakāśa*, ch. 1, p. 5.
64. The very routine of the poet visualized by Rājaśekhara in *Kāvyamīmāṁsā* (chapter 10) and Kṣemendra in *Kavikaṇṭhābharaṇa* makes the writing of *kāvya* an elite activity. The stress is on the poet in complete command over 'his time', a leisure which only an elite man could have, one who had no work to do both inside and outside the house.
65. Pollock, 2004: 117–18.
66. Ibid.
67. *Kāvyamīmāṁsā*, ch. 10, p. 132.
68. B.S. Miller and R. Eaton (eds.), 1992: 2.
69. Henning (in M.C. Albrecht, J.H. Barnett and M. Griff, eds., 1982: 356–7) points out that the work of art can be influenced by patronage in at least three ways—by stipulation or direct order of the patron, as for instance Kokkokā's *Ratirahasya*; by attraction, that is the ability of patron groups to attract artists to their point of view by providing economic support and a sympathetic intellectual climate (as, for instance, was true of Bāṇa and Mayūra who were given sustenance by Harṣa of Kannauj, and of Bilhaṇa who was financially supported by the Cālukyas of Kalyāṇa); and by selection, which involves the choosing of the work of art, because writers working for economic and social reward tended to follow the lead of the successful among them. In the case of the later classical Sanskrit writers, one can say that many were tempted to follow a rewarding style and content, particularly the erotic theme.
70. S.K. De, 1969: 17.
71. The growing rigidity of the style also had to do with the increasing standardization fostered by the science of poetics. In fact, poetics converted literature into a *śāstra*. This led to the neglect of content and theme (which could often be threadbare as in Subandhu's *Vāsavadattā*), and engendered a love for customary descriptions (such as moonrise, sunrise, drinking party, water-sport) no matter how digressive they may be, as in *Veṇī-saṁhāra* and *Śiśupālavadha*.
72. S. Bhattacharji (1993: 12, 145) talks of the artificiality which came to dominate literature, particularly the craze for *śleṣa* in literary writings. Bhaṭṭī in his seventh-century *Rāvaṇavadha* says that the book 'is like a lamp to those who have an eye for words; those without knowledge of grammar will grope with their hands like the blind. This poem can only be understood with the help of annotations, it is a feast for the learned. I have slaughtered the stupid in it because of my fondness for learning.' Poetry was a peg on which grammar, rhetoric and prosody were hung.

73. D.D. Kosambi, 1957: lxi.
74. Jayadeva's *Gītagovinda* is virtually an exception, in that it transcends its class base to appeal to a wider and popular audience.
75. Lienhard, 1984: 17.
76. In *Vikramāṅkadevacarita* (1.26-7) Bilhaṇa asks how a king who does not have a good poet with him can become famous.
77. *Kāvyaprakāśa*, ch. 1, p. 5.
78. *SRK*, section 32, 41, 46.
79. Bāṇa in *Harṣacarita*, says that all courtly service is hateful and the court itself is full of dangers. When he meets with Harṣa's disapproval at the very first meeting he can only plead with the king and appeal to his wisdom.
80. *SM*, 434.16.
81. *Śatakatrayam*, verse 166.
82. S.K. De, 1969: 17.
83. A.K. Warder, vol. 3, 1990: 2.
84. S. Pollock, 1996: 197–8.
85. K.K. Handiqui (1949: 21-2, 33); *Vikramāṅkadevacarita*, 1.115; *Rājataraṅgiṇī*, 1.58 and 2.8.
86. *CII*, vol. IV, pt. 1, no. 45, verse 24, p. 218.
EI, vol. IV, no. 40, verse 33, p. 289.
EI, vol. XVIII, no. 26, verse 10, p. 252.
South Indian Inscriptions, vol. III, pt. 3, no. 205, verse 45, p. 418.
87. *Mayūraśataka*, p. 234.
88. Cited in D. Desai, 1975: 165.
89. Cited in B.N.S. Yadava, 1973: 114.
90. Daud Ali, 2004: 240.
91. Handiqui, 1949: 100.
92. *CII*, vol. IV, pt. I, no. 24, line 20, p. 108.
93. *CII*, vol. IV, pt. I, no. 44, verse 10, p. 203.
94. *CII*, vol. IV, pt. I, no. 48, verse 11, pp. 246–7.
95. *CII*, vol. IV, pt. I, no. 31, line 18, p. 152; no. 16, line 23, p. 65.
96. *CII*, vol. IV, pt. I, no. 16, line 20, p. 64.
97. *Nāṭyaśāstra*, 34.2,16.
98. *Sāhityadarpaṇa*, ch. 3, p. 162.
99. *Mṛcchakaṭika*, *Ratnāvalī*, *Priyadarśikā*.
100. *Haravijaya*, *Jānakīharaṇa* (*mahākāvya*); *Amaruśataka*, *Āryāsaptaśatī* (*muktaka*).
101. *Vāsavadattā*, *Kādambarī*.
102. *Vikaramāṅkadevacarita*.
103. *Ratirahasya*, *Nāgarasarvasvam*.
104. Cited in A.K. Warder, vol 1, 1989: 189.
105. *Kāvyādarśa*, 1.16–17.
106. Cited in S.K. De, 1969: 17.
107. S. Lienhard, 1984: 73–4.

108. With the exception of Bhavabhūti who talks in terms of the primacy of *karuṇarasa* (*Uttararāmacarita*, Act 3.47), and Viśvanātha who in *Sāhityadarpaṇa* (ch. 3, p. 106) talks of the importance of *adbhuta rasa*, virtually the entire range of theoreticians from Bharata to Bhoja talk of the primacy of *śṛṅgāra rasa*. Furthermore, *kāma* in the sense of *rati* (sexual love between men and women) is the defining feature of this *śṛṅgāra rasa*. As Raghavan (Bhoja's *Śṛṅgāraprakāśa*, p. 476) points out, in the 36 chapters of *Śṛṅgāraprakāśa*, 19 deal with *ratiśṛṅgāra*. In chapter 22 of *Śṛṅgāraprakāśa* Bhoja talks of *dharma*, *artha*, and *kāma* as the three *puruṣārtha* sought after by all men as householders. Of these, *dharma* and *artha* are the means and *kāma* is the end, with the last being the most important. In his *Daśarūpakam* (ch. 3, p. 234) Dhanañjaya, declares that one sentiment, either heroic (*vīra*) or erotic (*śṛṅgāra*), is to be made the principal one, all others should be subordinate. But even among these two sentiments, the latter is considered predominant. Dhanañjáya devotes 23 verses to the importance of erotic sentiments and only one verse each to the other sentiments. The side-tracking of *vīra* by *śṛṅgāra* is particularly clear in Māgha's *mahākāvya Śiśupālavadha*.
109. V.M. Kulkarni, 1993: 169.
110. V. Raghavȧn, 1940: 144–6.
111. *Gāthāsattasaī*, 3.38.
112. Daud Ali, 2004: 67–8.
113. Cited in K. Krishnamoorthy, 1964: 125–6.
114. The Indian cultural tradition, whether the *Kāmasūtra* or the Jain philosophical treatises, does not reject the possibility of a person being sexually aroused even by an animal (Vanita and Kidwai, 2001: 25).
115. Perhaps for this reason, in classical Sanskrit literature we do not find fairy tales of the European kind, like Beauty and the Beast, Frog Prince or The Little Mermaid (even though they do exist in the folk tales). Critic Śāradātanaya says that a repulsive person's love would get categorized as *vībhatsa rasa* and would not be *śṛṅgāra* at all (cited in Krishnamoorthy, 1964: 130).
116. K.S. Srinivasan, 1985: 25, 37.
117. R.P. Poddar, 1974: 36, fn. 2.
118. The philosophy of love as elaborated in *Karpūramañjarī* is that of love as grossly physical passion, and it is a philosophy which is under the influence of tantric *kaula*. The *kaulācārya* Bhairavānanda (Act 1.21–3) valorizes sexual union. It is also important to remember that tantricism as a philosophy had always been more respectful of women.
119. Cited in V.M. Kulkarni, 1993: 154.
120. In fact, the description of women's poetry has some merit. German scholar Will Brandt noted that in *Gāthāsattasaī* verses 'feelings that are most tender and most sensuous are often frankly expressed; the tender feelings dominate. It is not a man who often speaks but it is a female voice that we

hear more and more; the women who speak are old, young, friend, mother, daughter and aunt. They speak to young men and girls who are in love, to other girls or to their own selves. They probably talk about so many things, yet the theme of the talk is always love' (cited in M. Winternitz, vol. 3, pt. 1, 1963: 109).

121. *Gāthāsattasaī*, 1.2.
122. *Āryāsaptaśatī*, 1.52.
123. Govardhana wrote in the *Āryā* metre, which was unquestionably borrowed by Sanskrit from Prakrit (A.B. Keith, 1920: 202).
124. *Kāvyaprakāśa*, ch. 1, p. 5.
125. *Kāvyādarśa*, 1.62–4.
126. Krishnamoorthy, 1964: 130.
127. For instance, love that courted apathy, such as Rāvaṇa's outpouring of love for Sītā.
128. D.H. Ingalls, tr. of *SRK*, 1965: 198–9.
129. Cited in J. Brough, 1968: 40–1.
130. S.K. De, 1969: 16.
131. Monier-Williams, 1994: 922, col. 3.
132. *SM*, 26.59.
133. Ibid., 239.2.
134. Ibid., 228.16.
135. *Saduktikarṇāmṛta*, verse 2039.
136. Ibid., verse 367.
137. Although it has not been possible to make a statistical analysis of the *upameya* in the vast corpus of Sanskrit texts, it would seem that a woman's breasts are the most common of the *upameya*, and a woman's heavy smooth thighs and tiny waist come a close second.
138. *Kāvyamīmāṁsā*, ch. 3, p. 20.
139. Warder, vol. IV, 1983: 427–8.
140. *Kāvyamīmāṁsā*, ch. 10, p. 142.
141. Pollock, 2006: 84–5.
142. *Kāvyaprakāśa*, ch. 1, p. 12.
143. *SM*, 47.91.
144. Ibid., 47.93.
145. Both the *pāñcālī rīti* and *vaidarbhī rīti* are styles of Sanskrit poetry that are specific arrangements of words and the cause of charm in the poetry (Keith 1920: 381).
146. Cited in Krishnamchariar, 1970: 391.
147. *SM*, 47.94–5.
148. *Kāvyamīmāṁsā*, ch. 10, p. 138.
149. Ibid.
150. Although Rājaśekhara in *Kāvyamīmāṁsā* (ch. 10, p. 131) talks of the need for women of the inner quarters (*antaḥpurikā*) to be well-versed (*bhāṣāvid*)

in both Sanskrit and Prakrit languages, this is not reflected in the literary output that we get.

151. *Nāṭyaśāstra*, 15.5–6; 18.39–46.
152. Raghavan, 1934–5: 64.
153. *SM*, 47.96.
154. Raghavan, 1934–5: 55–6.
155. Ibid.: 54.
156. *Śṛṅgāraprakāsā*, p. 833.
157. *SM*, 47.92.
158. *Śṛṅgāraprakāśa*, pp. 833–4.
159. M. Winternitz, 1963: 225, n. 2.
160. Indu Shekhar, 1960: 115.
161. *Kāvyālaṁkārasūtra*, 3.2.4.
162. S.K. De, 1960: 78–9.
163. P.V. Kane, 1961: 146–7.
164. Cited in I. Shekhar, 1960: 118.
165. Cited in M. Winternitz, 1963; 225, n. 2.
166. Manomohan Ghosh, 1958: 44.
167. Robert Padgug, 1979: 12.
168. Maurice Godelier, 1981: 17.
169. Halperin, Zietlin and Winkler (eds.), 1990: 3.
170. David Halperin, 1989: 257.
171. J. Weeks, 1981: 1.
172. Ibid.: 2-3.
173. J.H. Gagnon and W. Simon, 1973: 26.
174. Feminist criticism of Gagnon and Simon, who rely on socialization as an explanation of male sexuality, is that it lacks the concept of power. They fail to explain where these 'sexual scripts' come from, why they differ for men and women, why they take the form they do, and what functions this may serve.
175. Cited in Padgug, 1979: 10.
176. M. Foucault, 1978, 1985 and 1986.
177. J. Weeks, 1981: 3.
178. F. Engels, 1948.
179. R. Padgug, 1979: 5.
180. R. Coward, 1983.
181. G. Rubin, 1975: 167.
182. R. Padgug, 1979: 15.
183. Joan Kelly Godol, 1979: 216–27.
184. J.W. Scott, 1988: 35.
185. R. Padgug, 1979: 16.
186. Ibid.: 5–6.
187. Ste. Croix, 1981: 100.

188. G. Lerner, 1986: 9, 100.
189. C. Mackinnon, 1982: 533.
190. Ibid.: 515.
191. Ibid.: 515–16.
192. J.W. Scott, 1988: 34.
193. A. Rich, 1980: 631–60.
194. With what R. Coward (1983: 1–2) calls an 'informed gaze', a gaze that arises from the politics of feminism that illumine the social position of women.
195. Ann Ferguson et al., 1984: 106–35.
196. Carol Vance (ed.), 1984: 1.
197. Ann Ferguson, 1984: 110.
198. Gayle Rubin, 1984: 307–9.
199. Pat Caplan (ed.), 1987: 10.

1

The Philosophy of *Kāma*

The philosophical ideas of a given culture are a significant medium through which sexual behaviour is represented. In fact, as Simon[1] argues quite pertinently, 'all discourses of sexuality are inherently discourses about something else; sexuality rather than serving as a continuous thread that unifies the totality of human experience, is the ultimate dependent variable requiring explanation more often than it provides explanation.' When we use the term sexuality we are not referring to the sexual act by itself but to the attitudes, values, and beliefs as also behaviours that may be seen to have sexual significance in society. All societies prescribe and codify sexual activity and thereby legitimize some sexual practices and not others. While in all cultures this codification of sexuality has been linked to gender, the nature of the link between gender and sexuality is by no means universal. From this starting point it becomes possible to establish the rationale for theorizing about various philosophical ideas that provide the framework in which female sexuality may be better understood.

This chapter will analyse the philosophy of the *dharmaśāstra* insofar as it had a role to play in regulating erotic life by laying down ideal norms. More importantly, going beyond the ethical concerns of the *dharmaśāstra*, it analyses the problematization of *kāma* (that is, the *trivarga* debate) within not just the *dharmaśāstra* but the ayurvedic and *kāmaśāstra* discourses as well. Another important philosophical strand within the Indian tradition which was inextricably linked with the *kāma* tradition was the ascetic discourse (*vairāgya*). We shall examine how this discourse had no autonomy of existence and can be understood only within the context of *kāma* (and its linkages to the women). The Cārvāka or Lokāyata philosophy and the tantric philosophies were the other systems in which an analysis of *kāma* played an important role. Last, we shall deal with the cult of Kāmadeva, presiding deity of erotic literature, where he is constantly invoked as an icon/symbol of libidinal freedom.

Sexuality is learned and in a societal context. Sexuality is thus neither natural nor wholly individualistic but a societal outcome. The *Kāmasūtra*[2] tells us that women, unlike the female of other species, do not have a specific mating season; consequently union between the sexes is governed by considerations that need to be regulated. Thus, human sexuality even in ancient texts was never viewed as rooted in the natural order. And if sexuality is a social construct, it is only to be expected that society will expend its intellectual energy on theorizing about it. Let us, therefore, examine the notion of *kāma* as it was debated in the *trivarga* debate.

Since very ancient times, *kāma* or desire has had legitimacy in the Indian tradition. In the *Ṛgveda*[3] it is crucially linked to the very process of creation. The text tells us that at first there was a complete void and indiscriminate chaos and thereafter arose desire, *kāma* or the primal seed and germ of spirit. In fact, in early primitive societies sexuality and procreation were ideas which were never conceptually distinguished. The emphasis on procreation also necessarily led to a heterosexual concept of *kāma*. Vedic literature is replete with the heterosexual pairing (*mithuna*) in the description of sacrificial rituals. At the same time heterosexual relationships were increasingly construed as one of superordination and subordination for men and women, respectively.[4] The *dharmaśāstra* as a continuation of this ideology also conceived of *kāma* in these terms. Nevertheless, there was by now a move towards conceptually distinguishing *kāma* from *artha* and *dharma* (subsuming *mokṣa* in itself) and the latter was the sole concern of the *dharmaśāstra*. The three *puruṣārtha* were now three different goals of human life, hierarchically positioned.

For the *dharmaśāstra* writers[5] there was a definite gradation of value with regard to *trivarga*. This hierarchy was something that was established in the epics themselves. The *Mahābhārata*[6] states that 'a wise man tries to secure all three but if all three cannot be attained he secures *dharma* or *artha* or only *dharma* if he has a choice of only one'. The *Śāntiparvan* of the *Mahābhārata*[7] says that '*dharma* is the best, *artha* is the middling and *kāma* is the lowest and the man should so act that *dharma* would be the principal goal of his life'.

The *Rāmāyaṇa*[8] too regards *dharma* as the highest of the *trivarga*. Echoing this philosophy, Manu[9] states and Medhātithi agrees that what is best (*śreyas*) is the triad as a whole. Nonetheless, while striving for all three, says Manu,[10] if *artha* or *kāma* are in conflict with *dharma*, one should give up the former two. Commenting on this Medhātithi[11] says that Manu emphasizes the greater importance of righteousness or *dharma*.

Interestingly, the non-*dharmaśāstrīya* tradition as well, such as the *Kāmasūtra* and *Arthaśāstra*, in spite of the inherent valorization of *kāma* and *artha*, could not remain completely unaffected by the hegemonic position of the *dharma puruṣārtha*. Although Yaśodhara[12] in the very beginning of his *Jayamaṅgalā* commentary is of the view that since *dharma* and *artha* are the means (*hetu*) for the realization of *kāma*, which is the fruit (*phalabhūta*) of *dharma* and *artha*, therefore *kāma* is truly the chief (*param*) *puruṣārtha*. Nonetheless, he echoes that out of *dharma*, *artha* and *kāma* each preceding one is superior to each following one.[13] At yet another place[14] the usual *dharmaśāstrīya* refrain on the primacy of *dharma* is echoed and men warned against disaster resulting from the undue pursuit of *kāma*. Nonetheless, the *kamaśāstrīya* texts differ from the *dharmaśāstra* in conceptualizing *kāma* in many crucial ways. In the *Jayamaṅgalā* commentary[15] *kāma* is understood to be basic to human existence, comparable to food. This analogy with food is significant for, unlike Vedic literature and the *dharmaśāstra* which talk of *kāma* only in the context of procreation (which is crucial for the perpetuation of the specie), here the emphasis is on the physicality of sexual love (and in this sense on the individual rather than society). As Yaśodhara[16] explains, if one desists from realizing one's desire, the force of increasing desire (*rāga*) would lead to a state of frenzy (*unmāda*), endangering the body. Further, in contrast to the prescriptive texts like the *dharmaśāstra*, what is unique about the *Kāmasūtra*[17] is that its several injunctions are rarely backed up by suggesting rewards for conforming to, or punishments for violating, norms. Thus, provisions for enforcing norms are not explicitly laid down. Kauṭilya in his *Arthaśāstra*[18] says about the *trivarga* debate that in his opinion *artha* is the principal of the three *puruṣārtha*, as *dharma* and *kāma* both spring from *artha*. However, it must be remembered that this was being stated about a king.[19]

The *trivarga* debate was carried on in the ayurvedic discourse as well. In the *Carakasaṁhitā*[20] it was said that a sound mind and body (*ārogya*) were a pre-requisite for the attainment of the *puruṣārtha*. Given the fact that the focus of these texts was the science of life, it was only logical that in *Carakasaṁhitā*[21] the order of life's goals be reversed, with the desire for life (*prāṇeṣṇā*)[22] coming before the desire for wealth (*dhaneṣṇā*) and the desire for the other world (*paralokeṣṇeti*)[23] positioned at the end. Caraka gives reasons for the reversal of the order. He says[24] that 'out of all these desires one should follow the desire to live first. Why (*kasmāta*)? Because with the departure of life, everything departs. So one should maintain life by observing the code of conduct for the healthy, and be careful in alleviating disorders'. He also notes[25] that one should later pursue the desire for wealth. Next to life, it is wealth which should be sought. There is nothing more sinful than to have a long life without a means of sustenance. Caraka[26] then goes on to talk of the pursuit of the third desire, for the other world. He is well aware of the atheistic (*nāstika*) philosophy which dismisses the existence of the world beyond. For whatever is beyond the perception of the sense organs (*indriya*) is dismissed by the *nāstika*, but Caraka advises that a wise person should give up such a negative approach for the scope of perception is limited while that of the imperceptible is large and known by scriptures, by inference, and by reasoning. Moreover, the sense organs which are instruments of perceptions are themselves imperceptible. Caraka bemoans the fact that for the *nāstika* whose consciousness has been injured by accepting the theory of chance, there is no examination or one to be examined, there is also no doer, cause, god, sage, accomplished action, result of action, or self. Such negative beliefs (of the atheists) are the worst of sins (*pātakam*).

This remarkable reversal of the order of *puruṣārtha* by Caraka and his subsequent defence of the orthodox stand *vis-à-vis nāstika* (Lokāyata) can be better understood if we take into consideration the fact, as argued by Chattopadhyaya,[27] that the classical medical treatises of Caraka and Suśruta result from a grafting process whereby orthodox brahmanical ideas are superimposed on to a medical framework. As Zysk[28] too argues, 'what was fundamentally a heterodox body of knowledge was later rendered orthodox'. It was perhaps this brahminization of an initially heterodox tradition that resulted in the forced ascription[29] of an important advisory role to brahmin men well-versed in the *Atharvaveda* (*brāhmaṇaścatha-rvavedavido*) in child-birth, even though it was a practice that was located within the domain of female knowledge. In the *Caraka Saṁhitā*[30] there is an interesting description of the labour-room (*sautikagṛha*) where, as against a cursory precipitate reference to a knowledgeable brahmin, there is a detailed account of the number of experienced women (*bahuśaprajātaḥ*) who are involved in delivering the child. They are said to be solicitous (*sauhādryuktaḥ satatamanuraktā*), skilled (*pradakṣiṇācāraḥ*), with presence of mind (*pratipattikuśalaḥ*), and capable of tireless work (*kleśasahinyo-bhimataḥ*). Caraka also counsels that the advice of elderly women (*strīyścavṛdhāḥ*) be sought.

Thus we see that the *trivarga* debate was carried on in many different discourses, most of them part of a corpus of prescriptive literature within their respective fields. Narrative literature in our period also refers to this debate and this brings us closer to what men actually thought of the different goals of human life which tradition had prescribed for them. Perhaps it would not be wrong to say that ambivalence (regarding the three *puruṣārtha*) rather than a dogmatic stand on any one ideal characterized the evidence gleaned from the narrative literature. In Buddhasvāmin's *Bṛhatkathāśloka-saṁgraha*[31] it is asked: 'Who can be a greater sinner than he who rejects happiness which is the fruit of religious and worldly goods? How can a person who sacrifices the pleasures of this life (*tyakta-dṛṣṭasukha*) to attain happiness in the next life (*janmāntara-sukhaprāptye*) be called a wise one?' In another place in the same text[32] it is said that the absolute freedom of the soul, whether having a physical form or otherwise, from pleasures and passions (*sukharāga*) has been called final deliverance (*nirvāṇa*) by *Īśvara*. Throughout the *Śatakatrayam* Bhartṛhari considers the relative merits of life's alternatives: submission to passion (*kāma*), worldly success (*artha*), learning and virtue (*dharma*), and preparing in the forest for final release (*mokṣa*). All are separately commended, but finally all are deemed deficient. Desire for women and wealth breed anxiety, virtue, and wisdom are rare and of little avail either in the world or in the forest. Even the state of tranquillity so arduously won is threatened by sensuous beauty. In his confusion Bhartṛhari[33] thus oscillates between one extreme and the other realizing full well that none of life's possibilities are what they seem to be. This is what gives an edge to his tremendously evocative poetry.[34] In the story of *Siṁhāsanadvātrinśikā*[35] an ascetic is assailed by similar doubts, but unlike Bhartṛhari he is able to resolve them. Realizing the absence of pleasure in his life, the ascetic reflects that 'it is a fool's idea that joys that come to men from association with objects of the senses must be avoided because pain is connected with them', for 'who, pray, that has his own interest at heart would throw away rice, rich with fine white kernels, just because it is mixed with some particles of husk?' He therefore declares that 'the best thing of all is a gazelle-eyed woman'.

THE *DHARMAŚĀSTRĪYA* NOTION OF *KĀMA*

Laws have traditionally been intimately anociated with the practise of Eros. This brings us to the question as to why sexuality is an area of concern for the laying down of norms? The answer can be found in the words of Foucault:[36] 'sex was a means of access both to the life of the body and the life of the specie'; as a result, sex became a crucial target of power organized around the management of life.

Shastric texts such as the *dharmaśāstra* are storehouses of ethics dealing with a series of interdictions regarding human sexuality. By the seventh century the creative period of Indian law was over. What we have in our period of study are several commentaries and digests on the earlier *dharmaśāstra*, the most significant being Medhātithi's commentary *Manubhāṣya* on *Manusmṛti* written in the ninth century, and Vijñāneśvara's commentary, *Mitākṣarā,* on the *Yajñāvalkyasmṛti* composed in about the eleventh century. Important law digests of this period are *Kṛtyākalpataru* of Lakṣmīdhara (twelfth century) and *Smṛticandrikā* of Devannabhaṭṭa (early thirteenth century). What is evident from even a cursory glance at the *dharmaśāstra* material at our disposal is the diversity of opinions and interpretations. It also has a long chronological span and regional diversity (Gautama was from the north; Medhātithi from Kashmir; Baudhāyana, Āpastamba, Devannabhaṭṭa and Vijñaneśvara are generally placed in the south). Furthermore, the way every commentator uses his commentary to explain the original text itself has a historical rationale.[37] Given this reality it is not possible to postulate a unitary view of sexuality contained in these *dharmaśāstra*. I shall therefore draw only some conclusions about the shastric laws in general from a sociological and gender perspective, to arrive at the impact they may have had on the nature of female sexuality, for many women did live their lives circumscribed by shastric precepts. What one is attempting here is really to outline the shastric ideas that may have evolved over centuries. Many of them were accepted, some discarded, others reworked before being accepted. And this itself was a constant process. For instance, we have seven commentaries for just one text of *Manusmṛti*. Given the enormity of the task, I do not attempt an analysis of these ideas in either chronological or spatial context. Besides, there is a limitation in subjecting these texts to any rigorous chronological and spatial analysis, for they are the products of a patriarchal brahmanical world-view which often transcended the particularities of its setting. The early law makers as well as their commentators and their compilers remained in many ways the inheritors and disseminators of a fairly cohesive tradition (that is why we talk of a *dharmaśāstra* discourse). There is, therefore, a need to recognize and understand the complex link between an evolving society and its enduring patriarchal psychic structures.

The *dharmaśāstras* dominated by the householders' code of the reproduction of the people at its core, were given to glorifying the status of the *gṛhastha*[38] and pushing to the background the *āśrama* of *vānaprastha* and *sanyāsa*.[39] Certain *dharmaśāstra* even state that the latter *āśramas* are forbidden in the *kali* age. Manu[40] makes it clear that *gṛhasthāśrama* should not be passed over, but Medhātithi[41] qualifies this by stating that this injunction is deprecatory and not prohibitive. Views that valorised householders' lives also did not regard marriage and sexual life as impure or inferior to asceticism.[42] However, in Medhātithi's commentary[43] we notice a more ambivalent position. Like Manu, he too supported the *samuccaya* theory of *āśramas* (that is, one should resort to the *āśramas* one after another, not omitting any one) but he was not unreservedly laudatory of the *gṛhasthāśrama*. In analysing Manu's phrase that 'the *gṛhastha* is the best of all', Medhātithi says that the superiority belongs to the state itself and not to the man. Medhātithi's ambivalence regarding the householder stage was perhaps due to historical reasons.[44]

The *dharmaśāstrīya* laws were concerned with laying down norms for regulating society and not with its pleasures. Hence, in the man–woman sexual relationship it was the procreative and not the erotic angle that was the focus. In fact, the erotic was subordinated to the procreative. Cohabitation was a duty enjoined upon both men and women and there were penalties if that did not happen. It was men's duty to see that women's *ṛtu* was not wasted.[45] The centrality of procreation in the *dharmaśāstra* left a deep imprint on the conception of a sexual love that did not bring forth progeny or did not have procreation as its aim. Such love was deplored—*śocyam maithunam aprajām* in the *Mahābhārata*.[46] There was a gender implication of this *dharmaśāstrīya* norm as well. The patriarchal normative tradition[47] justified man taking another wife if his first one could not give him children particularly sons.[48] This practice of abandoning the spouse was not extended to women. It is true that Manu[49] states and Medhātithi[50] agrees that a wife is not to blame if she shows an aversion to a husband who is impotent (*klībaṁbījam*). *Nāradasmṛti*[51] allows a woman to desert her husband if he is impotent and sexually unite with another. But since the trend in the *dharmaśāstra* tradition is to disallow the remarriage of women[52] the medieval commentators and digests tend to interpret such practices as forbidden in the present kali age. The testimony of Kṣemendra[53] shows that the prohibition of remarriage began to be extended to child widows also. Devannabhaṭṭa in *Smṛticandrikā*[54] stated that texts sanctioning remarriage in such cases had no applicability in his age.

The notion of sex that was driven for the reproduction of the species had heterosexual coitus as the ideal form of sexual experience. Any deviance in the form of homosexuality (tellingly referred to as *klībya*, impotence) and lesbianism earned the ire of the *dharmaśāstra* writers. According to Manu,[55] one who unites in sexual union with a man loses his caste. Medhātithi[56] agrees: such a man should perform atonement for this sin. As for lesbian lovers, Manu[57] says that if the offender is a maiden she can get away with a lighter punishment (of lashes) without her crime being publicized. But if she is a mature woman, her guilt is to be publicly proclaimed and she is to be paraded on a donkey. Perhaps this was because a more mature and active partner was seen as directly threatening the patriarchal family and the conjugal rights of men. Medhātithi,[58] however, notes that there being no authority for such a view (punishment), it should be ignored. Referring to lesbian relations, the *Arthaśāstra*,[59] says that if the mature woman seduces a willing maiden both will be liable to a fine, the former paying twofold. But if the maiden was unwilling only the mature woman would be fined a hundred *paṇa* and a dowry for the girl. Yet again, it was the *śāstrīya* obsession with procreative sexuality which resulted in nearly all *dharmaśāstra* writers unanimously branding a *rajasvalā* (menstruating) woman as inauspicious and declaring that a man who sexually united with such a woman was guilty of grave sin. Leslie[60] says that since a menstruating woman was temporarily barren, for the *dharmaśāstra* writers the extreme inauspiciousness of infertility resided in her and this explains the revulsion.

Another point which comes through from the reading of the shastric laws is that the control mechanism operated at two levels. First, at an ideological level female sexual prowess was greatly exaggerated. Women were projected as possessed of insatiable and threatening in-born sexuality. In other words, they were predatory nymphomaniacs. Manu[61] said, and Medhātithi[62] confirmed, that this was women's inherent nature; they were wanton (*pramadā*). Given this *strīsvabhāva*, women were dangerous and therefore to be controlled and defended against. Yet, at another level women were depicted as *abalā*, forever needing the protection of the males in the family, father, husband, or son and under whose tutelage, says Manu,[63] they had to remain all the time. Medhātithi[64] says that women must always be guarded even when they are dependent. Here we notice the juvenilization of woman; she was forever a ward. Her autonomy, particularly her sexual autonomy, was non-existent. A woman could not exist in this setup as a woman but only as a 'type'. The *dharmaśāstra* talk of two types of women. The first was the *pativratā* who was chaste in thought, word and deed. As Manu[65] says, 'she alone is *sādhvī*'. This *pativratā* ideology with the weight of cultural force behind it was quite powerful in its insidious omnipotence. The second type of woman, described at length in the *Nāradasmṛti*,[66] was the *svairiṇī/bandhakī*: loose, promiscuous woman. Medhātithi[67] describes the term inconstant (*anavastithā*) as that woman who behaving like prostitute has intercourse with many men.

A patriarchal brahmanical society concerned with the purity of the patrilineage and caste was bound to treat adultery as a sin. Thus, we find that the *dharmaśāstrīya* writers were obsessively concerned with the upper-caste women's sexuality, be it a wife or a widow. Within brahmanical patriarchy a widow was enjoined to be patient of hardships, self-controlled and chaste.[68] Some later *dharmaśāstra* authorities were even more explicit in laying down norms for a widow's existence. Vṛddhaharita[69] states that she should 'give up chewing betel nut, wearing perfume, flowers, ornaments and dyed clothes, taking food from a vessel of bronze, taking two meals a day, and applying collyrium to the eyes; she should wear only a white garment, curb her senses and anger, and sleep on the ground.' The *dharmaśāstra* advocated a living *satī* who became an ascetic within the home.[70] Once the husband had died, the wife's sexuality, which in marriage had served familial and social goals, was of no use to the patrilocal household. Even more than the unmarried menstruating girl or nubile wife whose husband was away, the widow, says Chakravarty,[71] was the object of moral panic. While the sexuality of the former categories could be held in abeyance, the sexuality of the widow could not be similarly treated. She thus had to be completely unsexed. Although a widow was permitted procreation for the continuation of the patrilineage in an earlier period, the trend of the later *dharmaśāstrīya*[72] writers was to prohibit the practice of *niyoga*, particularly for the *dvija* caste. Medhātithi,[73] for instance, permits *niyoga* only if the widow undertook it under the instruction of elders of the husband's family. Furthermore, while Medhātithi[74] is not completely dismissive of a girl who is born of *niyoga* (*niyogotpanna*), at the same time he takes the view that one should not voluntarily marry such a girl. On the other hand a widow as a *punarbhū* is an accepted *nāyikā* within non-*dharmaśāstrīya* texts. Yaśodhara[75] talks about her, as does Bhoja in his treatise on Sanskrit poetics. In his *Śṛṅgāraprakāśa*[76] Bhoja enumerates four types of *punarbhū nāyīka*, viz., *kṣata*, *akṣata*, *yātāyāta*, and *yāyāvara*.

Medhātithi[77] says that a man who guards his wife well will be able to keep his progeny pure, his family free of blemish or ill-fame, his own self-protected (no paramour of the wife to murder him) and his religion too would be protected. Vijñāneśvara in his *Mitākṣarā* commentary on *Yājñavalkya Smṛti* also takes the view that an unchaste wife was not entitled to perform religious rites.[78] But it was the sin of the wife and her paramour which was the focus of the *dharmaśāstra* writers.[79]

The *dharmaśāstrīya* texts are conceptually incapable of discussing the adultery of the husband from the point of view of the wife. While most writers[80] take up the issue of adultery (*strīsaṁgrahaṇa*), they do not hold a unanimous view. Some prescribe harsher punitive measures against male adulterers (keeping the *varṇa* distinction in mind) than against women. They also make a distinction between mental and physical adultery, as also between rape and a wilful adulterous union.[81] Some writers hold that though woman transgresses, her menstruation is the mark of an all-encompassing purity unique to woman. As Leslie[82] points out, 'at no time are they defiled, for menstruation sweeps away their sins month after month'. It was essentially woman's procreative role which was at the root of many *dharmaśāstra* writers taking a lenient view of female adultery. Manu[83] views the *strī* as a possession that could be re-claimed by her original owner after being enjoyed by another. Medhātithi[84] refers to this *strī* as either a wife or a slave-girl, and if she remains in possession of someone else for ten years, then the husband's/master's right over her lapses. The *Yājñavalkya Smṛti* says that an adulterous woman should be abandoned only if she conceives, and Aparāraka in his commentary agrees.[85]

In brahmanical society there was also a caste connotation to female sexuality. Although ideally *dharmaśāstra* writers wanted a same-caste union and *varṇasaṁkara* (the progeny of miscegenation) was anathema to them, in practical life the *dharmaśāstra* accommodated *anuloma* (hypergamous) unions. They were, however, vehemently opposed to *pratiloma* (hypogamous) unions, where low-caste men sexually united with higher caste women.[86] This was because caste status was perceived as being contingent on the purity of the women in brahmanical patriarchy.[87] Yet another theoretical formulation on the control of female sexuality in a class/caste-based society is advanced by Sherry Ortner,[88] who argues that emphasis on female purity has to be seen in the context of the practice of hypergamy (vertical alliance system) within a stratified society. It is not so much that women maintained the kin group's actual status that they were controlled, but because women, in a stratified society, were oriented upwards and, therefore, represented the 'ideal' higher status of the group. For this reason, notions of virginity and chastity (proof of woman's worthiness for a hypergamous alliance) were particularly apt to symbolize her exclusiveness and status.[89] Manu[90] recognized both the *anuloma* and *pratiloma* forms as forms of *varṇasaṁkara*. His commentator Medhātithi,[91] even while waxing eloquent on the danger of inter-*varṇa* union, defines *varṇasaṁkara* only in the context of *pratiloma* union. Sociologically speaking, the *pratiloma* union was more of a taboo, says Kamla Ganesh,[92] because it ran contrary to the social arrangements that were based on patrilineal descent, patrilocality, and male authority. In a *pratiloma* marriage the wife could not live with her parents since her children were of a lower ritual status. She could move into the husband's patrilineage, but as a member of a superior caste she would upset the hierarchy of domestic relations based on male dominance and female subordination. Since both inter-sex and inter-caste relations were equally hierarchized and expressed in a similar language of subordination, a direct conflict between the two was avoided by banning *pratiloma*. Interestingly, a system with negative implications for the sexuality of elite women[93] had a positive one for the women of lower castes. Śūdra women always had a greater sexual autonomy, for the risk of pollution through defilement was not present. And since it is reasonable to surmise that the śūdras far outnumbered brāhmaṇas, relatively independent women were also more numerous. However, the notion of independent śūdra women needs to be qualified. While such women were free in the context of their family, they were unfree as they were sexually violated at will by upper caste/class men.[94] Men of higher caste control the sexuality of their own women, while at the same time denying the low caste men this right. This was done because low caste women's participation was required in production and they were also required to reproduce more workers.[95] Seen in this material context, the so-called sexual freedom of śūdra women cannot be overly valorized.

In spite of the *dharmaśāstra* essentially presenting a picture of a patriarchal society, we can discover spaces or niches within these shastric traditions where either patriarchy was not functional at all or was greatly diluted. Thus, we find eight forms of marriage listed in the *dharmaśāstra*.[96] The more acceptable forms of marriage (*brahma, daiva, ārṣa* and *prājāpatya*) were those in which men's (father's/husband's) *svāmya* or authority over women was established. The other four forms (*rākṣasa, asura, paiśāca* and *gāndharva*) were not excluded by the law makers and these were relatively non-patriarchal forms of marriage, where property rights and consent agency all point towards greater if not absolute control by women and their kin.[97]

The shastras also note the presence of a variety of sons:[98] *aurasa* (one's own), *dattaka* (adopted) and *kṣetraja* (in one's territory) sons were desirable and high in the hierarchy with patrilineal property devolving to them; others like *kānīna* (son of a maiden), *sahoḍha* (son of a pregnant bride) and *paunarbhava* (son of a twice-married woman) were all accepted as part of a family (*bāndhava*). The very manner of the birth of these sons allows a lenient view of female sexuality within patriarchal society. It also leads us to believe that in spite of constraining norms, women could negotiate the consequences of their desires.

The fact that women in spite of the ideology of control (the *pativrata dharma*, punitive penalties[99] and the social opprobrium) continued to exercise sexual choice is evident from a *dharmaśāstrīya* text like the *Nāradasmṛti*.[100] This text defines different categories of *svairiṇī* as follows: one who 'leaves for love and lives with another man; second, after her husband's death refuses his male kin but unites with a stranger for love; third, for want of money the woman gives herself to another man; fourth, one who after lawful marriage becomes the wife of another'. It is very clear from these definitions that women did challenge the male right to their sexuality directly or indirectly. The very fact that the *dharmaśāstra* were recognizing the reality of *svairiṇī*'s existence shows that in spite of the *dharmaśāstrīya* norms, at least some women managed to exercise choice.

Not only was there a social scripting of sexuality but an economic scripting as well. Women's economic freedom and unfreedom also had a lot to do with their social/sexual behaviour. I have in another context[101] established how communal control over resources also spelt greater sexual freedom for women. That economic considerations were crucial in constraining female sexuality is particularly noteworthy in the context of widow's property rights, as enumerated in the *dharmaśāstra*. *Kātyāyanasmṛti*[102] states that a sonless widow preserving the bed of her dead husband unsullied and residing with her elders and being self-controlled could enjoy her husband's property till her death. Kullūka, a commentator on the *Manusmṛti*, opines that a chaste widow could never be deprived of her right to inherit the property of her husband.[103] In Kauṭilya's *Arthaśāstra*,[104] in all the cases where a widow re-married against the wishes of her late husband's family particularly her father-in-law (*śvasura*), she forfeited the claim to her *strīdhana*.

The *dharmaśāstra* writers granted women *strīdhana*, said to be women's exclusive property.[105] Among the various categories of *strīdhana* which have been enumerated there is one called *prītidattā*, interpreted by Manu[106] as what women receive as a token of affection. Under this category, Manu includes the gifts a wife receives from her husband (*bhartṛdāya*). No wonder, then, that wives, particularly those in the elite polygamous households, were specifically advised to perfect their art of *kāmaśāstra*, for in this way says Yaśodhara,[107] they were likely to win and retain the affection of the husband (*svavaśe atmānovaśe*) even in an *antaḥpura* where many co-wives were present.[108]

Kauṭilya[109] among law-givers is unique in that he allows divorce by mutual consent if both husband and wife were disaffected with each other. But his sense of fairness deserts him when he grapples with the economic implications of divorce. He states[110] that a wife disliking her husband and not adorning herself (for fulfilment of the marital duty, that is sexual intimacy) during a period of seven *ṛtu* (menstrual cycle) shall forthwith set down her endowment and ornaments and consent to her husband lying with another woman. In other words, withdrawing from the husband sexually, the wife stood to lose her *strīdhana* as well. Furthermore, if the wife sought divorce on her own, says Kauṭilya,[111] 'her husband shall not give her whatever may have been received'. It is only when the husband took a second wife on his own that the *dharmaśāstra* writers provided for compensation to the first wife in the form of *adhivedanikā*, which too was classified under *strīdhana*.[112]

THE MATERIALIST PHILOSOPHY OF *KĀMA*

In the period of our study, Lokāyata was an important school of thought. Jaina scholar Siddharṣi in his allegorical romance *Upamitibhāvaprapañcakathā*, includes the Lokāyata amongst the principal non-Jaina systems, and in a CE 963 inscription of the Gaṅga king Narasiṁha, a famous Jaina teacher is described as *Lokasammatamatin* or one whose talents are appreciated by adherents of the Lokāyata system.[113] In the *Harṣacarita*,[114] Lokāyata are mentioned among the adherents of diverse schools of thought who studied and taught in the hermitage of Divākaramitra in the Vindhya forest. Bāṇa in his *Kādambarī* refers to the teachings of this system as promoting sinful tendencies (*lokāyatikavidye-vādharmaruceḥ*). What exactly was the *nāstika* Lokāyata (literally *lokeṣu āyataḥ*, that is, what is prevalent among people) philosophy, alternatively called Cārvāka and Bārhaspatya? This philosophy identified the self with the senses and talked of satisfaction of the senses.[115] The materialists were of the view that pleasure in this world is the only thing that is true and good. The only reasonable end for men is enjoyment or gratification of their senses (*kamevaika puruṣārtha*). Actually the philosophical system of the Cārvāka stands on the theory of knowledge which maintains that perception is the only means of knowing the truth. That which is amenable to the perception of the senses is true, and beyond perception everything is doubtful.[116] So the pleasure produced by sensation is the only goal which ought to be realized.

The *Bhagavadagītā*[117] describes the Lokāyata view as an *asura* view and is contemptuous of it. The *Gītā*[118] sums up the cosmogony of the *asura* thus—*aparasparasaṁbhūtam kimnyatkāmahaitukaṁ*: the world originated from the union of the male and female and could not have any other cause than *kāma* or the sexual urge. Chattopadhyaya[119] says that this identification of *asura* with the Lokāyata was quite well established and sources as old as the *Chāndogya* and *Maitrayāṇī Upaniṣad* and the *Viṣṇu Purāṇa* persistently attributed the Lokāyata views to the *asura*. In the *Mahābhārata*,[120] Cārvāka is called a *rākṣasa* and this appellation occurs also in Bhaṭṭanārāyaṇa's play, *Veṇīsaṁhāra*.[121] What is interesting about this *asura/rākṣasa* appellation to a sensual philosophy is that traditionally the *asura/rākṣasa* culture has had a positive empowering sexual image of women which stands in contrast to the misogyny of the brahmanic tradition.[122]

The association of a positive sexual image of women and lack of misogyny within the materialist philosophy is well brought out in Śrīharṣa's *Naiṣadhacarita*. Here the materialists say, 'Fie on those who boast of family dignity! They hold women in check out of jealousy; but do not likewise restrain men, though the blindness of passion is common to both.'[123] The materialists categorically declare, 'spurn all censorious statements about women as not worth a straw!'[124] The double standards of patriarchal society are exposed even more clearly when it is pointed out[125] that the 'norms' were never followed even by those who lay them in the first place. In one very telling verse the Cārvāka jeeringly ask[126] whether 'those other-worldly fellows, ready to perform sacrifices renounced their passion? For even after death they long for heaven, the quintessence of which lies in its gazelle-eyed nymphs'. In a more serious vein the materialists say that the body should be revered[127] for that alone is real and there is nothing beyond it. Therefore, bodily pleasures are not something to be deprecated.[128]

The brahmanic ideology which castigated the Cārvāka also singled out the *kāma puruṣārtha* for criticism. Thus, in brahmin Krishna Misra's eleventh-century allegorical play *Prabodhacandrodaya*, the Cārvāka as the representatives of the materialist forces are criticized.[129] Personified Kāma is depicted as the main assistant of antagonist Mahāmoha (great delusion) who is opposed to the protagonist Viveka (conscience/wisdom). We notice here the dichotomizing of mind (*viveka*) and body (*kāma* in its corporeality, which is nothing but delusion). It is interesting to note that the above feature was a recurring theme in the patriarchal ascetic traditions of all hues, brahmanic, Buddhist, and Jaina. It is also significant that in the *Prabodhcandrodaya*,[130] while *viveka* is born of *nivṛtti* (which is synonymous with *sanyāsa/sanyāsī*), *moha* is born of *pravṛtti* (natural inclination).

The orthodox opposition never allowed the Lokāyata philosophy as a systematic body of work to be passed on. In spite of being an important system of thought, its knowledge has to be gleaned from secondary sources that contain aphorisms rather than actual analysis. Yadava[131] points out that while the Lokāyata system occupied a significant place in ancient Indian thought, the evidence of *Prabodha-candrodaya* suggests a deepening of conflict between its followers and the dominant class and culture during the early medieval period. A tradition avers that Bhoja Paramāra destroyed the Nīlapaṭa who represented a section of the Lokāyatika.

TANTRIC DOCTRINE AND THE VENERATION OF *KĀMA*

The Lokāyata was not the only philosophy to lay stress on *kāma* or to have a positive gender imagery. Tantricism, which had emerged as a major force in our period of study, needs to be analysed in detail for its impact on the conceptualization of *kāma* with particular reference to women. In fact, tantricism was unique in that it did not have an in-built androcentrism under which other religious systems in ancient India laboured. The Kaula attitude towards women is described in *Śaktisaṅgama Tantra*[132] thus:

> Woman is the mother of the three worlds, the representative of the three worlds, the container of the three worlds and the body of the three worlds. Whether the form is male or female, all the best forms are those of women. All the beauty the world contains is created by woman. There is no friend better than a woman, no way better than a woman, no luck better than a woman, no kingdom better than a woman, no *tapa* better than a woman, no *tīrtha* better than a woman, no *yoga* better than a woman and no *japa* better than a woman.

This grand valorization of women had to do with a world-view or cosmogony in which female sexuality (and the generative organ or *bhaga*) had a life-giving symbolism.[133]

Madhu Khanna[134] points out that the *Śāktatantra* highly valued the body and the senses. More importantly, the woman's body and her five senses were made the locus of purity (in complete contrast to the somatophobia of the ascetic tradition). All the physical processes such as woman's breath, her postures and gestures, biological processes like the menstrual cycle, were considered sacred, energy-bestowing, and a manifestation of the goddess herself. It is held in the *tantra* that we do not experience consciousness external to our bodies. In fact, the human body is a miniature cosmos (*kṣudrabrahmāṇḍa*). Among the *pañcamakāra* of tantricism was *maithuna* (sexual intercourse), viewed as the human counterpart of the cosmic creative process. According to *Kaulāvalī Nirṇaya,*[135] *maithuna* was the only means by which a person could become a *siddha*. Sexual intercourse was thus looked upon with reverence and was not associated with guilt or sin. Here sex was salvation as opposed to the ascetic tradition where it was the eternal damnation.

Tantricism as a philosophical system can be seen as rejecting the ascetic doctrine of renunciation. The *dharamaśāstra* texts talk of continence as the *mahāvrata* for the ascetic,[136] and Manu[137] even refers to an ascetic as one who is indifferent to objects of sensual pleasure, experiencing delight in the soul (*adhyātmarati*) instead. The tantrics, on the other hand, were deeply connected to the corporeality of material existence. To quote a text of the Kaula 'for the adept let that be drunk which should not be drunk and that food which should not be eaten, and that which should not be the object of intercourse – let it be so'.[138] Dumont[139] talks of tantricism transcending the opposition between *yoga* (discipline) and *bhoga* (enjoyment). In fact, the expression *kaulayogī* is frequently used.[140] Miranda Shaw in her study of tantric Buddhism points out how within this philosophical system the enlightenment (she aptly calls it 'passionate enlightenment') was possible through heterosexual coupling. This was a major break from the early Buddhist tradition within which the renunciation of sexual relations was a prerequisite for attaining *nirvāṇa*.

Also, within the philosophy of *śākta tantra* while the *puruṣa* (male) was passive, *prakṛti* (female) was dynamic. This was a reversal of the traditional hierarchy in the heterosexual coupling as conceived in most other discourses. In fact, in the tantric *maithuna*, the reverse posture (*viparītarata*) was the norm. Gordon White[141] points out that in the *haṭhayoga*[142] practice of *Cakravedhana* (which is a sexual penetration of sorts), it is the female *kuṇḍalinī* which awakens, stiffens, rises and rushes upwards towards the cranial vault, the cavity which is the place of the passive male Śiva. As the *kuṇḍalinī* pierces each of the *cakra* great quantities of heat are produced which refine and transmute the seed that becomes the nectar which immortalizes the *yogī* who holds it in his cranium.

Not only was the usual hierarchy of the heterosexual coupling, but also perhaps heterosexual love itself, was challenged within the tantric system. As Bhandarkar[143] observed, 'the ambition of every pious follower of the Śākta system is to become identical with the *tripurasundarī*, and one of his religious training is to habituate himself to think that he is a woman. Thus, the followers of the Śākta school justify their appellation by the belief that god is a woman and it ought to be the aim of all to become a woman.' Similarly, speaking of Sahajīyā, Bose[144] remarked that 'the Sahajīyā believed that at a certain stage of spiritual culture the man should transform into a woman, and remember he cannot have the experience of true love so long as he cannot realize the nature of the woman in him'. The divine principle is the feminine, and the worshipper, even a man, in order to be considered a true devotee must try to invoke in himself his latent femininity. From the gender perspective this was truly liberating. For this meant as far as men were concerned a reversal of the normal status. From the point of view of sexual love, the tantric system of belief can be interpreted as encouraging lesbian love, if not in the physical sense most definitely in the conceptual sense.

This completely radical notion of *kāma* as well as the valorization of the female gender in tantric discourse perhaps had to do with the fact that tantric beliefs originated in non-brahmanized tribal areas where women had traditionally been held in high esteem and the mother goddess was worshipped.[145] In *Gauḍavāho* of Vākapatirāja,[146] a text of the eighth century, Kolī women and the Śabara are called worshippers of Kālī.[147] Within the tantric belief system not only was the female principle the very cause of the universe, but women themselves were the legitimate revealers of this knowledge. They functioned as priestesses—*yoginī* and *bhairavī*. *Rājataraṅgiṇī*, a text of the twelfth century, refers to women participating in the tantric rights of *gurudīkṣā*.[148] In tantricism women as spiritual preceptors could initiate lineages and were thus 'a source of spiritual power'.[149]

Tantric doctrine with its concept of *maithuna* and lack of misogyny became a target of criticism by the orthodox. In Rājaśekhara's *Karpūramañjarī*,[150] the tantric rituals involving women are ridiculed. In the eleventh-century *Daśāvatāracarita*, the tantric *cakrapūjā* and dalliance with women is described contemptuously.[151] A verse in *Daśāvatāracarita* also suggests that owing to tantric influence women took undue liberty.[152] The *Yaśastilakacampū* describes with contempt the tantric practice of drinking wine and union with women.[153] The radicalization of the tantric theology extended to the questioning of the brahmanical social hierarchy as well.[154] In *Daśāvatāracarita*, Kṣemendra questions the concept of liberation achieved by the drinking of wine from the same pot as the washer-woman or weaver, and is highly contemptuous of it. Tantricism obviously had a popular social base. These views seem more an effort to understand what was essentially an esoteric religious system rather than to explain its basic philosophy. Although there were variants within the tantric system too, the left hand (*vāmācāra*) was the earlier and the more original tantra system, later a more conformist right hand tantricism emerged.

ASCETICISM AND REVULSION FOR *KĀMA*

The ascetic traditions of all hues,[155] Jaina and brahmanical in particular, in this period opposed the materialist and tantric philosophy which had a significant doctrinal presence among people. In the ninth century Śaṁkarācārya was one of the greatest representatives of the ascetic tradition. In his commentary on the *Brahmasūtras* he equated the crude mob (*prākṛta janaḥ*) with followers of Lokāyata.[156] The Kāpālikas who had a strong likeness to many of the activities and practices of the tantrics, were also condemned by Śaṁkara, who accused them of sexual licentiousness among other things.[157]

Śaṁkara's Advaita Vedānta philosophy[158] also took the lead in undermining the feminine principle. For Śaṁkara women symbolized ignorance; therefore, in the Advaita philosophy at the cosmic level *māyā*[159] was the feminine principle of ignorance (*avidyā*) which caused people to be enveloped in a web of names and forms (*prapañca*). The *brahma*, on the other hand, was pure consciousness; it was free, without qualities and forms. It was the source of creation and growth, as also destruction. It was a dynamic principle, whereas *māyā* was completely passive. In fact, she was nothing more than the creation of *brahma*, who is called *māyin*. *Māyā* was only a playful enjoyment of the god.

In the pursuit of ascetic life (Śaṁkara never married and his monastic order was for men) women were a snare. It is interesting that Bhartṛhari with an entire *Vairāgyaśataka* to his credit also established a similar equation between woman, passion and ignorance. He says:

> When the darkness of passion wove a web of ignorance about me,
> Then a woman seemed to fill the world's expanse.
> But now that I am favoured with the salve of keener discernment,
> My tranquil sight sees Brahman ubiquitous in the world.[160]

Among the renouncers active in the period were many Śaiva, which was not surprising since within the brahmanic mythology Śiva is projected as a great ascetic.[161] Śaṁkarācārya helped to organize these Śaiva renouncers who had by the ninth century emerged as a distinctive group, the Daśanāmī *sanyāsī*. They took permanent residence in monasteries, practised austerities and celibacy, and subsisted on alms.[162] A careful analysis of the history of this sect shows that while the renunciation of *kāma* and the practice of celibacy may have continued, renunciation of *artha* was soon foregone, in spite of the fact that the renunciation of all wealth and taking to the begging bowl was an important rite at the time of entering *sanyasāśrama*.[163] Thapar[164] points out that the Daśanāmī sects not only competed with the Buddhist and Jain monks as regards proselytizing but also for power (political patronage) and economic control. The *sanyāsī maṭha*, Jaina *basadī* and Buddhist *saṁgha* developed into tax-free units which added to their economic viability. In fact, it is an interesting feature of the ascetic tradition that while ideally renunciation implied not just a celibate existence but renunciation of wealth[165] as well, the crux of the renunciatory doctrine emphasized the denunciation of *kāma* alone.[166] J.M. Masson in his interesting essay 'Psychology of the Ascetic'[167] also notes that the ascetic discourse is pre-occupied with sexual purity, more than with any other single topic. The ascetic exists because he is tempted and not once, but over and over. The only role of women in ascetic literature is as degraded objects, inspirers of lust and of the horror of that lust. Masson correctly surmises that this phobic avoidance of women bespeaks an unusually intense desire for contact.[168] As Bhartṛhari[169] says

> Two worlds alone are worth a man's devotion,
> the youth of beautiful women wearied by heavy breasts and full of fresh wine's heady ardour for sport
> Or the forest.

In another verse Bhartṛhari[170] notes,

> I do indeed speak without bias,
> This is acknowledged as truth among men:
> nothing enthrals us like an ample hipped woman,
> Nothing else causes such pain.

The Jaina monk Somaprabha Sūri, in *Yaśastilaka,*[171] underlines the same dilemma when he states in a more didactic vein that 'women when heard of deprive one of the faculty of hearing, looked at they deprive one of the power of seeing, remembered they captivate the mind, and embraced they disable the limbs. When in love, they take away one's life, and when separated, they take away one's joy. Yet women are the goal of all efforts in the world'.

In none of the mainstream discourses was *kāma* renounced as a *puruṣārtha* or goal of human life. It may have a lower hierarchy in the *dharamaśāstra* and *Arthaśāstra* but it was nonetheless seen as one of the essential aspects of human endeavour. It was accepted as such, even if grudgingly framed within procreative necessities of *gṛhasthāśrama.* But the ascetic tradition was unique in that it developed as an antithesis to *kāma* in all its aspects but most specially the erotic aspect. And since sexual desire was conceived essentially in heterosexual terms, the renunciatory ideology had a gendered aspect as well. Dumont[172] in fact sees renunciation as a sort of universal language of India and the renouncer has been identified by him as a creator of values. Thapar presents[173] the ascetic renouncer as a representative of a counter-culture who, as against the *gṛhastha,* exercised a great deal of moral authority in society. Viewed from the gender perspective, however, the ascetic and his philosophy of renunciation was not a counter-culture but very much within the mainstream of patriarchal society whose norms had misogyny as its leitmotif.

The ascetic tradition indulged in wholesale woman-bashing—woman as *kāminī* (lustful mistress) was seen as the temptress of man. In Jalhaṇa's *Sūktimuktāvalī,*[174] the verses under the *vairāgya-paddhati* underline the notion that because of woman there is desire (*puṁsā durvāsanā rajjunārī*); if one abandons woman one abandons desire for this world, and leaving this entitles one to happiness (*yasya strī tasya bhogecchā*; *strīyaṁ tyaktvā jagatyaktaṁ, jagatyaktvā sukhī bhavet*). A similar sentiment echoes through Bhartṛhari's poetry as well. In his verses,[175] women are called 'Kāma's victorious seal'; who casts them as a lure, and fools are caught like fish, only to be broiled on the flame of passion. Women, therefore, must be scrupulously avoided. Bhartṛhari says[176] that 'a man may tread the righteous path, be master of his senses, retire in timidity or cling to modest ways, only until the seductive arrow glances of amorous women fall on his heart'. In fact, the vehemence of Bhartṛhari's denunciation of women is a measure of the terrible fascination they hold for him.[177] Bhartṛhari curses woman not because she is repugnant but because of the desire for possession and enjoyment of her beauty. In a moment of self-realization he says[178] that 'a deceiver of himself and his peers is the pompous *paṇḍita* who reviles young women. The fruit of his austerity is heaven and even heaven is full of nymphs'. It is in such a moment of candour that Bhartṛhari finally unmasks the hypocrisy of the misogynistic ascetic tradition. D.D. Kosambi[179] says that there seems in Bhartṛhari not even the consciousness of the fact that woman is herself a human being, has her share of this world's suffering, and might also feel the need for renunciation, for freedom from her own peculiar sorrows and problems.[180]

If Bhartṛhari, a devout follower of the great ascetic god Śiva, felt this about women, Jaina Somaprabha Sūri was no different. Salvation for this Jaina was for men alone and only if they could denounce love for women. In his cleverly crafted forty-six stanzas of *Śṛṅgāra-vairāgyataraṅgiṇī*[181] using the device of punning (*śleṣa*) the poet has sought to convey the idea of renunciation even while the first reading of the verses gives an impression of erotic poetry. The message of these verses was that the sentiment of *śṛṅgāra* is transient and the desire for *mokṣa* is the ideal to be realized. In the Jaina *Kathākoṣa,*[182] a monk tells his pupil that 'it is not fitting for hermits to look at women, as even a small jungle fire consumes a whole forest of bamboos; so even the name of young women drives away severe penance'. Somadeva Sūri[183] echoes similar sentiments when he states, 'The body undergoes austerities and the mind meditates on the truth, and perfect calm prevails over the senses only as long man does not behold the visage of fair woman'. In Jaina thought it is underlined that study, meditation and practice of virtue are all out of question as long as the fire of sexual desire (*kāmaśuśukṣaṇī*)[184] burns.

Actually the conundrum of male celibacy within ascetic ideology derives from the fact that it is not problematized in the context of the male subject, but the object of his craving and desire, namely women. Furthermore, women were seen as representing through their reproduction, the hold of the family, and are thus disruptive and threatening *vis-à-vis* the male ascetic's quest for liberation. The focus here is not on desire or *kāma* as a problematic in itself, and conceptualized as such in the *trivarga* debate, but on the object of desire. Therefore, it is women who are considered more detrimental than *kāma*. Perhaps it will be easier to understand the misogyny of the ascetic tradition if we link it to somatophobia. The body was seen as a source of all the undesirable traits a human being could have and women's lives were seen as manifesting those traits.[185] As Bhartṛhari says in his *Vairāgyaśataka*, 'still unborn, man suffers a painful confinement in woman's foul womb'.[186] He goes on, 'With all her emotions woman enchains us'.[187] The ascetic perspective thus made woman a symbol of re-birth. And the ascetic in order to attain the ultimate goal of *mokṣa/nirvāṇa* had to transcend this rebirth cycle. This was the reiteration of the patriarchal dichotomy between men/ masculinity and transcendence and the woman/femininity and immanence.

The philosophy of the Digambara sect of the Jaina also underlines this belief. The Digambara say that a female body 'is not able to destroy the hosts of *karma*; because it is produced in association with that evil *karma* called wrong-view (*mithyātva*)'.[188]

The somatophobia of the masculine ascetic ideology had another aspect to it. Here the soul/mind was extolled and the body or passion was denounced by comparison. Since the phenomenal world with sensual pleasures was typified by women, they were relegated to the bodily/passionate sphere of existence and became the focus of vitriolic chastisement. This was the foremost way of cultivating aversion to the life of the senses. Bhartṛhari[189] says:

> Her breasts, those fleshy protuberances, are compared to golden bowls;
> Her face, a vile receptacle of phlegm is likened to the moon;
> Her thighs, dank with urine are said to rival the elephants' trunk.
> Mark how this despicable form (*nindyaṁrūpam*) is flourished by the poets.

Bhartṛhari therefore declares that 'the body of woman is a 'concoction of skin and flesh and bones'.[190] A verse in Jalhaṇa's anthology[191] under the *vairāgyapaddhati*, reads, 'On what ground do you support taking to the ordure regions of women for pleasure? Indeed that region is to be discarded even as the region of excretion.' This aversion for the female body is even more marked in the Digambara Jaina ascetic discourse of the early medieval period. Women's genitals (linked to menstruation) and breasts are described as prime sources of impurity, swarmed by microscopic creatures (*aparyāpta*) who are constantly destroyed. Thus, women are a sight and source of *hiṁsā* against living beings. Female physiology is cited in the Jaina debates as a principal reason for the alleged incapacity of women to achieve spiritual salvation.[192] However, the Yāpanīyas among the Jainas were in the forefront of denying asymmetry in the male and the female body which made women incapable of attaining *mokṣa* simply on account of their physiology. The Yāpanīya *ācārya* Śākaṭāyana (*c.* 814–67) argued that 'it is not the case that a woman's body is any different from the symmetrical (*samacaturasa*) configuration that characterize male bodies'.[193]

One only has to contrast this somatophobia of the ascetic tradition with the tantric tradition which had a liberating potential for women. We find evidence of many female *siddhas* who played a significant role in preaching and popularizing tantric Buddhism of Sahajayāna in the early medieval period. Of these, Bhagavatī Lakṣmīṁkara in the eighth century is foremost.[194] She boldly projected the new theory of Sahajayāna in her work entitled *Advyasiddhi Sādhanā*, declaring that truth can only be realized by 'reverence for the body' which is the abode of all gods, through the concentration of the mind, the *Sahajayoga*. Here we do not notice any dichotomy of body and mind; one is not valorized at the expense of the other. The ascetic tradition, which sets so much store by fierce vows about eating and drinking (Jainas in particular), is of no consequence in the tantric tradition. Lakṣmīṁkara declared that there were no restrictions regarding eating and drinking. Furthermore, as against the misogyny of the ascetic tradition, Lakṣmīṁkara forcefully underlined the need to venerate women. She says that no hatred should be expressed towards those who were the embodiment of the goddess Prajñā.[195]

Another early-medieval discourse in which we notice a positive valuation of *kāma* is in the theistic[196] religions like Vaiṣṇavism and Śaiva Siddhānta. In these communities, sensual pleasure when occurring as part of the relationship between god and devotee, was actually valorized. This was in contrast to the ascetic discourse in which pleasure was counter-posed to the world of monastic discipline. Historically, the reason why the southern theistic cults of the ninth century adopted a different notion of *kāma* was perhaps because they were engaged in a theological contest with Buddhism and Jainism and were, therefore, interested in popularizing a theological context that was at variance with the negative notion of desire and pleasure within these systems. In north India in particular, the Vaiṣṇava *bhakti* ideology took this devotion-hued *kāma* to an open celebration of Rādhā-Kṛṣṇa love (as symbolized in the *Gītagovinda*).

Apart from the tantrics and the Lokāyata, within mainstream ancient Indian society, Varāhamihira is virtually an exception in questioning the misogyny of the ascetic tradition. He says,[197] 'it is my conviction that those who, as a result of their following the path of renunciation, overlook the virtues of women and wax eloquent on their flaws, are indeed wicked and cynical'. Critiquing the notions of women's unbridled sexuality as the reason for their seducing men, Varāhamihira says[198] that 'even after a hundred years men's sexual craving does not subside; but they refrain from the act because of their physical incapacity, whereas women do so by conviction and courage'. He exclaims,[199] 'how bold and impudent are the immoral fellows who slander blameless women! They are like the thieves actually found stealing and yet crying, thief, stop!'

We have referred to Dumont's view about the renouncer as a creator of values in the Indian tradition. But this spiritual generosity was not extended to women and śūdra.[200] If renunciation was truly a value it was both gendered and casteist. This is not to say that historically śūdra and women have not renounced,[201] but they never enjoyed any legitimacy in the eyes of *dharma*. The *Atrismṛti* of about CE 800 lists renunciation among the six causes that degrades śūdras and women. Olivelle thus points out that it is 'safe to assume that at least the mainstream of the shastric tradition considered the renunciation by women as illegitimate'.[202] The position was the same within the Buddhist and Jaina religions, in spite of both of them having orders of nuns. Digambara Jaina monks were of the view that the presence of minute organisms in the vagina caused an itch that never allowed a cessation of sexual desire in women. They were, therefore, physiologically incapable of being free of sexual desire.[203] An interesting example of the lack of legitimacy of the female renouncer in popular thinking is furnished by a tale in Buddhasvāmin's *Bṛhatkathāślokasaṁgraha*.[204] A Jaina nun (*pravrajyakā*) Ṛṣidattā is expelled from the order for the sin of entertaining sexual desire for her beau Gomukha whom she subsequently married. However, in spite of her happy marital state she was still ashamed[205] of having left the mendicant's life (*pravrajyātyāgalajjitā*). She is lectured by Naravāhanadatta, the hero of this epic tale, to free herself of this shame. He tells her she had attained final emancipation (*mokṣa*) in every way by the removal of unbearable sorrow in the form of separation from Gomukha. In fact, Naravāhanadatta proclaims[206] that women who conquer their husbands with a glance are a source of satisfaction to their mothers and friends. This story illustrates in a very telling manner the redundancy of ascetism in a woman's life. The victory for woman is to capture the heart of her man with her charms and not conquest of the senses. In the patriarchal social world-view what was of ultimate significance and, therefore, lauded, was the role of women as propagators and sustainers of the family. Women were taught to prolong and value the household, whereas men could devalue it and escape it altogether.

If a woman's renunciation had no legitimacy, it was because theoretically she was perceived as not in a position to renounce. Given that she was seen as a ward of men at all stages of her life, she had nothing of 'her own' to renounce—neither wealth nor sexual relations. The 'renouncer leaves the world behind in order to consecrate himself to his own liberation',[207] but this was not a freedom women could have. Thus if women still became ascetics, their status remained very low. Throughout the period of study, a wide variety of sources project the ascetic woman as loose, promiscuous, or pitiable.

Medhātithi[208] says that ascetic women hide their lascivious tendencies.[209] While commenting on the six things that corrupt women, Medhātithi[210] refers to 'wandering about' as one of them. As Clementin-Ojha[211] in her sociological study of women ascetics remarks, 'she who has walked out of society tends to be suspected of wanting to misuse her freedom'. In Daṇḍin's *Daśakumāracarita*[212] Śākyabhikṣuṇī, Dharmarakṣitā and Śramaṇikā are described as procurers (*dūtīs*). In Kṣemendra's *Kalāvilāsa,*[213] old nuns (*vṛddha śramaṇā*) are among those who are said to rob women of good families (*kulanārī*) of their reputation (*śīlahāriṇya*).[214] In Vararuchi's *bhāṇa Ubhayabhisārikā,*[215] the *viṭa* charges that an ascetic woman (*parivrājikā*) sarcastically called Vilāsakauṇḍinī indulges in sexual intercourse (*suratotsava*). The *viṭa* states that she establishes *yoga* (relations) with desirable young men (*abhilāṣitataruṇa*) and takes *mokṣa* from undesirable ones! Interestingly, in Pāṇiṇī's *Aṣṭādhyāyī*[216] the *kulaṭā* is one who wanders from one family (*kula*) to another. At some point this word came to mean an unchaste woman and the texts of our period equate the ascetic woman with *kulaṭā*. In Kokkokā's *Ratirahasya*,[217] *yoginī* and *bhikṣukī* are classified as *kulaṭās* with whom the chaste wife should not interact. Yaśodhara[218] also describes the *bhikṣukī* who wanders from house to house as *kulaṭā,* and a bad character (*khaṇḍita caritra*).

What explains this great distrust of ascetic women by men? It would seem that what was feared was the subversive influence of ascetic women on wives. Kauṭilya[219] echoes this fear when he states that it would be considered a crime to induce a woman to renounce her role as a wife. It was greatly feared that woman's sexual, procreative, and sustenance services would no longer be available if she took to asceticism. As Megasthenes also noted, 'Indian (men) did not communicate their metaphysical doctrines to women, thinking that if their wives understood these doctrines and learned to be indifferent to pleasure and pain, and to consider life and death as the same, they would no longer continue to be the slaves of others.'[220]

The literary sources of our period talk of *tapasvinī* not as female renouncers of the world but as pitiable women in distress. Thus, in Harṣa's *Ratnāvalī*[221] the missing heroine Sāgarikā, who had incurred the wrath of the queen Vāsavadattā, is described as *tavassinī* (Prakrit form of *tapasvinī*). Similarly, Āraṇyakā is described by her friend Manoramā in the play *Priyadarśikā*[222] as 'that *tavassinī* (miserable girl) who is not so tormented by the hardships of imprisonment as by the hopelessness of seeing her beloved lord'. In the play *Veṇīsaṁhāra*,[223] Draupadī too is described by Yudhiṣṭhira to Bhīmasena as *tapasvinī* in the same sense. It is thus clear that the adjective *tapasvinī* describes the woman in distress, spoken of sympathetically. The term *tapasvinī* has the semantic value of pitiable, miserable, and poor.[224] For women certainly *tapa* was equivalent to patience and endurance rather than the heat of asceticism, which made the ascetic a figure of power or an alternative centre of authority.

The third image of the ascetic woman that is furnished by the literary sources of our period is that of woman performing penance for finding the right husband (or for his benefit). This Gaurī/Pārvatī model of asceticism (who at the end of her fierce *tapa* got Śiva for her husband) alone had social legitimacy and is much referred to in the literature. In Bāṇa's *Kādambarī,*[225] Mahāśvetā is depicted as engaged in an austere *tapa*—which Candrapīḍa sees as hard for women to perform (*vanitājanaduṣkaramapi*)—only to attain reunion with her beloved Puṇḍarīka. *Kathāsaritsāgara*[226] also makes copious references to girls performing austerities and asceticism only to gain a husband. In one such reference we come across a young princess Padmāvatī who expresses her desire to practice asceticism to which her lady-in-waiting says 'for whose sake, my friend, do you seek to perform asceticism?' To which Padmāvatī replies that it is to ensure the victory of her father and her future bridegroom who had already been chosen for her.[227]

In the perception of the classical poets too, it is the woman in separation (*viyoginī*) who can be likened to a woman in a mystic trance (*yoginī*), a woman who is meditating on her absent beloved. A verse by Rājaśekhara in Vidyākara's anthology[228] reads:

> Averse from eating, turned from every object of the senses
> And this too, that your eye is fixed in a trance;
> Again your mind is single-pointed, and then this silence;
> And the fact that all the world to you seems empty
> Tell me, gentle friend
> Are you a *yoginī* or a *viyoginī*?

THE CULT OF KĀMADEVA

Kāmadeva, the god of erotic love, is the presiding deity of the courtly *śṛṅgāra rasa* literature of our period. He is invoked in the *maṅgalācaraṇa* by Padmaśrī in *Nāgarasarvasvam*. Verses celebrating his erotic victory over mortals and gods alike are given in Bhartṛhari's *Śṛṅgāraśataka*, Vidyākara's *Subhāṣitaratnakoṣa,* and numerous other texts. From a historian's point of view it would be worthwhile to trace a short history of the cult of Kāmadeva, his deification and subsequent marginalization within brahmanical literature. This was also, as we shall see, linked to the more restricted or circumscribed space for women within the society where the dominant norms were patriarchal and brahmanical. Reference to *kāma* occurs for the first time in the *Ṛgveda.*[229] In the hymn of creation, all creation was said to be the result of the first seed which was *kāma*. By the time the *Atharvaveda*[230] was written, Kāma was no longer an amorphous sexual impulse, but appears in anthropomorphic form. He was now deified[231] and perceived to fulfil all desires.[232] In fact, in these verses Kāma was not conceived as the god of sexual enjoyment but a god in general and was lauded as a great power superior to all.[233] A verse in the *Atharvaveda*[234] states that 'first before all sprang Kāma into being. Gods, fathers, mortal men have never matched him. Stronger than these are thou, and great forever. Kāma, to thee I offer worship!' In another verse[235] Kāmadeva was addressed by two epithets, *ugraḥ* (mighty/powerful) and *īśānaḥ* (ruler/sovereign). Thus, Kāmadeva was a supreme deity and also the goal towards which all aspired. Nevertheless, in the *Atharvaveda*[236] itself there is a description of Kāmadeva which was to establish his credentials as a love god or fulfiller of the pleasure of the senses. It is wished that the arrow of Kāmadeva, feathered with longing, tipped with love, and necked with resolve, pierces the heart. And it is in this form that Kāmadeva appears in the *Purāṇa* where the sphere of his function gets narrower.

Bhattacharji[237] notes that in spite of the Ṛgvedic hymn of creation and the Atharvavedic prayers, Kāmadeva is a late and minor god in Indian mythology, 'rising to full stature only in the *Purāṇa*'. It is difficult to agree with Bhattacharji. If by full stature she means greater paraphernalia for Kāmadeva, her assessment may be accepted. In the *Purāṇa* Kāmadeva has many names—Madana (intoxicator), Manmatha (agitator of the mind), and Anaṅga (the bodiless). He has the parrot for his *vāhana* and *makara* as the emblem of his banner (*makaraketana*, *mīnadhvaja*). He has bows and arrows of flowers (*puṣpacāpa*, *kusumadhanvā*). Wherever he goes, the cuckoo, humming bees, and gentle breeze (*malayavāta*) accompany him. His friend is *vasanta* (spring) and *Rati* (sexual delight) and *Prīti* (affection) are his wives. In spite of such a detailed delineation that fleshes out Kāmadeva's figure as far as his status, power and function were concerned Kāmadeva was actually emasculated in the Puranic mythology. His greatest put down is from that great ascetic, Śiva. The *Śiva Purāṇa* celebrates the victory of Śiva over Kāmadeva who is burnt to death by the fire of Siva's third eye for trying to disrupt Śiva's *tapa*.[238] In fact, given the ascetic tradition's intense hostility to desire in all forms, particularly erotic desire, ascetic ideology tends to view Kāmadeva negatively as Māra or death.[239] Even the fertility symbolism of *kāma* is completely ignored here. The contrast between the Vedic perception of *kāma* (sexual instinct) and the later ascetic tradition is that while in the Vedas generative power was regarded quite ingenuously as the creator of new life and, therefore, deserving honour and worship, now the ascetic ideal across the sects saw *kāma* as unspiritual, something that needed to be conquered by spirit or *ātmā*[240] lest it grew into a wild exuberance that dwarfed all expression of spirituality. In this process of changeover, the instinct of *kāma* was no longer venerated as promoting fertility. At the inter-section of desire and terror, Kāmadeva was now conceived as Mara or a 'figure of the repressed'.[241] It is symptomatic of the emasculated status of Kāmadeva that he gets inextricably linked to other such emasculated groups. Kāmadeva is depicted with the *gaṇa* of the *gandharva* and *apsarā*,[242] of whom the *Harivaṁśa Purāṇa* recognizes him as the lord.[243]

In the courtly literature, where *śṛṅgāra* themes predominates, Kāmadeva and women have a pervasive presence. In Vidyākara's anthology[244] the poets often identify Kāmadeva with women in general. For instance, Rājaśekhara invokes Kāmadeva thus: 'Hail to the family priest of womankind' and 'Hail to the stage director of the play of sex!' In the invocatory verse of *bhāṇa*, *Padma-prabhṛtakam*,[245] Kāmadeva is described as *strīṇām vilāsamūrti*. In *Ratirahasya*[246] it is said that Kāmadeva who, though bodiless, conquered the three worlds with the help of women. The slim (*kṛśatanu*) women are really the bow of *kāma* and women's coquettish side-glances (*kaṭākṣa*) are the arrows with which Kāmadeva gains victory. Bhartṛhari[247] says, 'Kāmadeva must be the vassal of fair browed woman. He moves to conquer any man marked by the course of her glance.' The *Śṛṅgārī* poets[248] also took delight in questioning the efficacy of the ascetic Śiva's triumph over Kāmadeva. For, in the ultimate analysis, they point out tongue-in-cheek that Śiva was forced to pledge his troth to Pārvatī and even give her a permanent place by his side in the form of *ardhanarīśvara*. However, it is difficult to view this Kāmadeva–women connection as an empowering one for women. Given the heterosexual bias of the *śṛṅgārī* court poetry it was imperative that women as sexual objects *par excellence* of the male gaze be valorized, and this explains their inevitable connection with the love god Kāmadeva. Woman was Kamadeva's instrument in winning erotic battles. She was to be used as a weapon (*astra*) the way men used feminine beauty for arousal. This argument is best illustrated by a verse from Govardhanācārya's *Āryāsaptaśatī,*[249] where through the clever use of *virodhābhāsa alaṁkāra,* the poet points out that while women provide the bodiless Kāmadeva (*anaṅga*) with form (*sāṅgīkṛta*), Kāmadeva in turn made woman a weapon (*astrīkṛta*). Furthermore, from the patriarchal point of view the Kāmadeva–woman connection was the most natural one, for Kāmadeva was the god of sexual love and women were perceived as possessed of an uncontrollable sexuality. The *Manusmṛti*[250] underlines this again and again. Dumont[251] points out that in the *dharamaśāstra* ideal of the hierarchically graded *dharma*, *artha* and *kāma*, the analogy with the hierarchy of *varṇa* is apparent. *Dharma* here is the domain of the brāhmaṇa, *artha* of the *kṣatriya,* and *kāma* is associated with the rest, *vaiśya*, *śūdra* and women.

Linked inextricably with the figure of Kāmadeva was the festival of spring,[252] *Vasantotsava*[253] which was really *Kāmotsava* and was observed on the thirteenth day of the *śuklapakṣa* in the month of *caitra.*[254] A Chauhana inscription from Rajasthan[255] of the early medieval period also refers to the festival of spring celebrated in honour of Madana. *Kādambarī*[256] refers to *Vasantotsava* along with the worship of Kāmadeva. In a number of early medieval texts, *Vasantotsava* was the occasion for enormously free behaviour transcending class/caste distinctions.[257] The play *Ratnāvalī*[258] refers to the rejoicing of the citizens of the city of Kauśāmbī thus: 'the pavement in front is reddened by the people with the tread of their feet, pink with vermilion tints that drop from the cheeks of boisterous women in the yard which is flooded all over with a ceaseless flow of water[259] spouted by fountain jets, and where they are sporting in mud that is created by the heavy crush of hurrying feet'. The play also talks about the month of spring (*madhumāsa*) as one where when the heart is softened and desire (*kāma*) seizes the opportunity. In Dāmodaragupta's *Kuṭṭanīmatam,*[260] there is a reference to the spring festival of Kāmadeva (*kusumāyudhaparva*) in which even *kulavadhūs* participated openly in festivities with women who were not confined to houses, i.e. prostitutes. All women played the game of dice and did not shrink from using obscene words (*aślīlokti*) in public.

A sexually charged atmosphere is conveyed by the description of *Vasantotsava* in a twelfth-century text, *Pārijātamañjarī*.[261] It states that 'the ladies of the town, with their bodies made charming by flowery ornaments ... and dancing in an intoxicating and faltering manner so as to cause confusion in the lilt (of music) look smilingly at the faces of their lovers, the drummers in sports'. Anderson[262] notes that here in the setting of the spring festival the 'conventional boundaries and social distinctions dissolve into ambiguity'. Men and women smear each others' bodies with mud and water. By 'shedding of their established skins and by the assumption of unconventional[263] behaviour the participants in these rituals, position themselves outside normative values and constrictions ... sexual licentiousness points to dissolution in its contravention of social mores.'

Ratnāvalī[264] refers to women dancing the *vasantābhinaya* or spring dance. According to the *Nāṭyaśāstra*,[265] the spring dance is *lāsya* and *lāsya* is one which is imitative of the activities of the ordinary people (*laukikavṛtta*).[266] *Daśakumāracarita*[267] particularizes the nature of the spring dance by suggesting that the *lāsya* is a dance of love, in which emotions of love are expressed through gesture and postures that suggest enticement and beckoning. *Saṅgītaratnākara*[268] (of the twelfth century) considers the songs of the spring festival as Prakrit songs, and according to *Mānasollāsa*[269] the mass dancing and mass singing of vulgar songs typical of this occasion were performed most often by women (*yoṣitā*). *Ratnāvalī*[270] in its description of *Madanotsava* refers to roads ringing with the swelling music of wild songs (*carcarī*). Two conclusions can be reached after analysing the above data. First, *Vasantotsava* had a popular[271] origin and second, female erotic desire had a legitimate outlet during this festival. A lack of class/caste and sexual constraints must have outraged the sensibilities of orthodox brahmans.

There was an attempt to marginalize *Vasantotsava* and Kāmadeva himself through appropriation, as we shall see. In *Virupākṣava-santotsavacampū* (fifteenth century, Vijayanagara empire) we see that the spring festival is now celebrated as a temple festival. It depicts, says Anderson,[272] the transition of *Vasantotsava* as a popular festival centring on the figure of Kāmadeva to the *Vasantotsava* as a brahmanical temple festival whose major concern is the worship of Śiva. According to the myths, Śiva is the destroyer of Kāmadeva. Also, in a brahmin temple low castes would not be given entry, and women who could never be priests, would only be mere spectators of the festival rather than active participants in it.

Interestingly, in the thirteenth-century *Siṁhāsanadvātrinśikā,*[273] there is reference to the celebration of the spring festival (southern recension of the sixteenth tale) but Kāmadeva does not figure anywhere[274] in the preparations made for the rites in honour of Vasanta. It states,

> a beautiful assembly pavilion was constructed and brahmins who were skilled in Vedas and law books were summoned, as also dancers and, among them, charming women acquainted with song and music. In that assembly pavilion a throne was set up . . . upon the throne were placed two statues of Lakṣmī and Nārāyaṇa. To pay honour to the images all manner of substances were brought in . . . and the king himself had the sixteen-fold services performed to Nārāyaṇa and presented the brāhmaṇas and other people trained in the various arts with garments and gifts.

In this description we notice a distinct brahminization of the ceremony. Kāmadeva is singularly absent and patriarchal brahmanical deities preside over the celebrations. The plebian and erotic content of the festival is also markedly absent.

Not only was Kāmadeva marginalized in the brahmanical sources, his worship by women too was sought to be appropriated within the patriarchal setting.[275] As Anderson notes,[276] the concatenation of these *kāma* rituals with rites of fertility directed towards getting, keeping, and satisfying husbands is much in evidence. The *Bhaviṣya Purāṇa*[277] states that 'a woman should honour her husband with ornaments, garlands and clothes, thinking of him as Kāmadeva with her mind full of happiness'. Thus, in *Ratnāvalī,*[278] Vāsavadattā offers worship to Kāmadeva and her husband king Udayana simultaneously.

The purpose of *ratikāmavrata* as detailed in the *Nārada Purāṇa*[279] is to achieve a long married life and prolific progeny. In Rājaśekhara's *Kāvyamīmāṁsā,*[280] Kāmadeva is venerated by women only alongside Gaurī (a deity inextricably linked with women who worship her to secure a husband). Rājaśekhara also talks of married women (*vadhūnām*) who fill red ochre in the parting of their hair (*sīmantasindūrajuṣāṁ*) and worship their husbands as if they were Kāmadeva in the season of *vasanta.*[281] This suggests that shrinkage in the significance of Kāmadeva is linked to shrinkage in social spaces for women. Although women and Kāmadeva continued to be linked, this association was becoming quite frivolous.

NOTES

1. W. Simon, 1996: xvii.
2. *Kāmasūtra*, 1.2.20.
3. *Ṛgveda*, 10.129.3–4.
4. K. Roy, 1994: 247, 255–8.
5. P.V. Kane, 1974: 8–9.
6. *Mahābhārata*, 5.124.34–8.
7. Ibid., 12.167.8–9.
8. *Rāmāyaṇa*, 2.21.57–8; 2.53.13; 4.38.20–2.
9. *Manusmṛti*, 2.224.
10. Ibid., 4.176.
11. *Manubhāṣya*, 4.176.
12. *Jayamaṅgalā*, 1.1.1.
13. Ibid., 1.2.14–15.
14. Ibid., 1.2.32–6; 7.2.58–9.
15. Ibid., 1.2.37.
16. Ibid.
17. K. Roy, 1996: 155–70.
18. *Arthaśāstra*, 1.7.12
19. Somadeva Sūri (Handiqui, 1949: 115) says that a king who devotes himself only to *dharma*, overriding the claims of *artha* and *kāma*, is like a man who tills a forest abandoning a ripe corn-field.
20. *CS*, *Sūtrasthāna*, 1.15–16.
21. *CS*, *Sūtrasthāna*, 11.3.
22. *Kāma* would be subsumed within it.
23. *Dharma* and *mokṣa* would be subsumed within it.
24. *CS*, *Sūtrasthāna*, 11.4.
25. *CS*, *Sūtrasthāna*, 11.5.
26. *CS*, *Sūtrasthāna*, 11.6–15.
27. D.P. Chattopadhyaya, 1977.
28. K.G. Zysk, 1991: 4.
29. *CS*, *Śārīrasthāna*, 8.32–3.
30. CS, *Śārīrasthāna*, 8.33–4.
31. *Bṛhatkathāślokasaṁgraha*, 18.18–19.
32. Ibid., 21.17.
33. *Śatakatrayam*, verses 147, 172.
34. Ibid.: xxiv.
35. *Siṁhāsanadvātrinśikā*, p. 81.
36. M. Foucault, vol. 1, 1979: 146.
37. K. Roy (1994: 3-17), for instance, has shown that Medhātithi through his commentary succeeded in achieving a substantial reworking of the original text of *Manusmṛti*.
38. *Manusmṛti*, 3.77.

39. P.V. Kane, 1974: 424.
40. *Manusmṛti*, 4.1; 6.1, 34–7.
41. *Manubhāṣya*, 4.36.
42. *Manusmṛti*, 6.87–9.
43. *Manubhāṣya*, 6.89.
44. One possible explanation for this may have been the influence of Śaṁkara, who is known to have graduated to *sanyāsa* without going through the *gṛhastha* stage. However, Medhātithi's view was not universally shared. Lakṣmīdhara in his twelfth-century law digest *Kṛtyākalpataru*, upheld the ideal of *gṛhasthāśramadharma*. He deliberately omitted in his *mokṣakāṇḍa* the authorities who permitted *sanyāsa* immediately after the *brahmacarya āśrama* and consciously emphasized the superiority of the life of a householder to that of an anchorite (cited in B.N.S. Yadava, 1973: 75).
45. *Manubhāṣya*, 3.45; 9.4.
46. *Mahābhārata*, 5.39.62.
47. P.V. Kane, 1974: 561.
48. An ayurvedic text defining nine types of *vandhyā* or infertile women, lists women who give birth to only girls (*strīprasūti*) among them (*Mādhavanidāna*, *Nidānapariśiṣṭa*, 27).
49. *Manusmṛti*, 9.79.
50. *Manubhāṣya*, 9.79.
51. *Nāradasmṛti*, 12.62.
52. P.V. Kane, 1974: 619–20.
53. Cited in B.N.S. Yadava, 1973: 70–1.
54. *Smṛticandrikā*, 1948, p. 221.
55. *Manusmṛti*, 11.68.
56. *Manubhāṣya*, 11.174.
57. *Manusmṛti*, 8.369–70.
58. *Manubhāṣya*, 8.370.
59. *Arthaśāstra*, 4.12.20–1.
60. Cited in R. Porter and M. Teich (eds.), 1994: 75.
61. *Manusmṛti*, 2.213.
62. *Manubhāṣya*, 2.213.
63. *Manusmṛti*, 5.148.
64. *Manubhāṣya*, 9.3.
65. *Manusmṛti*, 9.29.
66. *Nāradasmṛti*, 12.50–4.
67. *Manubhāṣya*, 11.138.
68. Ibid., 5.156–60.
69. P.V. Kane, 1974: 584.
70. This comes through quite forcefully in the *Kāśīkhaṇḍa* of *Skandapurāṇa* as well, where a widow is advised never to sleep on a cot, never to wash her body with fragrant unguents, nor enjoy the fragrance of sweet-smelling things (P.V. Kane, 1974: 585).

71. U. Chakravarti, 1995: 2248–56.
72. P.V. Kane, 1974: 599–607.
73. *Manubhāṣya*, 9.59.
74. Ibid., 3.5.
75. *Jayamaṅgalā*, 3.2.39; 4.2.44.
76. *Śṛṅgāraprakāśa*, p. 32.
77. *Manubhāṣya*, 9.7
78. A.S. Altekar, 1962: 313.
79. While the husband's patriarchal view on adultery was developed in the *dharmaśāstra*, that of the lover was discussed in the *kāmaśāstra* (section on *paradārā*). As for the woman herself, her subjectivity in the adulterous union was reflected only in narratives such as *Kathāsaritsāgara* and *Śukāsaptatī* and the verses in anthologies. These works depict a different reality and a different fantasy. From the lover's point of view, adultery was fun, from that of the husband it was terrifying, and from the woman's point of view there was an element of both pleasure and fear.
80. P.V. Kane, 1974: 531–7.
81. *Manubhāṣya*, 8.364.
82. Cited in R. Porter and M. Teich (eds.), 1994: 76.
83. *Manusmṛti*, 8.149.
84. *Manubhāṣya*, 8.149.
85. A.S. Altekar, 1938: 313.
86. *Smṛticandrikā*, 1950: 478–85.
87. U. Chakravarti, 1993: 579–85.
88. S. Ortner, 1978: 19–36.
89. Ibid.: 32.
90. *Manusmṛti*, 5.88–9.
91. *Manubhāṣya*, 5.88.
92. K. Ganesh in M. Krishnaraja and K. Chanana (eds.), 1989: 89.
93. As Gananath Obeyesekere (1984: 431) notes, the brahmanical ideal for high-caste women insisted on virginity in a bride, chastity in a wife and continence in a widow. This had the effect of extreme repression and such side effects as 'sexual frigidity . . . propensity to hysteria and masochistic tendencies owing to the internalisation of aggression'.
94. Yaśodhara in his *Jayamaṅgalā* commentary (5.5.5–6) informs us that women of the lower classes (*carṣaṇī*) performing forced labour (*viṣṭi*) for high-status men could be made the target of sexual advances. In fact, within a feudal polity low caste/class men were encouraged to buy protection through the sexual gift of their women (5.5.25). For *dharmaśāstra* writers the sons of *kṣatriya* or *vaiśya* men born of a *śūdra* wife/mistress could not inherit their father's property as a right. *Manubhāṣya* (9.155) states that they were only entitled to whatever their father may choose to offer them.

95. U. Chakravarti, 1995: 2248.
96. *Smṛticandrikā*, 1946: 149–53.
97. K. Roy, 1992: 55–60.
98. *Manubhāṣya*, 9.158–60.
99. *Arthaśāstra* (3.3.7–10, 27) recommended fines and corporal punishment for straying women.
100. *Nāradasmṛti*, 12.50–3.
101. S. Shah, 2002: 29–30.
102. P.V. Kane, 1974: 584.
103. Cited in A.S. Altekar, 1938: 257.
104. *Arthaśāstra*, 3.2.20–6.
105. P.V. Kane, 1974: 770–802.
106. *Manusmṛti*, 9.194–5.
107. *Jayamaṅgalā*, 1.3.19.
108. Ibid., 4.2.72.
109. *Arthaśāstra*, 3.3.16.
110. Ibid., 3.3.12.
111. Ibid., 3.3.18.
112. P.V. Kane, 1974: 773–80.
113. Handiqui, 1949: 230.
114. *Harṣacarita*, Book VIII.
115. S. Radhakrishnan, 1953: 133–8.
116. *Jayamaṅgalā*, 1.2.22–4.
117. *Bhagavadagītā*, ch. 16.
118. Ibid.: 16.8.
119. D.P. Chattopadhyaya, 1959: 49.
120. *Mahābhārata*, 12.38.22.
121. *Veṇīsaṁhāra*, Act VI, p. 270.
122. S. Shah, 2002: 30–1.
123. *Naiṣadhacarita*, 17.42.
124. Ibid., 17.58.
125. Ibid., 17.43–4.
126. Ibid., 17.68.
127. Ibid., 17.54.
128. Ibid., 17.48, 50–1.
129. *Prabodhacandrodaya*, Act II, p. 62.
130. Ibid., Act I, p. 21.
131. B.N.S Yadava, 1973: 325.
132. N.N. Bhattacharyya, 1982: 346.
133. Ibid.: 128.
134. M. Khanna, 2000: 116.
135. Ibid., p. 121.
136. *Baudhāyana Dharmasūtra* (2.10.41) states that for an ascetic sexual intercourse is forbidden—*maithunasya ca varjanam*.

137. *Manusmṛti*, 6.41, 49.
138. Cited in L. Dumont, 1960: 53.
139. Ibid.
140. The *Kaularṇavātantra* describes a kaula devotee as a man free of desires (*nispṛha*), ever-content (*nityasaṁtuṣṭa*), impartial (*samdarśī*), and chaste (*jitendriya*)—cited in K.K. Handiqui, 1949: 205, fn. 3.
141. D. White, 1996: 308, 320.
142. A major off-shoot of the tantrics in the twelfth and thirteenth centuries were the *siddhas* like Matsyendra and Gorakhanāth. However, the vernacularized *siddhabānī* (*Gorakhabānī* and *Gopīcandreragāna*) is misogynistic. Here a woman's vulva is identified as a vampire and tigress. In fact, the popular legend tells us that Gorakhanāth rescued his guru Matsyendranāth, who had become too deeply involved in tantric practices with women disciples. For this reason, the followers of the nātha sect held Gorakhanāth in greater esteem. Hazariprasad Dwivedi and Govinda Trigunayat (1961: 266) refer to the fact that nātha literature was not an independent philosophy, but developed from the confluence of many streams of thought. Apart from *śākta* tantricism there was also the influence of Shaivism and *yogamārga*, and it is this which may have contributed to the misogynistic streak in *Gorakhabānī*.
143. Cited in D.P. Chattopadhyaya, 1959: 284.
144. Ibid.: 284.
145. R.S. Sharma, 1977: 180–3.
146. Cited in R.S. Sharma, 1977: 180.
147. At Bherāghāṭ the 81 *yoginī* temple built by the Kalachuri of Tripurī in CE 1000, each of the *yoginī* has her name inscribed along the base of the slab. Some of these names reveal autochthonous origins – Teramva, Parovi, Erudi, Takari (cited in Vidya Dehejia, 1988: 83–4).
148. *Rājataraṅgiṇī*, 6.12.
149. Miranda Shaw, 1994: 6, 11.
150. *Karpūramañjarī*, Act I.22.
151. Cited in N.N. Bhattacharyya, 1982: 122.
152. Cited in B.N.S. Yadava, 1973: 107, fn. 799.
153. K.K. Handiqui, 1949: 204–6, 208.
154. *Rājataraṅgiṇī*, 7.282.
155. Although Buddhism had the Vedic and Upanisadic philosophies to contend with, where sexual symbolism was also ubiquitous, in early Buddhism renunciation took centre-stage with Gautama himself as the first renouncer. For the Buddhist monks too, desire (particularly sexual desire) had to be overcome, and most rules for the monks deal with punishment for sexual transgression. The female in the early Buddhist discourse was seen as a snare of the Māra (Allan Sponberg, 1992: 20).
156. Cited in D.P. Chattopadhyaya, 1959: 2.
157. R. Thapar, 1979: 66.

158. Meena Kelkar, 1999: 75–6.
159. In the Jaina discourse too, cheating and crookedness, referred to as *māyā*, are the fundamental causes of re-birth as a woman (P.S. Jaini, 1992: 15).
160. *Śatakatrayam*, verse 6.
161. The paradox here is that although in human terms an ascetic is opposed to sexuality and fertility, in mythological terms *tapa* is itself a powerful creative force. The generative power of ascetic heat is commonly associated here with virility and increased potency. The myth of Śiva illustrates this connection. Śiva is *ūrdhvaretas*, the great ascetic, and yet it is impossible to find a myth in which Śiva remains chaste throughout, although many myths are based upon the initial premise of his chastity. O'Flaherty also points out that the very act of burning Kāma betrays Śiva's vulnerability and his innately erotic nature (O'Flaherty, 1975: 41, 143, 148).
162. R. Thapar, 1979: 67.
163. P. Olivelle, 1984: 116–19.
164. R. Thapar, 1979: 67.
165. The apparent resolution of this paradox was that material wealth was possessed not by the individuals but by the institutions of which they were a part.
166. R.N. Nandi (1977: 193–4), however, refers to the interesting case of Kālāmukha in the Deccan in the early medieval period who did not insist on celibacy for their monks. In fact, the heads of the Belurmaṭha of the Kālāmukha were all married men and, as a result, the Belur pontificate became hereditary. Actually, this dilution of the celibacy principal was a strategic move to make the sect more attractive to the Jainas who were also competing for religious, political, and economic space in the same area and were more puritanical regarding celibacy.
167. J.M. Masson, 1976: 616.
168. This fact is brought out by Rousselle (1983: 141–59) in her study of the early Christian monks in the desert of Egypt.
169. *Śatakatrayam*, verse 85.
170. Ibid., verse 81.
171. Handiqui, 1949: 176.
172. L. Dumont, 1960: 53.
173. R. Thapar, 1979: 70–1.
174. *SM*, 449.24–5.
175. *Śatakatrayam*, verses 113–14.
176. Ibid., verse 95.
177. There is a paradox here. The male spiritual aspirant reverses the sexual metaphor of women as the hunted prey and the man as the pursuing hunter (as in *kāmaśāstra*). In the spiritual realm it is the woman who hunts, ensnares, and eventually destroys man. Thus the secular metaphor of male = pursuer and female = pursued becomes reversed in the spiritual realm

(V. Ramaswamy, 1991: 14). It is also interesting to note that when women ascetics who had internalized the masculine misogynous ideology of asceticism are assailed by sexual temptations and are unable to practise self-control, never castigate men as tempters; rather, they admit to their own weakness. When faced with the temptations offered by Māra, the Buddhist *therī* heap no violent reproaches on the head of men, but try to avert them by portraying the utter worthlessness and contemptibleness of sensuous passion and lust. They even go to the extent of self-mutilation to turn lusting suitors away (J.B. Chaudhuri, 1941: lxxxviii–lxxxix).

178. *Śatakatrayam*, verse 120.
179. D.D. Kosambi, 1986: 83–4.
180. I.D. Serebryakov (1972: 290–1) tends to view Bhartṛhari's renunciation of the world not in the traditional Hindu or Buddhist sense, but as a 'form of expression of protest'. He believes that only he who has renounced the world (the inequitable world of class and caste divisions) in which he is made to live can remain in it with his conscience. However, Serebryakov's unique view of Bhartṛhari's asceticism seems wanting when viewed from a gender perspective. If Bhartṛhari's renunciation is a protest against the inequitable world in which he is made to live, it certainly does not take gender inequality into account.
181. *Śṛṅgāravairāgyataraṅgiṇī*, Kavyamala series, V.124.
182. *Kathākoṣa*, p. 181.
183. Handiqui, 1949: 176.
184. Ibid.: 266.
185. E.V. Spelman, 1982: 118.
186. *Śatakatrayam*, verse 199.
187. Ibid., verse 79.
188. P.S. Jaini, 1992: 13.
189. *Satakatrayam*, verse 159.
190. Ibid., verse 108.
191. *SM*, 450.29.
192. P.S. Jaini, 1992: 13–14.
193. Ibid., 1992: 74.
194. N.N. Bhattacharyya (ed.), 1999: 239.
195. Ibid.
196. Daud Ali, 2000: 170.
197. *Bṛhatsaṁhitā*, 74.5.
198. Ibid., 74.14.
199. Ibid., 74.15.
200. In the *Rāmāyaṇa* (7.76.3–4) *śūdra* Śambūka was killed (*vadha*) by Rāma for practising asceticism, to which he was not entitled.
201. P. Olivelle, 1984: 114–15.
202. Ibid.

203. P.S. Jaini, 1992: 13.
204. *Bṛhatkathāślokasaṁgraha*, canto 25.
205. Ibid., 25.106.
206. Ibid., 25.109.
207. L. Dumont, 1960: 46.
208. *Manubhāṣya*, 8.363.
209. P. Olivelle, 1984: 115.
210. *Manubhāṣya*, 9.13.
211. Clementine-Ojha, 1988: 34–6.
212. *Daśakumāracarita*, pp. 175, 368.
213. L. Sternbach, 1953: 116.
214. Bloomfield (1924: 238) refers to tales from *Kathākoṣa* and *Daśakumāracarita* to describe nuns as either bawds or go-betweens among lovers. They are hypocritical female ascetics skilled in deception.
215. *Śṛṅgārahāṭa*, pp. 129–32.
216. *Aṣṭādhyāyī*, 4.1.127.
217. *Ratirahasya*, 12.4.
218. *Jayamaṅgalā*, 4.1.9.
219. *Arthaśāstra*, 2.1.29.
220. Cited by Max Müller, 1968: 24.
221. *Ratnāvalī*, Act IV, p. 138.
222. *Priyadarśikā*, Act IV, p. 39.
223. *Veṇīsaṁhāra*, Act VI, p. 319.
224. Minoru Hara, 1977–8: 153.
225. *Kādaṁbarī*, p. 227.
226. *KSS*, vol. III, p. 147; vol. VI, p. 130; vol. VIII, p. 176.
227. *KSS*, vol. VIII, pp. 157–8.
228. *SRK*, verse 703.
229. *Ṛgveda*, 10.129.4.
230. *Atharvaveda*, 3.21.4.
231. Ibid., 9.2.16; 19.52.1–4.
232. As in *Taittirīya Saṁhitā* 2.2.3.1.
233. The memory of this power of *kāma* was contained in the *Mahābhārata* (14.13.11) where Kāmadeva says in his *Kāmagītāgāthā*, 'none can destroy me . . . I am the one immortal and indestructible though *yoga* power may overcome this pervasive power.'
234. *Atharvaveda*, 9.2.19.
235. Ibid., 9.2.3.
236. Ibid., 3.25.1–2.
237. S. Bhattacharji, 1970: 107.
238. This episode finds mention in various other *Purāṇa* as well, such as the *Matsya*, *Bhāgavata* and *Bhaviṣya Purāṇa*.
239. As in Buddhism; also, *Kuṭṭanīmatam* (verse 302) refers to *kāma* as Māra.

240. *Ātmā* was conceived entirely in masculine terms.
241. To borrow the phrase of Borgeaud for the god Pan (Halperin, Zietlin, Winkler, eds., 1990: 16).
242. I have shown elsewhere that *apsarā* had the status of the mother goddess at one point of time. In the *Mahābhārata*, and most certainly the *Purāṇa*, they were completely emasculated figures (Shalini Shah, 1995: 122–5).
243. Bhoja in his *Śṛṅgāraprakāśa* (p. 61) refers to his *madanatrayodaśī* where Manmatha was worshipped on the thirteenth day of the first month of spring. The ladies would bathe and wear fine saffron-coloured clothes, and worship the god of love. Yet the same saffron colour was the most visible symbol of renunciation among the ascetics of all hues.
244. *SRK*, verse 327.
245. *Śṛṅgārahāṭa*, p. 1.
246. *Ratirahasya*, 1.1, 3.
247. *Śatakatrayam*, verse 127.
248. *SRK*, verses 323, 326.
249. *Āryāsaptaśatī*, verse 29.
250. *Manusmṛti*, 9.14–17; 2.213–15.
251. L. Dumont, 1960: 41.
252. In the text on poetics, love festivals are treated as *uddīpana vibhāva*, which strengthens the sentiment of *śṛṅgāra*.
253. V.R. Raghavan, 1979: 87. A. Chattopadhyaya, 1967: 137–41.
254. *SS*, *Sūtrasthāna*, 2.10.
255. Cited in A. Chattopadhyaya, 1967: 138–9.
256. *Kādambarī*, ed. R. Shastri, 1964: 713.
257. L. Anderson, 1993.
258. *Ratnāvalī*, Act I.11.
259. *Jayamaṅgalā* (1.4.27–8) while describing a group game refers to *śṛṅgakrīḍā* where water is thrown with a syringe.
260. *Kuṭṭanīmatam*, verses 886–95.
261. Cited in Anderson, 1993: 39–40.
262. Ibid.: 41.
263. Lakṣmīdhara in his *Kṛtyākalpataru*, talks of yet another love festival, *udakasevā mahotsava*, which was celebrated after the full moon day *aśvina*. Giving the details of the festivities, Lakṣmīdhara notes that men and women indiscriminately indulged in indecent pranks, casting to the winds all sense of shame (B.P. Mazumdar, 1960: 373).
264. *Ratnāvalī*, Act I, p. 14.
265. Cited in Anderson, 1993: 31.
266. V.R. Raghvan (1979: 198) suggests that unbridled behaviour during the *Vasantotsava* underlines the fact that the festival is in special vogue among the lower castes.
267. Cited in Anderson, 1993: 31.
268. Ibid.

269. Ibid.: 35.
270. *Ratnāvalī*, Act I, p. 13.
271. Jīmūtavāhana, in his *Kalāviveka*, cites the festival *Śavarotsava* celebrated around October. It too had its origins in folk festivities of the *śavara* tribal people and was also characterized by free sexual behaviour of men and women.
272. L. Anderson, 1993: 203.
273. *Siṁhāsanadvātrinśikā*, p. 146.
274. In the metrical recension (ibid.: 148) of this tale the king pays homage to Umā, Maheśvara, Lakṣmī and Nārāyaṇa, to spring and to Kāmadeva and Rati. The latter two are, thus, among the other more exalted gods who are placed before them.
275. Although this was not the case in the narrative texts where the setting of Kāmadeva worship by women is more ambiguous. Thus even prostitutes worship Kāmadeva, as Vasantasenā in *Mṛcchakaṭika* and Hāralatā in *Kuṭṭanīmatam*.
276. Anderson, 1993: 66.
277. Ibid.: 67.
278. *Ratnāvalī*, Act I, p. 30.
279. Cited in L. Anderson, 1993: 67.
280. *Kāvyamīmāṁsā*, ch. 18, p. 262.
281. Ibid.

2

The Physiology of *Kāma*

In this chapter we shall focus on the body, with particular reference to the female body as conceived in two types of literary discourses, the ayurvedic texts and the *kāmaśāstrīya* texts, to analyse the nature of sexuality in its bodily manifestations. From a gender perspective there is a need to study the female body, because that gives us an idea of social relations. In anthropology[1] the physical body is not seen as a mere biological given, but is perceived as a code or metaphor for society. Encoded in this biological body are social meanings; for if gender identity is a 'constructed' identity, it is neither biology nor psychology but really, as Judith Butler[2] remarks, culture that becomes destiny. A body is perceived as an instrument or medium of culture. Culture's grip on the body is a fact, so that a woman's relation to her body is dominated by the culture. In the movement from sex to gender, there occurs a sculpting of the original body into a cultured form. We shall therefore focus on analysing the cultural elaborations of physiological facts.

In both the ayurvedic and *kāmaśāstrīya* discourses, we see that woman is perceived only as a body. This objectification is linked to sexuality to the extent that it is the woman's body as a sex object as well as the presentation of her embodied self as an expression of her sexuality, that take precedence over everything else. It is, therefore, important to emphasize the all-pervasive nature of sexuality which, as MacKinnon[3] points out, is a dimension along which gender occurs and through which gender is socially constituted. Thus, the restriction and constraint, the servility and the display, the requisite presentation of the self as a beautiful thing and enforced passivity, all constitute the content of sex in the case of women.

THE AYURVEDIC DISCOURSE

In its analysis of what the physiological discussion initiated by the ayurvedic writers implies about the sexual lives of women, this study has made use of treatises such as Vāgbhaṭṭa's[4] *Aṣṭāṅgasaṁgraha* dated to the seventh century, *Mādhavanidāna* of Mādhavakar also of the same period, Dṛḍhabala's[5] ninth-century redaction of the *Caraka Saṁhitā*, and Ḍalhaṇa's twelfth-century commentary on the *Suśruta Saṁhitā*.

Within this medical discourse women were marginalized, if not altogether excluded. For instance the *Caraka Saṁhitā* is addressed to the learned man (*buddhimāna, paṇḍita, vidvāna*), or male physician (*bhiṣaja*). Ḍalhaṇa[6] refers to the *vaidya* as a reliable, sincere person (*viśvāsabhājanmiti*), aware of his duties to the public. He has to study constantly, think hard to improve his knowledge, and teach. Many women, on the other hand, are dismissed by Ḍalhaṇa[7] as thoughtless (*avivekinogrāhyaḥ*). Apart from the low intellectual development of women which would have prevented them from being the initiators of this discourse, there was also a practical problem about gathering authentic knowledge about women. Given the social code of conduct, it was very difficult for the male physician to gain access to women's bodies. The *Vimānasthāna* of *Caraka Saṁhitā*, which deals with the training, duties, and privileges of the physician, informs us that 'a physician must not enter a private house without permission or proper introduction, nor attend to a woman in the absence of her husband (*bhartā*) or guardian (*adhyakṣa*)'.[8] And where physicians gained entry it was always possible that they may abuse this access rather than honour it. Kṣemendra in his satirical tract *Narmamālā*[9] talks of a *vaidya* who, when called upon to attend to a woman patient, came and sat beside her, touched her breasts and quickly gave his diagnosis. In the *Āryāsaptaśatī*[10] there is the description of a lovesick *nāyikā* whose paramour is a *vaidya*, and unmindful of public scandal (*aganitajanāpavāda*) she acted feverish so that she could get to meet him. And so men of the household tried to restrict the entry of medical men.

Given this social reality, the woman's body, both in health and pleasure, had no autonomy of expression, but was dependent on the male guardian or physician for its manifestation. The only depiction of the female body (framed within the male discourse), that we get is what was of significance to the men. When these ayurvedic treatises deal exclusively with women's pathology, it is with diseases pertaining to the uterus or *garbhavyāpta*, as they are referred to in the *Śārīrasthāna* chapter of *Aṣṭāṅgasaṁgraha*. Also referred to are the diseases of the women's genitals called *yonivyāpta* by Caraka,[11] Ḍalhaṇa,[12] and Vāgbhaṭṭa.[13] The *Mādhavanidāna*[14] deals with female diseases of the genital tract, abortion, diseases of the post-natal period, lactation, and infertility. Of the *aṣṭāṅga* or eight branches of medicine enumerated by Vāgbhaṭṭa, there is one devoted to *bāla-cikitsā* (paediatrics), and another to *vṛṣacikitsā* which deals with virilification therapy for men, but females do not figure as a subject anywhere in this specialized list. We thus notice a basic gender asymmetry about the health of men and women. Men are advised to balance their diet in order to maintain good health, while women's health is dominated by their sexual function. Furthermore, if at all ayurvedic texts expressed concern for diseases of the uterus it was not because of concern for women but because a healthy uterus was crucial for the birth and health of the progeny. Vāgbhaṭṭa[15] underlines the procreative reasons for safeguarding women's health: *strī hi mūlapatyānāma strī hi rakṣati rakṣitā* – woman is the chief cause for progeny; if she is protected even the progeny is protected. One might say here, that the stance of the ayurvedic writers is pro-antenatalistic. Their intent is to protect women's fertility and the fruit of that fertility. As Vāgbhaṭṭa[16] and Caraka[17] also note, 'the genital tract afflicted by defects does not hold semen, and as such the woman does not conceive and gets infected by various disorders like tumours (*gulma*), piles (*arśa*), and menorrhagia (*pradārā*).' It is evident, then, that for ancient physicians all symptoms of women's disorders were to be considered in relation to the genital area. Āyurveda may have been the science of longevity, but women's longevity was hardly of any concern to it.

Given the gendered nature of the sources where woman as woman is not considered, the issues regarding female sexuality have to be grasped only by inference while reading about men.[18] In this context it is worth examining how the ayurvedic discourse had framed the question of sexual pleasure. Caraka, Ḍalhaṇa, and Vāgbhaṭṭa talk in terms of a virile model (the missionary coital position) of the sexual act. There is no ambivalence regarding who is the giver and who the receiver in this act. They also tend to reinforce in medical terms, the desirability of this practice. Caraka[19] tells us that

> one should not perform coitus with the female partner in the bending down or side positions. In the former, the *vāta* (wind) humour being strong inflicts the genital tract. In the latter, if she is on her right side the *kapha* humour blocks the uterus, and if on her left side, the *pitta* humour afflicts both ovum and sperm with a burning sensation. Hence, she should receive the seed, i.e. semen, while in the supine position, because in that condition the *doṣa* remain in their normal positions.

This statement is repeated by Vāgbhaṭṭa.[20] Ḍalhaṇa[21] while listing the 'don'ts' for a man during intercourse, talks of an act of coition enjoyed by lying flat and holding the woman on one's bosom (that is, where the woman is on top of the man). At that moment, the man must not ejaculate (*uttānaśayanepi retaso visargaḥ parivarjayet*). In another place Ḍalhaṇa[22] describes an impotent or *ṣaṇḍha* person and says that he is the offspring of parents who have intercourse with the woman on top. The impotent son or *ṣaṇḍha* behaves like a woman and is incapable of discharging semen. Ḍalhaṇa notes that if coitus in this manner produces a girl, her sexual behaviour will be that of a man. Vāgbhaṭṭa[23] concurs with this opinion. It follows that 'masculinity' according to the ayurvedic writers was an achieved state and not an anatomical fact, and in order to achieve the correct proportion of masculinity it was necessary to follow the virile model of the sexual act.

Since the correct posture of the sexual act was perceived as virile it was but natural that alternative models of sexual gratification for women, like lesbian love and auto-eroticism, were denounced.[24] Thus, Ḍalhaṇa[25] tells us that a boneless monstrosity (*alpakomalāsthi*) is the outcome of a sexual act in which both partners are female and their *śukra* (sexual secretions) unite somehow or the other in the womb of one of them. Ḍalhaṇa[26] states that if a lady who has had a bath after her menstrual period and then, in a dream, experiences the pleasure of intercourse, the *vāyu* pushes menstrual blood (*ārtava*) into the uterus and converts it into a foetus. Such a foetus (*kalalaṁ*) is devoid of features inherited from father. Ḍalhaṇa,[27] therefore, declares that all such foetuses should be considered as the outcome of deadly sin and atheism (maternal and paternal). It is thus clear that Ḍalhaṇa's intention was to denounce the undesirable sexual acts of people in general, and of women in particular. Vāgbhaṭṭa[28] opines that at the time of sexual intercourse with men, women secrete *śukra* (his reference to woman reaching orgasm), but since to him it had no significance in the formation of the foetus, he does not elaborate on it any further. He also claims[29] that birth anomalies could result if a woman reached orgasm before the man – for then the *śukra* (male seed) is deposited in the woman who is no longer attentive (to its reception) due to the ecstasy of sex. Then *vāta* brings about abnormalities leading to the birth of a person who is without semen. So it follows that for the ayurvedic authors woman is nothing more than a uterus, who has a reproductive life but nothing beyond it.

But even while the correct model of the sexual act is virile, the question of 'desire' of the female partner in the sexual act is not discounted altogether, and is alluded to at least in the context of procreation if not for its own sake. It is interesting to note that the description of a woman's role in intercourse appears in the chapter entitled *Śārīrasthāna* which deals with embryo formation. Caraka[30] points out that it is the mother's lack of desire for coitus that is one of the reasons for the birth of deformed progeny. Desire on the part of both partners is underlined as an important element in the formation of the foetus in the first place. Caraka[31] says that 'when they are stimulated well and are favourably disposed for coitus (*saṁjātaharṣa-maithune*) they should go to bed well-perfumed'. Vāgbhaṭṭa[32] also opines that in the process of begetting children it is important that the man and woman be healthy, in love with each other, and desirous of sexual intercourse. Ḍalhaṇa[33] says men should not have coitus with woman (*agamyā*), who is not amorously disposed (*akāmā*), inimical (*kṣubdhacitta*), or one who leads the life of a nun (*pravrajyakā*). Having sexual relations with such women leads to a waste of semen (*śukrakṣaya*). Thus, medically speaking, women's desire and sexual pleasure were seen as aids to the conception.

Interestingly, where female desire transcends the virile model it usually gets classified under the diseases of the genital tract (*yonivyāpta*). Vāgbhaṭṭa[34] says that one of the twenty diseases of the genital tract is caused by the use of an unnatural thing (*apadravya*) for coition. Ḍalhaṇa[35] describes nymphomania (*atyānandayoni*) as a kind of uterus that does not know satiation by ordinary intercourse (*grāmyadharma*). The woman takes longer to get excited and requires intercourse many times (*bahuśoaticaraṇāta maithunāta*). Mādhavakara,[36] Ḍalhaṇa,[37] and Caraka[38] refer to the *aticaraṇāyoni/ acaraṇāyoni* as one which is unable to retain semen (*bījamgarbh-āṅkurjananaṁ na vindati*), suffering pain due to overindulgence in sex. Caraka[39] describes satyriasis in women when he refers to *acaraṇāyoni* which is characterized by intense itching of the genitals, and women afflicted by this ailment constantly desire sexual intercourse. Ḍalhaṇa's[40] description of the *acaraṇāyoni* is an illustration of a woman experiencing orgasm before male ejaculation is complete (*puruṣāt pūrvamatiricyate*). Referring to *acaraṇā* as *prākcaraṇā*, the *Madhukoṣa* commentary on *Mādhavanidāna*[41] says that such a woman cannot be impregnated. Thus we see that what can be construed as sexual pleasure for women is associated in the ayurvedic treatises with difficulty in procreation. Perhaps the control of women's sexuality was also sought by instilling in them a fear of genital disease.

The medical discourse also represented very clearly the valorization of semen (*vīrya, śukra, retas*), and the male organ penis (*liṅga, meḍhra, śiśna*), both of which were at the heart of the discussion in the *vājikaraṇa* section of the works of Caraka,[42] Ḍalhaṇa,[43] and Vāgbhaṭṭa,[44] that comprise knowledge about increasing male virility. This valorization of the male secretion is reflected in many ways – first, in terms of the pre-eminence given to semen; second, in terms of the focus on disease that afflicts semen and the penis;[45] third, in terms of the diet that one should take to enhance semen; fourth, by focusing on old age (*vārdhakya*) as one of the causes of semen-loss[46] and steps that could enhance virility (whereas, in contrast, women's menopausal stage is completely ignored); fifth, through the discussion of continence primarily in the context of men; and last, through discussion of the season and time of the sexual act solely in male terms.

Caraka[47] says that the wise one in order to protect his body should protect his semen, because it is the final and best product of food, and its diminution leads to many diseases, even death. Suśruta[48] gives an elaborate description of the origin of semen:

the *rasa* or the lymph chyle exercises a soothing effect upon the entire organism and tends to contribute to the increased formation of blood. ... The bones in their turn contribute to the formation of marrow. The marrow contributes towards the formation and increase of semen and fills the internal cavities of the bones and forms the chief source of strength, amorous feelings and hilarity. The semen gives rise to valour and courageousness making a man amorously disposed to the female sex, increases his strength and amativeness, and is the sole impregnating principal in the male organism.

Ḍalhaṇa[49] commenting on this verse of Suśruta, contrasts the capabilities of potent (*śukravāna*) and impotent (*klība*) men. We do not find a similar valorization of menstrual blood (*ārtava*) of the female. In fact, we notice in the *Caraka Saṁhitā* a basic homology of blood and semen, thereby suggesting the generating power of men and exclusion of women from the symbolic control of blood.[50]

There is great emphasis on the kind of diet one should take to preserve semen. Caraka[51] tells us that while bitter (*kaṭu*), pungent (*tikta*), and *kāṣāya* fluids taken in excess tend to be damaging, sweet (*madhura*) fluids tend to increase semen production (*śukravardhaka*). Suśruta says, and Ḍalhaṇa[52] agrees, that the excessive intake of articles of bitter (*kaṭu*), acidic (*amla*), or saline (*lavaṇa*) taste, or heat (*ūṣṇa*) inducing articles, leads to the loss of the watery principal of semen.[53] Caraka[54] lists many herbal roots which are semen-promoting, as well as those that are semen depurants. Various aphrodisiac preparations are listed by him.[55] While there are suggestions that aphrodisiacs increase male virility even in old age, menopause and its sexual implications are completely ignored. Only the bare physiological fact of menopause is stated. Thus, *Suśruta Saṁhitā*[56] makes a passing reference to it: 'the *rasa* or lymph chyle coloured through the effect of the healthy, normal dyeing heat of the body becomes blood. This blood is transformed into the catamenial flow in women which commences at the age of twelve and ceases at the age of fifty.' Vāgbhaṭṭa[57] also refers to menopause in women aged fifty years.

The predominant male view in the literary sources of our period is that a menopausal woman is 'diseased'. In Śyāmilaka's *bhāṇa Pādataḍitaka*[58] we find an old prostitute, Madayantī, who at menopause (*rajoprodhāta*) lost her sexual urges (*nivṛtakāma*). It was only for the sake of sustaining her family that she indulged in some salacious talk (*śabdakāmāmanuvartate*) with clients. The sexual mores of a patriarchal culture treated a menopausal woman as sexually dysfunctional even though there was little physiological and cultural justification for it, as Leick[59] has shown in the context of ancient Mesopotamian literature. He cites the case of an old woman who is shown as saying that 'my vulva is still fine although people say that it is finished with you'. Anthropological data seem to confirm this view. Among the Amatanago tribe of the Maya, after menopause women actually became the sexual initiators of young men. Freed of the compulsions of modesty required of younger women, their personalities flowered.[60]

While an old woman could be condemned as sexually dysfunctional, men were never similarly old, they only had to undergo virilification therapy. The very definition of an aphrodisiac (*vājikaraṇa)* in the ayurvedic discourse underlines the extent to which male desire is privileged over that of the female. There is virtually no focus on the production of woman's orgasm. Caraka[61] says that '*vājikaraṇa* is that which potentiates man to traffic into woman like a horse and which makes him capable of sustaining excessive sexual intercourse'. This definition is repeated by Ḍalhaṇa[62] and Vāgbhaṭṭa.[63] Ḍalhaṇa[64] says that a youth in sound health taking some sort of aphrodisiac regularly, may enjoy the pleasures of youth every night during all the seasons of the year. Old men suffering from senile decay or sexual incapacity and persons weakened by sexual excesses should take a course of *vājikaraṇa* or virilification therapy. Virility was prized not only in terms of sexual prowess but also in terms of fertility which it enabled. Caraka[65] says that 'a man alone without progeny looks like a tree having only one branch, shadeless . . . like a pond dried up . . . (whereas) a man having numerous progeny is praised as auspicious . . . hence those desirous of progeny as well as sexual pleasure should use an aphrodisiac regularly'.

Women, on the other hand, were not the focus of aphrodisiac prescriptions. Rather they themselves were presented as the 'object' of consumption for the desiring subject who was always an ostentatiously virile male. Vāgbhaṭṭa[66] states that *strī vṛṣyatamā mata*, that is, woman is the best aphrodisiac. Caraka[67] tells us that the foremost aphrodisiac is the (sexually) exhilarating woman who is beautiful (*surūpā*), youthful (*yauvanasthā*), endowed with auspicious features, submissive (*vaśyā*), and skilled (*śikṣitā*). The conception of woman as an aphrodisiac for man is something we note in all types of literary sources of our period such as *kāmaśāstra*[68] and even non-shastric narrative texts. For instance, in one of the verses of *Mayūraśataka*[69] there is a description of the beauty of a young woman (*dṛṣṭvā rūpam idaṁ*) whose beautiful limbs prompt arousal in even an old man (*vṛddho api kāmāyate*). In Vāgbhaṭṭa[70] we also come across a single line reference regarding the best aphrodisiac for a woman. Women do not look their best without pairing with men. 'For woman sexual union with man is the best aphrodisiac.' A woman is thus one whose sexuality exists for someone else (who is male). Woman's sexuality lies in her capacity to arouse desire in that someone. Can then one ask, as does Mackinnon,[71] 'Is woman's sexuality its absence, if being for another is the whole of woman's sexual construction?'

Perhaps this gender asymmetry concerning aphrodisiacs followed from a biological difference. The effect of sexual stimulation on a man is clearly visible (swollen penis, involuntary erection, nocturnal emissions) whereas in a woman it is not easily detected without circumstantial evidence.[72] Perhaps this is why Ayurvedists thought that the sexual feelings of men and women are different. However, this still does not take away from the patriarchal overevaluation of the male sex needs. Just because female desire was not physically visible this does not mean that it does not exist.

Diseases that were caused by the loss of semen or vice versa also occupied the attention of these medical treatises. Phthisis was one such disease.[73] The myth of the moon suffering from phthisis due to excessive sexual intercourse and its consequent loss of vital power (semen) is invoked many times. Ḍalhaṇa[74] refers to impotence resulting from loss of semen in a person addicted to excessive sexual pleasure and not using aphrodisiac remedies. As a result, he claims, there is a long-standing disease of the male generative organ or the destruction of the spermatic chord which destroys the power of coition altogether. Caraka[75] refers to herpes (*kakṣā*) and to sores of the penis (*liṅgapāka*) in the same context. Thus, on the one hand there is medical advice about *vājikaraṇa*[76] where the focus is to ensure the health and production of semen (*vīryavivardhana*) and penile strength,[77] to avoid looseness of the penis (*liṅgaśaithilya*), and destruction[78] of semen (*śukranāśa*). On the other hand, there is concern with the loss of semen (*retovagrahaṇa*)—in excess,[79] this is supposed to lead to diseases. As Caraka[80] cautions, 'man desirous of health (*ārogya*) should be greatly concerned about the discharge of semen'. Thus, both nocturnal emission (*śukrayoniśi*)[81] as well as masturbation are prohibited.[82] In fact, *Mādhavanidāna*[83] calls a person who indulges in masturbation a fool (*mūḍha*).

Linked to the issue of loss of semen and disease caused by sexual excesses was the frequency of sexual intercourse and the need for continence. Ḍalhaṇa[84] says that all sexual excess should be avoided. Caraka[85] says that there are three sub-pillars (of the body) – diet, sleep and celibacy (*brahmacarya*). If these are observed correctly and the body is supported well by them, it continues to be well-endowed with strength, complexion, and development till the completion of the life-span. Elsewhere Caraka[86] says celibacy is life-promoting (*brahmacarya āyuṣyanāma*), and also that the wise one is advised not to indulge in sexual intercourse even if he is accustomed to it.[87] For one who indulges excessively in such activities perishes suddenly, much like a lion pulling down an elephant.

In the *Caraka Saṁhitā*[88] the discussion on impotence caused by excessive intercourse explains that the remedy should deal with the cause itself (that is, total renunciation of coition). Nevertheless, the general tenor of the medical treatises regarding sexual activity is ambivalent. The *Caraka Saṁhitā*[89] warns against any retention of semen as a cause of impotence (*śukravega nirodha ṣaṇḍhyakāraṇaṁ*). Vāgbhaṭṭa[90] agrees with Caraka's statement. Ḍalhaṇa[91] also says that the repression of natural sexual desire from a sense of shame is undesirable. Besides, the whole purpose of *vājikaraṇa* therapy was to make man capable of greater and more frequent sexual intercourse. We notice that the ayurvedic texts discuss both the need to conserve semen and the efficacy of emitting it, from the point of view of health. This discourse does not concern itself with the morality of abstinence which men were required to conform to at least in two stages of life, viz., *brahmacarya āśrama*, and *vānaprastha/sanyāsa āśrama*.

As far as women were concerned, continence was never an issue. Medical men spoke of women's continence specifically at the time of menstruation and during the early stages of pregnancy,[92] when for the stabilization of the foetus (*garbhatiṣṭhati*) women were advised to refrain from intercourse (*vyāvāya*). Vāgbhaṭṭa[93] recommended less sexual activity during pregnancy in general, and the husband was advised to share the bed of his pregnant wife only once a month. Yet men's sexual desire could always make them ignore medical advice; thus, in the *kāmaśāstrīya* texts we see that if man's pleasure demanded sexual intercourse with women who were in the prohibited category in the ayurvedic texts,[94] it was to be still encouraged. For example, Kokkokā in *Ratirahasya*[95] says that a woman whose body has been fatigued by journey, who has recently been attacked by fever, who has given birth a month ago (*māsekaprasavā*), and who has been pregnant for six month (*ṣaṇamāsagarbhā*) gives pleasure during coitus (*dadatisuratesukham*). Within the *kāvya* poetry too, a pregnant woman does not seize to be the object of a man's scopophillic pleasure; only the metaphors change. Thus, Bilhaṇa in *Vikramāṅkadevacarita*[96] while delineating the breasts of a pregnant *nāyikā* talks of the darkening of her nipples and the breasts themselves are compared to earthen pots filled with milk, instead of the usual metaphor of hard, twin peaks. A woman's middle (*kaṭi*) continues to be eroticized, but instead of being tiny (*sūkṣma*), the emphasis now is on expansion, which leads to the disappearance of the three folds (*trivali*). We thus see that the overtly erotic gaze of the poet does not seem to be any less invasive even when looking at a pregnant (*garbhiṇī*) *nāyikā*.

Women who were menstruating[97] were enjoined to stay celibate (*brahmacāriṇī*). The most opportune time for sexual activity for women was considered to be just after the menstrual discharge. The rationale behind this advice to women had to do solely with harnessing female sexuality in the service of procreation. It was also this procreative concern which led medical writers to talk about the right age for females to have sexual intercourse. Vāgbhaṭṭa[98] and Ḍalhaṇa[99] recommended that the right age for initiation into intercourse was sixteen for a woman and for a man twenty five; and copulation before that age would only produce a child that would either die in the womb, or if born, would either have a short life or be plagued by ill-health. Girls of young age should not be allowed to conceive. Although in most matters the medical discourse is not contrary to the norms set by the *dharmaśāstra*,[100] as far as the age of sexually active girls is concerned they are quite clear in their stand. The section on *yonivyāpta* (diseases of the genital area) in the ayurvedic treatises refers to *phālinīyoni*[101] which is a reference to deflorative vaginitis. But nowhere among the remedies do we find specific instructions that women should not have intercourse. One is, therefore, forced to surmise that for the ancient Indian physicians coitus for women was thought to be a healthy activity overall. This conclusion is supported by the fact that in the ayurvedic discourse women are discussed only in the context of pregnancy, childbirth, and the case of the neonate.

As far as the right time for sexual intercourse is concerned, the ayurvedic treatises are in agreement[102] that winter and spring are best, and sex is positively recommended in these seasons. During summer it should be avoided altogether, while in the rainy season it should be infrequent, as the digestion is weak and *vāta* humour is aggravated at this time. Suśruta states, and Ḍalhaṇa[103] agrees, that sexual intercourse should not be performed in the early morning (*pratyūṣa*) or at midnight (*ardharātri*), because the *vāyu* and *pitta* humours are aggravated as a result.

Both in *Caraka Saṁhitā*[104] and in Ḍalhaṇa[105] we find a precipitate reference to the institution of *dhātrī* or the wet nurse, but there is no discussion of the reasons which led to the need for wet nurses. Did women (of the richer classes) as a rule not breast-feed their babies to maintain their erotic appeal, or did the wet nurses become important due to the mother's illness? While the ayurvedic texts do not provide an answer to this question, we can analyse other text of this period. We see that *kāmaśāstra* literature gives tips on cosmetic treatment to women for achieving a body which was the chief object of the male gaze. Kokkokā's *Ratirahasya*[106] tells us how a newly-delivered woman (*prasūtā*) can regain a smaller vulva (*smaramandira-saṁkucana*), and what diet she should follow to make her bloated and loose belly flat again (*kṛṣamudaram*).[107] Tips are also provided for making sagging breasts firm (*kuconnatikaraṇa*), and it is stated explicitly that by achieving the desired results women can entrap the hearts of men (*rasikahṛdaya*).[108] Conversely, loose or sagging breasts (*bhṛṣṭapayodhara*) are linked to the end of women's good luck (*saubhāgyaguṇoaṅganānāmnaṣṭa*).[109] Thus, an entire aesthetic of femininity was sought to be constructed which women were supposed to uphold, not for their own sakes but to conform to the ideal of the male gaze.

Catherine MacKinnon[110] once argued that 'under patriarchy the organized expropriation of the sexuality of some for the use of others defined the sex woman'. An analysis of the ayurvedic discourse leads us to draw a similar conclusion.

THE *KĀMAŚĀSTRĪYA* DISCOURSE

The three *kāmaśāstra* texts which we have taken up for our analysis are Kokkokā's *Ratirahasya* and Padmaśrī's *Nāgarasarvasvam,* both of about the tenth century, and Yaśodhara's *Jayamaṅgalā* commentary on the *Kāmasūtra,* datable to the thirteenth century. However, more than space and time, it would be relevant to examine these texts in terms of the class bias of their authors, which in itself was determined by the quality of patronage extended to them. Kokkokā states that his composition on the art of love was written in obedience to the wishes of the king Śrī Vainyadatta to satisfy his curiosity (*Kautūhala*) regarding sexual matters.[111] Yaśodhara wrote under the patronage of King Viśāladeva.

A cursory glance at these texts dispels the notion of female centrality within the erotic tradition. When we question the notion of female centrality we do not mean that the erotica can exist without the presence of a *nāyikā* (more so given the heterosexual bias of the Indian erotic texts); what we imply is that within the discussion on erotics the *nāyikā* is not the subject but the object. The erotic is presented as a sensation (for men) with direct reference to the female body which is perceived as an inert, fetishized object of the male gaze. The *kāmaśāstrīya* discourse was essentially meant for educating men on the mechanism of sexual principles that governed man–woman sexual relations. In other words, these texts intended to control through erotic knowledge the women themselves. Kokkokā, in his *Ratirahasya,*[112] says that the aim (*prayojana*) of the *kāmaśāstra* is the easy attainment of a woman who is difficult to obtain (*asādhya*), to erotically arouse the one who is already attained (*siddha*), and to enjoy complete sexual pleasure with her. A verse attributed to Vātsyāyana in Jalhaṇa's *Sūktimuktāvalī*[113] also states, that 'The winning of women who are very difficult to obtain (*asādhyāyāḥ*) keeping their attachment evergreen, exeriencing pleasing enjoyments with her who is devoted, are the purposes served by the science of love (*kāmaśāstraprayojanam*)'. At his most charitable, the author of *Nāgarasarvasvam*[114] visualized the purpose of this text to be the satisfaction of erotic fever (*madanajvara*) in wide-hipped women (*nitambinīnāṁ*) by men steeped in *kāmaśāstra* knowledge (*manmathaśāstravedī*) out of a sense of grace (*kṛpānvito*). Insofar as sex was conceived in heterosexual terms, women were cast only as the necessary supporting players in these sexual scripts, not participants in their own right. We thus see that in the *kāmaśāstrīya* discourse woman's body was largely depicted as colonized by the hegemony of male desire and it was masculine pleasure that was valorized above all.

The very title *Ratirahasya* is suggestive. Kokkokā is talking in terms of unravelling the mystery and secrets of sex *(rati)* relations which systematically and comprehensively progressed from attraction to consummation, covering embraces *(āliṅgana),* kisses *(cumbana),* love marks *(nakha* and *danta kṣata),* sexual positions, and so on. One can view such texts in the context of the male desire to classify in order to control. To borrow Parker's analysis[115] of classical Greek sexological literature, such texts were an 'anatomy' of sex, a cutting apart and naming of the components in an attempt to control them. They also had the effect of comforting the male reader that he would meet nothing unexpected in the sexual world. Such literature was thus produced by and for men, assuring them that what women really want is precisely what men want them to desire.

Male access to the knowledge of *kāmaśāstra* was also encouraged on more practical grounds. As Kokkokā[116] pithily states, 'a man puzzled about the nature, type, disposition and gestures according to the place of origin of a woman, and who is ignorant of the doctrines of sexual pleasures (*ratitantra mūḍaḥ*) will not know what to do even in the presence of a young woman, just as an ape does not know what to do after having acquired a coconut.'

Although *kāmaśāstra* theoretically gave knowledge to both men and women,[117] for the latter too were involved in its practice, women's access to this knowledge was circumscribed. As Das notes,[118]

> engaging in sexual relations is the means by which one discovers the body of the other. We may even say that the knowledge that a body possessed by one person may have its ego in another, emerged only through engagement with sexuality. Thus, sexual relations may be seen as not only satisfying desire but also as leading to carnal knowledge which, after all, is a form of knowing the

other. From the objective point of view a man and a woman may be seen as reciprocally possessing each other's bodies. The cultural discourse, however defines this possession asymmetrically.

This asymmetry follows from the restriction on the access of women to carnal knowledge.[119] Yaśodhara[120] tells us that a girl should learn the *kāmaśāstra* in her father's house, because after marriage she will not be independent and will not then be able to acquire this knowledge *(kuto'adhyayanam).* He also warns that if a married woman tries to gain knowledge of *kāmaśāstra* without her husband's permission, he is likely to doubt her virtues and might think of her as promiscuous *(svairiṇīśaṁkanīya).* Besides, girls/wives could gain such knowledge only from a select circle of women, mainly kinswomen. Thus, an entire 'network of control'[121] existed to regulate women's access to the knowledge of *kāmaśāstra.* As Yaśodhara[122] explains, men are independent and can find many to give them knowledge, but for women it is not so; they have only a handful to teach them these things. Partly it is so because women are shy[123] and only the presence of a confidante (*viśvasta*) could help them to learn. Women of a more privileged background, like the daughters of *sāmanta* and *mahāsāmanta,*[124] who were in a position to have independent or direct access to the texts, were in a way warned that women's intellect could be literally assaulted by the *śāstra*, tiring them (*śāstreṇa prahata khinna buddhiya*). Even if women learned the *kāmaśāstra* knowledge, that did not lead to their sexual liberation: women could not express their own desires or seek fulfilment; rather this knowledge for women was really perceived as an auxiliary skill which made them more desirable in the eyes of men.[125] No wonder that in these texts women are rarely selected for sexual roles on the basis of their own preferences; the texts hardly ever focus on women's orgasm.

It can be argued that inequity was central to these texts, which through their description of sexual relations were articulating a set of statements about social hierarchy and the power relations that existed between men and women. The society reflected in the *kāmaśāstra* texts was essentially feudal and patriarchal, a society with a polygynous household in which the *nāyaka* was the focus of socio-sexual relations and in control of them. Woman/*nāyikā* as the object of sexual relations came to be classified and objectified in a comprehensive way. The ideal woman was defined in terms of physical (viz., *mṛgī/hariṇī, vaḍvā, hastinī*) and psychological (viz., *padminī, citriṇī, śaṅkhinī, hastinī*) attributes, and also according to the region from which she hailed.[126] There was a striking contrast with the construct of the *nāyaka*, where the ideal seemed to be a universal man with a single, uniform, albeit with different-sized, penis (*śaśa, vṛṣa, aśva*).[127] *Nāyikā* were differentiated almost ad infinitum from men and from each other, and what was important in the classification were their sexual ties to the man. Whether they were accessible to a single man (*kanyā, bhāryā*), to two men (*paradārā, punarbhū*), to all men (*veśyā*), or inaccessible (*agamyā*) women barred on grounds of incest, taboo, class/caste considerations, and so on.[128] One suspects that the sheer diversity of women enumerated had not only to do with men's flight of erotic fancy but with the social context in which women were mere goods (*paṇyasadharma*) on display, fit to be sold (*vikretavyatulya*).[129]

In *Kathāsaritsāgara*[130] a number of queens in the king's harem discussing their husband's proclivity to marry women continuously and still not be satisfied, explain it by saying, that 'No woman possesses all the qualities. Some fair ones captivate by their faces, others by their breasts full and firm, and yet others by their limbs. One has limbs yellow as gold, another is dark . . . one is of budding beauty while another is of full-developed youth.'

The construction of *nāyaka* as the embodiment of 'hegemonic masculinity' (one who attempts to dominate, subordinate and feminize the rest) was reinforced by the classification of eunuchs defined as the *tṛtiyā prakṛti*,[131] the first two types being men and women. Eunuchs could be feminine or masculine in attire and manner, but were defined as feminine *vis-à-vis* the *nāyaka*. Although the *kāmaśāstra* texts do not elaborate[132] on the dynamics of sexual relations with the eunuch, there are interesting references in the narrative texts. In Vararuchi's *Bhāṇa Ubhayābhisārikā*,[133] the *viṭa* tells the eunuch Sukumārikā that she has a major advantage as compared to the other *nāyikā*. When she (i.e. Sukumārikā) embraces (the *nāyaka*) the breasts do not intervene. She is not afflicted with monthly periods (*ṛtu*), cause of loss of attachment (*rāgadhvaṁsa*). She does not get pregnant (*garbhiṇī*), cause of the destruction of beauty (*rūpa*), grace (*śrī*), and youth (*yauvana*) in the *nāyikā*/woman.

With so many advantages (*saguṇa*), if the man shows no affection for her then he is certainly not fit to celebrate the love festival (*ratyutsavaṁ*). But while eunuchs may be in a feminine position *vis-à-vis* the *nāyaka,* this is certainly not the case with relation to the *nāyikā.* In Bhavabhūti's play *Mālatī-Mādhava* and also in some stories in *Kathāsaritsāgara,*[134] cross-dressing (men can be treated as eunuchs in this state) is a narrative device for men to penetrate the confined space of secluded women. Once a man achieves this, he reverts to his masculine role and seduces the heroine. Transvestitism in such cases only serves to thinly cloak a somewhat aggressive male hetero-sexuality and the transvestite, rather than being read as a woman or being emotionally identified with her, is actually understood as a man. It is, therefore, not easy to automatically read the transvestite eunuch as a gender-bender.

We have said before that the social milieu of the *kāmaśāstra* texts was feudal and patriarchal, which left its impact on sexual relations. In order to understand sexual relations we will have to analyse the family and the socialization taking place within it, for the family was the arena in which sexual mores were fashioned. The sexual meaning is to be found in the context of social relations of power, a process by which gender is also produced. Thus, sexuality, particularly female sexuality, cannot be understood separately from the theory of gender inequality. Sexual desires were conceived, realized or thwarted in good measure within the domestic boundary. *Ratirahasya*[135] describes the duty of the wife (*bhāryā*): 'a young wife should give up unfavourable behaviour, and honouring her husband like a god, she should serve him devotedly through speech, mind and body'. Yaśodhara[136] also states that for women the husband is god (*bhartā tu devatā strīṇāma*). One kind of unfavourable behaviour which the wife was supposed to eschew was going out, even on a pilgrimage, since on such occasions she would be accessible to others, and there could be a possibility of sexual encounters. Yaśodhara,[137] aware of the liberating effect of mobility on women, comments that if a woman made visits to public gatherings, she was likely to be considered loose (*svairiṇī*) by her husband. A wife's confinement within the four walls of the house was necessary for her to remain chaste and virtuous.[138] The upholders of proprieties declared the front door to be the boundary of a good woman's territory.[139] Given such norms, a wife can be likened to a 'sexual serf' whose immobility subjected her to greater exploitation. Thus, a wife having freedom of will[140] was seen as an invitation to ruin (*nāśa*), for she was likely to become promiscuous. *Ratirahasya*[141] and *Jayamaṅgalā*[142] also state that wives should have a restricted lifestyle, focused on the husband's likes and dislikes: washing his feet, cooking for him, waking before he does, and sleeping after him. In other words, a wife should serve him like a maid. It is this kind of social setting which has made theorists like Catherine Mackinnon[143] define the institution of patriarchy as one whose structure is heterosexuality, gender and family being its congealed forms. Sex roles are its qualities, and are generalized to social persona. Furthermore, within this patriarchy, reproduction is a consequence, and its control a major issue.

Within this regimented domestic setting women had no mobility, friendships on associations of their own, and were permitted very little autonomy as far as emotions and sentiments were concerned. In such a milieu it is difficult to postulate that a woman would be culturally and psychologically capable of articulating sexual desires of her own. The sexual mastery of men over women had social legitimacy. If men were masters of women all the time and in all spheres, they had to be women's superiors in the erotic sphere as well. In Kumāradāsa's *Jānakīharaṇa*[144] it is said that 'women are not the cause/means of men's greatness (*strīyo na puṁsa abhyudyasya sādhanam*); rather it is men who are the cause (*hetu*) of women's prosperity (*vibhūti*) and strength (*dhyāmana*). For the clouds thunder even without lightning, but without clouds, lightning does not glitter.' This juvenilization of women makes female 'agency' in sexual relations a problematic issue. Although the *kāmaśāstra* texts do pay lip-service to women's pleasure during sexual intercourse as highly desirable,[145] it is more of a theoretical formulation and the sentiment is not echoed in the spirit of the *kāmaśāstra* texts.

Woman as a spouse may be valorized, but she is recognized not as an independent entity, but only in unity with her husband. Thus, if a woman is infertile or gives birth to only girls, she is supposed to request her husband to take another wife.[146] In fact, here we notice the blurring of an erotic procreative divide. The wife could also be called upon to arrange love assignations with other women for her husband.[147] Nowhere do we notice a husband performing this role for his wife. While the *kāmaśāstra* texts give tips on the wife's protection (*dārārakṣaṇa*), no such advice is forthcoming on saving husbands from such temptations. Thus, while for woman there was conjugalization of sexual life, the husband was not expected to reserve all his sexual pleasures for his wife. Highlighting the consequences for women of the prevalence of sexual double standards, Dorothy Dinnerstein[148] says that it 'injures the animal centre of self-respect, the brute sense of bodily prerogative of having a right to one's bodily feelings. A conviction that physical urges that one cannot help having are unjustified, undignified, presumptuous, undercuts the deepest, oldest basis for a sense of worth, it contaminates the original well-spring of subjective autonomy'.

Yaśodhara in *Jayamaṅgalā*[149] refers to an elaborate deception practised by men to gain sexual access to others' women (*paradārā*). A man well-versed in these stratagems of deception will not be fooled in the case of his own wife. In this sense, the *kāmaśāstra* texts were different from the *dharmaśāstra* texts[150] which harp on women's inherently deceptive nature. The *kāmaśāstra* texts[151] are emphatic in underlining the role of men in sexual transgression even to the extent of using force (*grāhyamāhubalenenāma*) on a woman who refuses to be deceived by elaborate lies.[152] In Daṇḍin's *Daśakumāracarita*[153] is told the pathetic tale of Nitambāvatī, who had refused to enter into an adulterous union. Through an elaborate criminal charade, the man who desired her managed to overpower her. The threat of force against an unwilling woman was thus very real. In fact, given the feudal setting of these texts, sexual access to women was presented as an index of male status. Yaśodhara's[154] description of women's sexual exploitation is distressing in its nakedness. He tells us that women of the lower classes (*Carṣaṇī*) who perform forced labour (*viṣṭi*) for high-status men could be made the target of sexual advances. We thus see a double exploitation of women. Their labour was appropriated through *viṣṭi*; at the same time they were made to render sexual services. Yaśodhara[155] goes on to list a number of state bureaucrats who could use their official position to gain sexual access to women. In fact, men who were at the receiving end in this feudal polity were encouraged to buy protection through the gift of their women.[156] In a feudal setup it was normal for the superior liegelord to demand favours from his subordinates.[157] Obviously, men of high status had regular access to women of lower strata, but the converse was not as common. Theoretically, lower class (*sādhāraṇa*) men could gain access[158] to royal apartments (*antaḥpura*). This was a possibility which was not perceived as desirable as it would have meant overturning of both social and sexual hierarchies. The solution consisted in guarding women.[159] To prevent the possibility of cuckoldry, Yaśodhara,[160] enumerating *agamyā* (that is, women who should not be visited sexually), lists royal women (*rājadārā*) among them. *Ratirahasya*[161] advises that *paradārā* should be from the non-*dvija* (*advija*) castes only, so that the class/caste hierarchy was not adversely affected.

Given the fact that the *kāmaśāstra* texts visualized men as initiating sexual relations and at the same time controlling them, it was only natural that primacy was given to the male desire. In the androcentric virile model of sexuality, woman's pleasure lay in being 'objectified' as the passive recipient of male desire. If she was to have sexual pleasure, it could only be constructed around her objectification. It could not be a pleasure that came from desire for the other (a subject position), rather her desire (within this model) was to 'be desired'. One form of male desire was that pleasure was gained by observing and using female beauty. Woman was the object par excellence of the male gaze. Ancient Indians treated sexual desire as a response to the stimulus of visual beauty. The narrative literature (the *śṛṅgārī* court poetry/prose texts) talks ad nauseam of *kṛśāṅgī, tanvaṅgī* (slim woman with small waist) and women with hard and high breasts. Yaśodhara[162] says that women should always go to their husbands appropriately dressed and made up, or else they would become indifferent. Women's bodies were thus 'subjected' in the sense that they were made to conform to the ideal of the male gaze. An entire aesthetic of femininity was thus built up which women were supposed to uphold, but not for her own sake. Thus, in Kumāradāsa's *Jānakīharaṇa*[163] we get a verse wherein Rāma decorates Sītā, but she does not evince any desire to see herself in the mirror, because for a woman the entire purpose of dressing is to please her husband.

Not only did women have to possess the right physical proportions, they also had to be the right age. An old menopausal woman (*vṛddhā*) was stated by *Nāgarasarvasvam*[164] to be prohibited for sexual intercourse (*suratotsavavarjitā*). Yaśodhara[165] states that women who are past youth (*gatayauvanā*) should not be visited sexually, for uniting with them negatively affects men's age (*āyu*) and strength (*teja*). *Ratirahasya*[166] even states that old women themselves do not care for sexual stimulation and are delighted by mere conversation and respect. But for the *kāmaśāstra* writers, while older women are sexually dysfunctional, men are never similarly old, they only have to undergo virilification therapy. In *Ratirahasya*[167] when the husband's old age is described as the reasons for the wife not desiring him, it is listed as a cause of her ruin (*nāśa*). While the ayurvedic texts talk of older women being menopausal and the *kāmaśāstra* texts harp on their undesirability, in the narrative texts this 'unfitness' is converted into an ethical one. In Bhavabhūti's *Mahāvīracarita*,[168] Jaṭāyu tells Sampāti that in Pañcavaṭī Śūrpanakhā approached Rāma with a desire for sexual relations (*vṛṣasyanti*). Sampāti expresses surprise at Śūrpanakhā's lack of ethics (*nirmaryādatā*) in desiring a mere youth (*kṣīrakaṇṭhakaṁ*) while she was a much older woman (*anekayugajīvinyāstretā*) and not being ashamed of it (*na lajjitā*). Although the male gaze cultivated within the patriarchal culture attributed a sexual negativism to older women, there was little actual justification for it.[169]

In the *kāmaśāstra* texts the heterosexual coitus prioritized male pleasure, so much so that even when the texts[170] focus on the details of woman making love to the *nāyaka*, the verses do not convey the pleasure of woman from the act. The emphasis was on what the woman should do to enhance the pleasure of man. It was expressly stated that she should give herself totally to the pleasure of man. Masculine heterosexual desire was valorized to the point that any variant was completely marginalized. There is no mention of homosexuality in *Ratirahasya* and *Nāgarasarvasvam* and there is only one direct reference to this behaviour in Yaśodhara's *Jayamaṅgalā*.[171] This text refers to several marginal groups, effeminate youth and servants (*paricāraka*), the less virile (*mandarāga*), those of advanced age (*gatavayas*), and those unable to find women[172] (*strīṣvalabdhavṛtyaḥ*), as indulging in oral sex (*auparișṭaka*), regarded as undesirable.[173] Another oblique reference to homosexuality in the *Jayamaṅgalā*[174] is where anal sex is referred to as the lower congress (*adhorataṁ*).

Masculine sexuality was also conceived as inherently violent. A *nāyikā* who was indifferent to sexual intercourse (*surata-parāṅgamukhī*) was to be forcibly made love to.[175] In fact, love was described as a sexual war[176] (*madanayuddha*) in *Ratirahasya*[177] and as *kalaharūpa* by Yaśodhara.[178] He also states that this was because both man and woman tried to accomplish[179] their own goals (*svārthasiddhaye*) by overcoming the other (*parasparābhibhavena*). Yet women do not seem to fight this battle on an equal footing. In this combat, men had the right to strike (*prahaṇan*) but women could only respond with shrieks or moaning sounds (*sītkāra*) the reason being that men are by nature rough (*kaṭhora*) and impetuous, but women are passive (*niṣprāṇa*) and weak (*abalā*).[180] What follows from this gender division is that a masochistic position is associated with the female and the sadistic one with the male. Yaśodhara[181] lists a number of instances where women had either died or were injured badly due to the violence perpetrated upon them during sexual intercourse. In the masochistic eroticization of female subordination, pleasure lies in the experience of conquest. Since the *kāmaśāstra* texts do not enlighten us about the female tendency to delight in pain and suffering, we can only turn to narrative texts. In Śūdraka's *Mṛcchakaṭika*[182] Vasantasenā says it is worth (*guṇa*) that is the cause of love (*anurāga*), not force (*balātkāra*). Perhaps it would not be wrong to say that this must have been the opinion of many women, if not all. In the *kāmaśāstrīya* discourse, the idea of love is a largely narcissistic and chauvinistic one (from the male viewpoint). It is also conceived in a gross physical sense of pursuit and capture of the *nāyikā*. The emotional reciprocity in the physical act is something that is alien to the spirit of the *kāmaśāstrīya* discourse.

In the realm of body language, the various ways of carrying oneself are culturally encoded, and can even define social status. Thus, in patriarchy, men are perceived (and even glorified) as predators while women in order to be sexually attractive must be passive, shy, and given to flight so that their pursuit becomes that much more desirable for men. The theme of chase as a metaphor for heterosexual coitus was intended to indicate dominance and submission as inherent in sexual activity. It is significant that in the classification of *nāyikā* according to nature, *padminī* is described as the best (*uttama*) while *citriṇī*, *śaṅkhinī* and *hastinī* have successively lower appeal.[183]

Padminī, the most desirable, is deeply shy (*gāḍalajjā*) while *hastinī,* the least desirable, is totally devoid of a sense of shame (*vītalajjā*). She is given to ugly behaviour (*krūraceṣṭā*) during copulation and is difficult to satisfy.[184] *Śaṅkhinī* too is sexually more forward[185] in her behaviour and is quick to make nail and tooth marks on her lover's body.[186] We thus see that female sexual appeal is supposed to lie in receptiveness and in being passive and submissive. This culturally constructed femininity became a matter of women's identity and the cause of male desirability. Thus, *padminī* women were more desirable than the *śaṅkhinī* and *hastinī nāyikā.*

Heterosexual sex in the *kāmaśāstra* literature was essentially conceived in terms of virile penetrative model which was the outcome of a patriarchal phallic culture (here the term phallic signifies the dominance of men over women. The issue of who derived greater pleasure during intercourse, the penetrator or the penetrated, became a matter of debate. Yaśodhara[187] comments on the Auddālaka Śvetaketu and Bābhravya debate, where Śvetaketu opined that since females do not emit (*visṛṣṭi*) semen (*śukra*), they do not feel the same kind of pleasure.[188] In Śvetaketu's judgement, a sharp and quick sensation is valued more, while the female sensation which is dull and a long-lasting one is devalued. Bābhravya, on the other hand, claims that the secretion of women continues in the course of copulation and they too experience pleasure. Vātsyāyana suggested and Yaśodhara[189] comments that the difference between the male and female in the sexual act is only that of 'consciousness' of the pleasure. The difference in the ways of working (*kriyābheda*) by which men are actors (*kartā*) and women are persons acted upon (*ādhāra*) or receptacles, is owing to the nature of the male and the female.[190] The one is he who eats (*grāsaka*), and the other is she who is eaten (*grāsya*). From this difference in the ways of working follows the difference in the consciousness of pleasure. For a man thinks that 'this woman is united with me (that is, I am pleasuring her) and woman thinks I am united with this man (I am the cause of his pleasure)'. Vātsyāyana, however, concludes and Yaśodhara[191] comments that both men and women experience pleasure in their complementary roles.

In spite of the concluding sentiments of this debate it is very clear that in the *kāmaśāstra* literature female pleasure is conceived in terms of successful and frequent sexual penetration. In other words, sex is an invitation to mount and the penis is seen as the primary organ of sexual pleasure for both sexes. Thus, men who have soft (*mṛdu*) and small (*hasvadhvaja*) penises, says *Nāgarasarvasvam*,[192] and ejaculate early can never satisfy women. Men are advised[193] to follow a regimen that would make their organs hard like iron (*lauhapama*) and such men become conquerors[194] of women (*narīṣu durjayo bhavati*). This emphasis on male genitals and on inexhaustible, voracious male appetite as the only formula for success in erotic relationships tends to devalue the notions of desire *per se* (with its emotional and mental connotations) and of reciprocity. *Ratirahasya*[195] gives various aphrodisiac preparations to increase semen and to prevent quick ejaculation (*vīryastambhana*). Both *Ratirahasya*[196] and Yaśodhara[197] describe various ways in which the size of the penis could be increased. This obsession with the size of the penis was an indication of their significance as weapons or symbols of male power in androcentric sexual model. The implication is that a man who is unable to penetrate a woman is also unable to exercise power over her.[198]

It was again the virile model which led the *kāmaśāstras*[199] to describe the efficacy and desirability of sexual intercourse in terms of the 'right size' of the male and female genitalia. We are told that *mṛgī* and *śaśa, vaḍvā* and *vṛṣa* and *hastinī* and *aśva* are equal sexual union (*samarata*) and are the best. All other permutations and combinations are unequal unions (*viṣamarata*) and though not as desirable, even here the higher congress (*uccarata*) is better than the lower (*nīcarata*). In the higher, the penis (*sādhana*) is bigger than the vulva (*yoni*) and is therefore capable of giving greater pleasure to the woman. Given the fact that the penetrative sexual model is seen as highly efficacious in inducing female orgasm, such approval of higher congress (*uccarata*) is expected. But even more significantly, since a sexual encounter also articulated a statement about social hierarchy, the social/gender hierarchy would have been greatly compromised in the lowest of the low union (*atinīcarata*) as between a *hastinī* woman and a *śaśa* man where the penetrator (that is, *śaśa* man) would presumably not have control of the *hastinī* woman during copulation. So it was the most undesirable of all unions.

In *Jayamaṅgalā* says Yaśodhara[200] women are in a permanent state of satyriasis (*kaṇḍūti*) or abnormally elevated sexual desire accompanied by itching and tension in the genitals. This can only be satisfied by penile penetration. This obsessive focus on penetration and the conceptualization of women's pleasure as dependent on it also explains why lesbian relations were all but invisible, outside the realm of sexuality. We do get references to lesbianism,[201] but it is not seen as a unique kind of sexual union, rather it is defined in terms of categories of heterosexual intercourse with one of the women involved being classified as *puruṣavat*,[202] or literally man-like. Thus at one level, says Roy,[203] such relations were either obliterated or marginalized[204] from discussion, while at another level recognition was accorded by assimilating them to heterosexual roles which were legitimized in the dominant tradition. But one need not dismiss the male-like woman (*puruṣavat*) in the lesbian coupling as mere assumption of the heterosexual role. It can also be seen as gender deviance. The very possibility of deviance casts doubt on the stability of gender categories man and woman. The masculine woman assumes a masculine role in sexually pursuing a woman partner. In such a case there is an abandonment of the culturally-constructed feminine identity in favour of a culturally-constructed masculine identity.

We notice marginalization of female desire at work again in the description of the *puruṣāyita* erotic posture in which the woman lies on top of the man during copulation. In this posture the virile model of sex was compromised[205] by the reversal of the penetrator-penetrated hierarchy and, therefore, it was described as *viparītarata*.[206] The very use of the term *viparīta* (opposite) is significant for it conveys departure from the norm. In such a case a man had a receptive rather than an insertive sexual role. Furthermore, his sexual precedence was jeopardized, and thus his power to initiate the sexual act and his right to obtain pleasure from it. Yaśodhara[207] state that in this posture women make their desires more apparent. It seems that in this position, women could finally 'own' desire. *Ratirahasya*[208] describes a woman atop a man who says that 'now you rogue, you have been laid down by me, I shall kill you, hide yourself, you have been rendered humble.' Recognizing this as subversive, Kokkokā points out in *Ratirahasya*[209] that becoming too used to this position and adopting it frequently is neither desirable nor cultured. While Yaśodhara[210] warns women that they should adopt this posture only if the *nāyaka* is tired and unsatisfied should she perform this act, otherwise she would be considered shameless. He further says[211] that a woman can initiate this posture on her own only if she is very sure of her man and knows that he enjoys this form of copulation.[212] Yaśodhara[213] barred women who were *ṛtusnātā* (immediately after menstrual cycle) from performing *puruṣāyita*, for it would not be instrumental in conception.[214] The *kāmaśāstra* texts make the case for an aggressive woman, but only for the aim of pleasing a man.

Interestingly, the *kāmaśāstra* texts betray an awareness of limitations on the pleasure of women in heterosexual intercourse. Thus, *Nagarasarvasvam*[215] suggests that by keeping women happy by a strategy of sexual relations that take female desire and pleasure into account, even impotent men (*klība*) can keep their loyalty intact. The *Ratirahasya*[216] describes the role of the clitoris in inducing female orgasm. Describing this erogenous zone, it says very clearly that in the middle of the vulva (*bhagamadhya*) there is a penis-like (*liṅgatulya*) nerve spot (*nāḍikā*) which is called the *madanagamandolā* and *manmathachatra.* When rubbed, it leads to orgasm in women. In fact, the anatomical paradox of heterosexual coitus is that while the lodging of the penis inside the vagina (*yoni*) is significant for the male orgasm, in women it is the clitoris which is the centre of sexual sensitivity and it is not necessarily stimulated sufficiently in the conventional sexual positions of heterosexual coitus. Autoeroticism was thus an important means for female orgasm but since women were defined sexually in terms of what pleases men, this aspect of female desire was ignored and even prohibited.[217]

Although an analysis of the *kāmaśāstra* reveals an essentially passive construction of female sexuality, there are certain descriptions, as in *puruṣāyita,* where we notice a more active participation of women. *Vāḍavaka* or mare-like coital position[218] was such an erotic position. Here the woman held a not-so-erect penis firmly. It is significant that *Ratirahasya*[219] refers to four types of erotic positions in the lower congress (*nīcarata*) which was between a more active woman with a less active man who had a smaller organ. Kāñcīnātha in his *Dīpikā* commentary on this verse of *Ratirahasya*[220] lists the *vāḍavaka*[221] position among them. Perhaps it was this 'active role' of woman which led Kokkokā to be critical of this position. He says in *Ratirahasya*[222] that women from Āndhra transgressed the limits of good conduct. Afflicted by a great desire for sexual pleasure, they were inclined to the *vāḍavaka* position.

Referring to orgies like *saṁghāṭakaṁ* and *goyūthikaṁ,* where one woman may also unite with two or more men, Yaśodhara[223] places such freedom of behaviour in lands like *grāmanārīviṣaya* adjacent to *strīrājya* and Vāhīka. These lands were traditionally associated with *svairiṇī* or free women in situations where political and social/ sexual hierarchy did not exist as it did in the brahmanical patriarchal *madhyadeśa.*[224] We thus see that while the reversal of sexual relations was recognized as a theoretical possibility in the *kāmaśāstra* texts, it was at the same time marginalized into a remote and obscure context. It is also significant that while courtly erotic *mahākāvya,*[225] which draw so much from the *kāmaśāstra* literature, give many descriptions of the male variants of the *saṁghāṭakaṁ* and *goyūthikaṁ,* they are silent about the female orgies. This may have been largely due to the essentially patriarchal and polygynous setting of the *mahākāvya.*

NOTES

1. Douglas, 1966.
2. Judith Butler,1990: 8.
3. C. MacKinnon, 1994: 260.
4. Vāgbhaṭṭa describes himself as a *Mahāyāna* Buddhist (AS, *Uttarasthāna,* 50.203–4).
5. *Siddhisthāna,* the last chapter of *Caraka Saṁhitā* was added by him.
6. *SS, Kalpasthāna,* 1.8.
7. *SS, Nidānasthāna,* 7.11.
8. *CS, Vimānasthāna,* 8.13.
9. Basham, 1976: 30–1.
10. *Āryāsaptaśatī,* verses 67, 240.
11. *CS, Cikitsāsthāna,* 30.
12. *SS, Uttaratantra,* 38.
13. *AS, Uttarasthāna,* 38.34.
14. *MN, Nidanapariṣiṣṭam,* 27.
15. *AS, Śārīrasthāna,* 2.40.
16. *AS, Uttarasthāna,* 38.57.
17. *CS, Cikitsāsthāna,* 30.37–8.
18. Men are the focus of discussion, and women have to be understood by deduction. For, as Derrida would argue, any identity is always already haunted by the other it seeks to exclude (see M. McQuilian, 2000: 22).
19. *CS, Śārīrasthāna,* 8.5–6.
20. *AS, Śārīrasthāna,* 1.30.

21. *SS*, *Cikitsāsthāna*, 24.120.
22. *SS*, *Śārīrasthāna*, 2.42–4.
23. *AS*, *Śārīrasthāna*, 1.30.
24. We notice the same attitude in the *dharmaśāstra* as well, since they too were concerned only with the reproduction of the species (*Manusmṛti*, 11.68; *Manubhāṣya*, 11.174; 8.369–70).
25. *SS*, *Śārīrasthāna*, 2.47.
26. *SS*, *Śārīrasthāna*, 2.48–9.
27. *SS*, *Śārīrasthāna*, 2.52.
28. *AS*, *Śārīrasthāna*, 1.44.
29. *AS*, *Śārīrasthāna*, 2.22.
30. *CS*, *Śārīrasthāna*, 2.20.
31. *CS*, *Śārīrasthāna*, 8.7.
32. *AS*, *Śārīrasthāna*, 1.12.
33. *SS*, *Cikitsāsthāna*, 24.114–16.
34. *AS*, *Uttarasthāna*, 38.34.
35. *SS*, *Uttaratantra*, 38.15.
36. *MN*, 62.9.
37. *SS*, *Uttaratantra*, 38.16.
38. *CS*, *Cikitsāsthāna*, 30.18.
39. *CS*, *Cikitsāsthāna*, 30.17.
40. *SS*, *Uttaratantra*, 38.16.
41. *MN*, vol. 2, pp. 828–9.
42. *CS*, *Cikitsāsthāna*, 2.1, 2.4.
43. *SS*, *Cikitsāsthāna*, 26.
44. *AS*, *Uttarasthāna*, 50.
45. Ḍalhaṇa (*SS*, *Sūtrasthāna*, 15.9) notes that while the semen pervades the whole body (*śukrasya sarvaśarīra vyāpino*), it is located particularly in the penis (*meḍhra*).
46. *MN*, *Nidānapariṣiṣta*, 22.6-9.
47. *CS*, *Cikitsāsthāna*, 30.185–7; *Nidanasthāna*, 6.8–9.
48. I have followed the English translation of *Suśruta Saṁhitā* (*Sūtrasthāna*, 15.6) by K.L. Bhishagratna.
49. *SS*, *Sūtrasthāna*, 15.4.
50. It is stated in the *Mahābhārata* (14.24.7), that from sexual desire is born the semen, and from semen menstrual blood (*kāmāta saṁjāyate śukram śukrāt saṁjāyate rajaḥ*). There is thus an appropriation of blood as a male reproductive fluid. On the other hand, in gynaecentric *tantra* literature, where menstrual blood is considered auspicious, it is stated that the 'blood in the womb is called the seed' (O. Flaherty, 1981: 34–5).
51. *CS*, *Sūtrasthāna*, 26.43, 60–1.
52. *SS*, *Cikitsāsthāna*, 26.10.
53. In the *Caraka Saṁhitā* (*Cikitsāsthāna*, 30.10.) we find a description of a diet that could cause problems with menstrual blood.

54. *CS*, *Sūtrasthāna*, 4.12.
55. *CS*, *Cikitsāthāna*, 2.1, 24–42.
56. *SS*, *Sūtrasthāna*, 14.6.
57. *AS*, *Śārīrasthāna*, 1.11.
58. Motichandra and Agrawala, 1960: 212.
59. G. Leick, 1994: 92.
60. Seaman and Seaman, 1978: 314.
61. *CS*, *Cikitsāsthāna*, 2.4.51.
62. *SS*, *Cikitsāsthāna*, 26.3–5.
63. *AS*, *Uttarasthāna*, 50.2–3.
64. *SS*, *Cikitsāsthāna*, 26.4–5.
65. *CS*, *Cikitsāsthāna*, 2.1.16–23.
66. *AS*, *Uttarasthāna*, 50.118–23.
67. *CS*, *Cikitsāsthāna*, 2.1.4–7.
68. S. Shah, 2003: 131–53.
69. *Mayūraśataka*, p. 74.
70. *AS*, *Uttarasthāna*, 50.6.
71. C. MacKinnon, 1982: 533.
72. S. Ardener, 1993: 2.
73. *CS*, *Nidānasthāna*, 6.12; 8.11.
74. *SS*, *Cikitsāsthāna*, 26.11.
75. *CS*, *Sūtrasthāna*, 20.14; *Cikitsāsthāna*, 30.168.
76. *CS*, *Cikitsāsthāna*, 2.1.23.
77. *CS*, *Cikitsāsthāna*, 30.154; 2.1.46.
78. *CS*, *Cikitsāsthāna*, 28.21; *Sūtrasthāna*, 26.62.
79. *CS*, *Sūtrasthāna*, 26.43.
80. *CS*, *Cikitsāsthāna*, 30.184–6.
81. *CS*, *Cikitsāsthāna*, 2.1.46; 2.3.13.
82. *CS*, *Cikitsāsthāna*, 30.165; *SS*, *Cikitsāsthāna*, 24.119–20.
83. *MN*, *Nidānapariśiṣṭa*, 24.1–5
84. *SS*, *Çikitsāsthāna*, 24.111–13.
85. *CS*, *Sūtrasthāna*, 11.34–5.
86. *CS*, *Sūtrasthāna*, 25.40.
87. *CS*, *Sūtrasthāna*, 7.34–5.
88. *CS*, *Cikitsāsthāna*, 30.193–4, 153.
89. *CS*, *Sūtrasthāna*, 25.40.
90. *AS*, *Sūtrasthāna*, 5.2, 21.
91. *SS*, *Cikitsāsthāna*, 24.110.
92. *SS*, *Śārīrasthāna*, 3.16–17; CS, *Śārīrasthāna*, 8.24; *AS*, *Śārīrasthāna*, 2.36.
93. *AS*, *Śārīrasthāna*, 1.35.
94. *AS*, *Śārīrasthāna*, 1.35; *SS*, *Cikitsāsthāna*, 24.114–16.
95. *Ratirahasya*, 4.28.
96. *Vikramāṅkadevacarita*, 2.63–9.

97. *SS*, *Śārīrasthāna*, 2.25, 28, 31; *AS*, *Śārīrasthāna*, 1.23.
98. *AS*, *Śārīrasthāna*, 1.3.
99. *SS*, *Śārīrasthāna*, 10.54–5.
100. Altekar, 1938: 58–72.
101. *SS*, *Uttaratantra*, 38.18; *CS*, *Cikitsāsthāna*, 30.19–20.
102. *CS*, *Sūtrasthāna*, 6; *AS*, *Sūtrasthāna*, 4.
103. *SS*, *Cikitsāsthāna*, 24.117.
104. *CS*, *Śārīrasthāna*, 8.52–4.
105. *SS*, *Śārīrasthāna*, 10.22–4.
106. *Ratirahasya*, 15.80.
107. *Ratirahasya*, 15.83.
108. *Ratirahasya*, 15.102–5.
109. *SM*, 226.5.
110. Catherine MacKinnon, 1982: 515–16.
111. *Ratirahasya*, 1.4.
112. *Ratirahasya*, 1.6.
113. *SM*, 395.77.
114. *Nāgarasarvasvam*, 1.4.
115. Cited in Porter and Teich, 1994, 32–3.
116. *Ratirahasya*, 1.8.
117. *Jayamaṅgalā*, 1.3.1–3.
118. Veena Das, 1988: 199.
119. Van Gulik (1961: 8) points out that in pre-patriarchal (1500–771 BCE) China, women were repositories of all sexual knowledge. All texts on sexual relations introduced women as initiators and men as ignorant pupils. However, the strictly patriarchal system of the Chou and the subsequent dynasties 'reversed' this position, Interestingly, Monier-Williams' *Sanskrit-English Dicitionary* (1994, col. 2, p. 867) defines the term *rataguru* as husband.
120. *Jayamaṅgalā*, 1.3.2.
121. Kumkum Roy, 1996: 162.
122. *Jayamaṅgalā*, 1.3.14.
123. Ibid., 1.3.12–13.
124. Ibid., 1.3.11.
125. Ibid., 1.3.19.
126. *Ratirahasya*, 5; *Nāgarasarvasvam*, 20; *Jayamaṅgalā*, 2.5.21–33.
127. Kumkum Roy, 1996: 158.
128. *Jayamaṅgalā*, 1.5.29.
129. Ibid., 3.1.14.
130. *KSS*, vol. IV, pp. 73–4.
131. *Jayamaṅgalā*, 2.9.1–2.
132. Both feminine and masculine types of eunuchs derive their sexual satisfaction from taking a receptive role in fellatio, but feminine ones earn

their livelihood by making a living from it. The more manly eunuchs acted as masseurs, thereby exciting their male clients, and performed oral sex on them (*Jayamaṅgalā*, 2.9.6–9).

133. *Śṛṅgārahāṭa*, 1960: 137.
134. *KSS*, vol. III, p. 16, vol. VIII, pp. 13–16.
135. *Ratirahasya*, 12.1.
136. *Jayamaṅgalā*, 4.1.1.
137. Ibid., 4.1.15.
138. *Ratirahasya*, 4.22; *Nāgarasarvasvam*, 15.6,12.
139. *Jayamaṅgalā*, 4.1.22.
140. *Ratirahasya*, 4.22.
141. Ibid., 12.4–7.
142. *Jayamaṅgalā*, 4.1.12, 16–17.
143. C. MacKinnon, 1982: 515–16.
144. *Jānakīharaṇa*, 9.5.
145. *Nāgarasarvasvam*, 3.10.
146. *Jayamaṅgalā*, 4.2.2.
147. *Ratirahasya*, 13.98.
148. Cited in Carol Vance, 1984: 367.
149. *Jayamaṅgalā*, 5.6.46.
150. *Manusmṛti*, 2.214–15.
151. *Ratirahasya*, 13.15–18.
152. *Ratirahasya*, 13.72; *Jayamaṅgalā*, 5.3.4.
153. *Daśakumāracarita*, pp. 368–74.
154. *Jayamaṅgalā*, 5.5.5–6.
155. Ibid., 5.5.7–10.
156. Ibid., 5.5.25.
157. Ibid., 5.5.31–2.
158. Ibid., 5.6.27.
159. Ibid., 5.6.39.
160. Ibid., 1.5.29.
161. *Ratirahasya*, 13.6.
162. *Jayamaṅgalā*, 4.1.13.
163. *Jānakīharaṇa*, 8.42.
164. *Nāgarasarvasvam*, 16.2–3.
165. *Jayamaṅgalā*, 1.5.29.
166. *Ratirahasya*, 4.4.
167. Ibid., 4.22.
168. *Mahāvīracaritam*, Act V.11.
169. G. Leick, 1994: 92; B. Seaman and G. Seaman 1978: 314.
170. *Nāgarasarvasvam*, 37.6–10.
171. *Jayamaṅgalā*, 2.9.35–6.
172. This is an interesting cause for homosexual behaviour: the insufficient

supply of sexually available women, as in the case of lesbianism in the context of the *antaḥpura* of polygynous households, where the non-availability of men is said to be responsible for leading women to seek sexual partners from other women (*Jayamaṅgalā* 5.6.1–2).

173. *Jayamaṅgalā*, 2.9.26.
174. Ibid., 2.6.49.
175. *Ratirahasya*, 10.4.
176. Van Gulik, 1961: 76 points out that in the ancient Chinese literature sexual congress was often referred to as a battle. In fact, some sexological books in ancient China worked out the details of coitus as military moves on the battlefield, and were therefore mistaken to be manuals of strategy and arts of war.
177. *Ratirahasya*, 10.53.
178. *Jayamaṅgalā*, 2.7.1.
179. Ibid.
180. *Jayamaṅgalā*, 2.7.22.
181. Ibid., 2.7.28–30.
182. *Mṛcchakaṭika*, Act I, p. 38.
183. *Ratirahasya*, 1.10.
184. Ibid., 1.18–19.
185. Ibid., 1.17.
186. For ancient Chinese sexologist literature (Van Gulik, 1961: 149–50), women best suited as sexual partners should be young, with smooth bodies, and be naturally tender and docile and of gentle mien. The woman unsuitable for coitus is the ugly one with a manly appearance and intercourse with her would rob the man of his health and vigour.
187. *Jayamaṅgalā*, 2.1.10–22.
188. In Monier-William's *English-Sanskrit Dictionary* (1985, p. 726, col. 1) semen is described as *ānandaprabhvaḥ*.
189. *Jayamaṅgalā*, 2.1.26.
190. Van Gulik (1961: 125–6) points out that in ancient Chinese sexological literature too, we come across this virile penetrative model of sex where it is said that 'man calls and woman follows, above these is action and below, compliance, this is the natural order of all things ... therefore man and woman must move according to their cosmic orientation, the man should thrust from above and the woman receive below. If they unite in this way, it can be called heaven and earth in even balance'.
191. *Jayamaṅgalā*, 2.1.27.
192. *Nāgarasarvasvam*, 12.1.
193. Ibid., 12.4.
194. Ibid., 12.7.
195. *Ratirahasya*, 15.11–13, 20.
196. Ibid., 15.28–34.

197. *Jayamaṅgalā*, 7.2.28–30.
198. Pat Caplan, 1987: 74.
199. *Ratirahasya*, 3.3–6; *Nāgarasarvasvam*, 14.10–12; *Jayamaṅgalā*, 2.1.2–4.
200. *Jayamaṅgalā*, 2.1.17.
201. Ibid., 5.6.1-2; 2.9.36.
202. Ibid., 5.6.2.
203. Kumkum Roy, 1996: 159.
204. Yaśodhara (*Jayamaṅgalā*, 2.5.27) refers to *strīrājya* as *apadravyapradhāna*. Here, a practice (using an artificial penis) associated with lesbian sex is attributed to a marginalized mythical land.
205. In an exceptional verse of *Amaruśataka* (verse 77) *puruṣāyita* is not conceived as a female initiating the coital posture. The verse states that 'he put me on his breast, and urged by passionate desire he firmly bit my lip, he pulled away my lip, he pulled away my garments with the toes of his feet as with a pair of tongs and started doing what for the rogue was the proper thing to do'.
206. *Ratirahasya*, 10.52.
207. *Jayamaṅgalā*, 2.8.39.
208. *Ratirahasya*, 10.49–50.
209. Ibid., 10.65.
210. *Jayamaṅgalā*, 2.8.1.
211. Ibid., 2.8.2–3.
212. In *SRK* (verses 581, 585, and 589) the *nāyikā* resorts to *puruṣāyita* to please her lover rather than herself.
213. *Jayamaṅgalā*, 2.8.41.
214. In *Āryāsaptaśatī* (verse 363) pregnant women are also advised against this form of copulation.
215. *Nāgarasarvasvam*, 6.12–16.
216. *Ratirahasya*, 10. 6 –7.
217. *Arthaśastra*, 4.12.22; SS, *Śārīrasthāna*. 2.48–9.
218. *Ratirahasya*, 10.20; *Nāgarasarvasvam*, 29.3; *Jayamaṅgalā*, 2.8.33.
219. *Ratirahasya*, 10.14.
220. Ibid.
221. O'Flaherty (1981: 163–4, 202, 207, 218) refers to certain Indo-European myths in which the mare is a symbol of active, hence threatening, female sexuality. *Padma Purāṇa* refers to a mare that devours the testicles of the husband and drinks his semen. *Devībhāgavata Purāṇa* refers to Lakṣmī becoming a mare because she was lustful. Thus, a mare was the symbol of a whore. This image of a sexually aggressive woman who rides astride like the castrating mare also occurs in the classical Greek mythology. Andromache rides Hector as a horse in an 'on-top' position (Porter and Teich, 1994: 38).
222. *Ratirahasya*, 5.14.

223. *Jayamaṅgalā*, 2.6.42–5.
224. S. Shah, 2002: 251.
225. Māgha's *Śiśupālavadha*; Ratnakara's *Haravijaya*, and Kumāradāsa's *Jānakīharaṇa*.

3

In the Business of *Kāma*

Prostitution, like other social institutions of the time, has to be studied in the context of the overarching patriarchy with which it was intimately linked. The terms *veśyā* and *gaṇikā* are, in the classical literature of the period, all gendered or gender-specific—they specifically refer to women prostitutes.[1] In none of our sources do we find any term referring to male prostitution.

In Yaśodhara's *Jayamaṅgalā* commentary on the *Kāmasūtra*, we can find references to nine types of prostitutes:[2]

kumbhadāsī: a slave woman assigned the duty of fetching water
paricārikā: female attendant
kulaṭā: unchaste woman
svairiṇī: sexually promiscuous woman
naṭī: a dancing girl or actress (*raṅgayoṣitā*) as Yaśodhara describes her.
śilpakārikā: a female artisan. Yaśodhara describes them as wives of dyers and weavers.
prakāśavinaṣṭā: a woman who leaves her family, says Yaśodhara, either when the husband dies or during his lifetime, to become someone's mistress.
rūpājīvā: a woman living on her beauty.
gaṇikā: regular courtesan.

A glance at this list shows that women workers were included in the category of prostitutes. This would reinforce the view that under patriarchy it was not possible for women to enter a profession or work for wages and thereby earn a livelihood, and at the same time maintain the integrity of their body. Not only did women workers get classified as prostitutes, many a prostitute upon the end of her earning phase ended up as a beggar who had to perform lowly jobs to subsist. It was thus a two-way traffic. In Kṣemendra's *Samaya-mātṛkā*,[3] an eleventh-century satirical tract on prostitutes, we can observe a significant statement that unlike men who can live on their knowledge and experience, old courtesans (*yauvananāśe veśyā*) can live only on charity (*bhikṣā*). The career of bawd Kaṅkālī in this text illustrates this aphorism. The cycle of the prostitute's existence in this social setup in historical times is also pithily summed up in a verse from an anthology[4] which says, courtesans are first servants (*pūrvam ceṭī*), then courtesans (*tato beṭī*), afterwards old procuresses (*paścāta bhavati kuṭṭanī*), and at the end when they are completely without funds (*sarvopāyaparīkṣīṇā*) they end up as ascetic nuns (*vṛddhā veśyā tapasvinī*).

Although the sources of our period put all kinds of women under the category of prostitutes, women who were forced to be sexually available to their masters, like *kumbhadāsī* and *paricārikā*, or women who were generous with their sexual favours of their own free will, such as *svairiṇī, kulaṭā* and *prakāśavinaṣṭā*, are not objects of analysis in this chapter. For the sake of clarity, I restrict the definition of the prostitute to those who accept payment in exchange for sexual favours. Otis[5] describes prostitution as an institution in which 'socially identified groups of women earn their living principally or exclusively from the commerce of their bodies'.

DEFINING THE PROSTITUTE

In classical Sanskrit literature, a prostitute is one of the *nāyikā* type and is discussed as such in all the poetic works from the time of Bharata's *Nāṭyaśāstra*[6] onwards (i.e. from the third and fourth centuries). She is variously described as a *bāhyā* in *Nāṭyaśāstra,* and *sāmānyā* in Rudraka's *Śṛṅgāratilaka* and *Śṛṅgāraprakāśa* of Bhoja. Dhanañjaya in *Daśarūpakam* describes her as *sādhāraṇa strī.* Since she was a *nāyikā* who was not exclusive[7] she could not, even if she was genuinely in love (*rakta*), be shown with a king or a noble as a *nāyaka* opposite her.[8] In the sources of our period we find her presiding mainly over forms of plays that are called *prahasana* and *bhāṇa.* Here she is depicted stereotypically as bold, cunning and mercenary.[9] In the *prahasana* she did not have to be depraved as in the stereotype—for instance, Vasantasenā's character in Śūdraka's

Mṛcchakaṭika. In the period of our study there is a specific class of works such as Rūpa Gosvāmin's *Ujjvalanīlamaṇī* datable to 1150, in which *sāmānyā* as a *nāyikā* type did not figure at all. *Ujjvalanīlamaṇī* was a leading text on the rhetoric of divine *śṛṅgāra* which dealt with love of Kṛṣṇa as a supreme *nāyaka.* According to Rūpa Gosvāmin there was no *sāmānyā nāyikā* in *Kṛṣṇarati.* Even a low-class woman like *sairandhrī* was subsumed within the *parakīyā* (another's woman), and within *Kṛṣṇabhakti parakīyā* as a *nāyikā* was considered superior.[10] The logic in dropping *sāmānyā* as *nāyikā* in these texts was that anyone in love with Kṛṣṇa (and no one can love God falsely) was automatically transformed into being uncommon and unique.

Three conclusions can be drawn from the above discussion. First, *veśyā nāyikā* is one who feigns love and sells her sexual favours for material gain. Second, she could be occasionally shown genuinely in love, but then she does not remain a prostitute; she either dies (Harlatā in Dāmodaragupta's *Kuṭṭanīmatam*) or gets royal permission to marry her *nāyaka* (Vasantasenā in *Mṛcchakaṭika*). Third, if any woman (even a prostitute) loves God, she could not remain a common woman.

PROSTITUTE—WHORE, VICTIM OR SUBVERSIVE?

Beyond the routine textual description of the *sāmānyā nāyikā* discussed above, we have to examine the social institution of prostitution as depicted in our sources. Was prostitution a 'safety valve' of patriarchal social life, an adjunct that preserved the stability of family life? An interesting verse in Dāmodaragupta's *Kuṭṭanīmatam*[11] states that 'sex with the wife is necessary for the sake of progeny, and intercourse with a prostitute for avoiding sickness' (*vyādhi*) or excessive sexual desire. This shows that the prostitute's sexuality, being non-marital and non-procreative, was considered dangerous. We also notice here the patriarchal idea of women as virtuous women or whores. Even in *Mṛcchakaṭika,* where *veśyā* Vasantasenā is an object of romantic love rather than a mere erotic object,[12] the *nāyaka* Cārudatta[13] is ashamed to admit that a courtesan is his friend (*mitra*). He qualifies his admission of friendship with Vasantasenā by saying that it is his youth (*yauvana*) which is at fault, not his character (*caritra*). In the same play[14] we find *viṭa* describing a courtesan's profession as one 'which is the birthplace (*janmabhūme*) of hypocrisy, deceit, treachery and falsehood, and one which consists of perfidy'.

There is a need to release the prostitute not only from this castigating and judgmental language in which she is embedded, but also from a certain kind of feminist counter-discourse which, too, is a negative construction that focuses on the undesirable suffering and oppression bound up with prostitution through the centuries. This approach, which tends to view the prostitute as a 'victim', is best illustrated in Bhattacharji's historical survey of prostitution in ancient India.[15] Simone de Beauvoir,[16] notwithstanding her perceptive comment about prostitutes in *Second Sex*, says that 'of all women they are the most submissive to the male and yet more able to escape him; this is that makes them take on so many varied meanings'. She does not pursue this insight further, and simply ends up with the 'prostitute as victim' approach. This is evident when she says that 'the greatest misfortune of the hetaira is not only that her independence is the deceptive obverse of a thousand dependencies, but also that this liberty is itself negative'.[17]

A more recent approach to the study of prostitutes/prostitution is represented by scholars like Oldenburg[18] and Bell.[19] Bell resorts to a 'reverse discourse', the discourse of the subjugated subject, to study the prostitute. Here the meaning and power of the dominant discourse are to some extent challenged. Like Bell, Oldenburg too tends to see prostitutes as social agents acting with relative autonomy within the confines of the male body politic. In fact, Oldenburg,[20] on the basis of her survey of the nineteenth-century Lucknow courtesans, talks of the 'self-perception of prostitutes' as powerful. Not only do they view themselves as an experienced lot, they even manage to create a counter-culture or ideology of their own, which subverts and mocks the existing positions and roles of the patriarchal culture. Oldenburg concludes that the courtesan tradition, far from reinforcing patriarchy, represents its circumvention. With this approach as a starting point, scholars have tried to recover a prostitute history which is 'herstory'. Wells[21] argues that the courtesans functioned outside the restrictions that the male state of Greco-Roman antiquity imposed on its wives and daughters. The hetairae could inhabit the public space, exchanging conversation and sexual interaction for payment. They had the most freedom. They were intelligent, witty, articulate, and educated, and they were the only women who were allowed to manage their own financial affairs. They were accomplished conversationalists and the intellectual equals of the men they entertained. They were poets, artists, and herbalists, a truly talented lot. Even de Beauvoir[22] grudgingly acknowledges that 'paradoxically enough those women (hetairae) who exploit their femininity to the hilt, create for themselves a situation almost equivalent to that of a man; beginning with that sex which gives them over to the males as objects, they came to be subjects. Not only do they make their own living like men, they exist in a circle that is almost exclusively masculine, free in behaviour and conversation, and they can attain the rarest intellectual liberty'.

THE *VEŚYĀ* HOUSEHOLD

In order to recover such a prostitute history from our sources we need to first of all analyse the prostitute household organized along lines which were distinct from patriarchal households. The role of the household in writing the history of any social institution is immense, for it is a truism that the household is the arena in which gender relations are structured and maintained. Unlike the patriarchal households surrounding it, prostitute households were rigorously matrifocal institutions. Our sources allow us to recover some of the characteristics of such households. The gender equations here were very different. For one, daughters were highly prized over sons. A woman says in *Kuṭṭanīmatam*[23] that 'the birth of a daughter is desirable (*duhitā eva ślāghya*) and to be satisfied with the birth of a son is worthy of criticism'. This disregard for sons in the prostitute household is strikingly brought out in the *Mṛcchakaṭika*. In this play, when Maitreya on his visit to a *veśyā* household asks his escorts who they are,[24] they respond by saying that 'we are *bandhulā* who sport about like the cubs of elephants, being reared in other peoples' houses (*paragṛhalalitā*) , fed on others' food (*parānnapuṣṭā*), begotten by other men upon stranger women (*parapuruṣearjanitā parāṅganāsu*), enjoying others' riches (*paradhananiratā*), and possessing no merit to speak of (*guṇeṣvavācyā*)'.[25]

Yet again when Maitreya is introduced to Vasantasenā's brother, he remarks,[26] 'I must not (think highly of him) for although he is gaily dressed, gentle, and well-perfumed, still he is to be shunned by the people just like a campaka tree growing in the enclosure of a cremation ground, although it may be bright, attractive and sweet-smelling.' In fact, children in the prostitute household were completely under their mother's control.[27] This is the reason why law givers ignore them completely. Medhātithi,[28] in his commentary on the *Manusmṛti,* says the progeny of miscegenation have no right to perform *uḍakakriyā,* i.e. the ritual offering of water to dead persons, and includes the offspring of the *veśyā* in this category. Evidently, then, such children were not claimed by fathers for ritual needs.

There was also a greater fluidity of domestic arrangements within such households. Srinivasan[29] in her study of the *devadāsī* household points out that *devadāsī* girls dedicated to the deity were not permitted to cook or perform mundane domestic tasks[30] either for the men of their own households or for their *guru.* Oldenburg's[31] data on courtesans also confirms that prostitutes take pride in being able to avoid the drudgery of housework which was the lot of 'respectable' household women. The household division of labour (the sexual division of labour) has an important bearing on the status of women in society. Familial relations shape women's access to work and other resources, and also play a key role in producing and maintaining gender ideologies.[32] Within the setup of the prostitute household, their labour was not subsumed within the category of housework and, therefore, was not marginalized; in fact, it can be designated as 'work'.

Within the prostitute household not only was her work 'the work', but also the 'space' was her own. Patriarchy relegated the wives and daughters solely to the sphere of the private, a space controlled and regulated by men. In this universe their very identities were defined by their ties to men as mother, wife, or daughter. Even if there was some dispersal of power to the suitable age group and category of women, it was according to male-defined rules. So while there could be room for women at every level, there was no 'room of her own'. The prostitute, on the other hand, was defined by a space of her own. She had her own place (*veśavāsa*), over which she had complete command. It is interesting to note that when Maitreya visits *gaṇikā* Vasantasenā's house[33] her maid introduces Vasantasenā's mother and brother in relation to her. In *Kathāsaritsāgara*[34] we read the tale of the *veśyā* Kumudikā who gives refuge to the defeated king Vikramasiṁha. It was because of this autonomy of the *veśyā* household and her subversive potential that it was perceived as dangerous. The *Smṛti* literature which represents the patriarchal brahmanical viewpoint[35] underlines this; Manu as well as his commentator Medhātithi[36] agree on the threat that the *veśyā* household represented.

It would not be an exaggeration to state that *veśavāsa* culture was considered dangerous enough by the patriarchal household, and the patriarchal state would not allow any transgression of the boundaries separating the patriarchal domain from that of the prostitute household. Prostitutes, as far as patriarchy was concerned, were located in the space of the erotic and were denied family space. The patriarchal household used the mechanism of purity and pollution to achieve this. In *Mṛcchakaṭika, gaṇikā* Vasantasenā visits Cārudatta's house twice but never gains entry into his inner apartments or meets his wife. Cārudatta himself[37] says that even Vasantasenā's ornaments cannot be taken into the inner apartments for safe keeping since they have been worn by a prostitute (*prakāśanārī*).

From *prakāśanārī* to a *kulavadhū* of the inner apartment was a rubicon that could not be crossed over with ease. In Buddhasvāmin's *Bṛhatkathāślokasaṁgraha*[38] it is said for a prostitute that the blemish of her appellation as a courtesan (*gaṇikāśabdadoṣāstu*) does not leave her even now. Śārvilaka tells Madanikā[39] that the title of a bride (*vadhū*) is hard (*durlabha*) to obtain. The prostitute tradition, with its evidently subversive potential, required the permission of the state as upholder of patriarchal ideology, if an individual prostitute was to achieve a change in her status to that of wife. In both *Mṛcchakaṭika*[40] and *Bṛhatkathāślokasaṁgraha*,[41] permission for a *gaṇikā* to become a *kulastrī* had to come from the king alone (*rājādeśa*). In Bhoja's *Śṛṅgāramañjarīkathā*,[42] again it is the king who gives *veśyā* Aśokavatī permission to become the wife of Caḍḍālaka who was a feudatory of the king. In *bhāṇa Padmaprabhṛtaka*[43] for a particularly loyal *veśyā* it is hoped that she soon earns a veil (*avaguṇṭhanabhāginī*) at the hands of the queen (*mahiṣī*). It is of course obvious that all these instances of royal permission[44] came after it was made sure that the *veśyā* in question had internalized the *pativrata* ideology of the patriarchal household. In Yaśodhara's commentary[45] we are told that a *veśyā* could be given in marriage to one who could provide special musical assistance to the establishment, for such a marriage leads to greater prosperity. The marriage bond here was not governed by patriarchal ideology, and marital ties were only notional.

The obverse side of this shutting out of the *veśyā*[46] from patriarchal domesticity was that prostitutes could create their own counter-culture with their own value system against the ethics of the dominant culture. Their ostracism simultaneously ensured their greater independence and autonomy within their own space. Prostitutes led an independent life (*svādhīna*) and though they took others' money, they did not become slaves. On the contrary, they were clever enough to overpower men (*vaśīkartum naram*). They had the whole world under their control and were, therefore, proverbial as persons who did not suffer under anybody's authority.[47]

MATRIARCHY OF THE VEŚAVĀSA

Within the boundary of the prostitute household it was the mother figure who reigned supreme. Her will was law. Yaśodhara[48] states that a *veśyā* should never disagree with the mother, who could be either real or adopted, and she should seek her advice on everything. Jalhaṇa's *Mugdhopadeśa* underlines this advisory role of the bawd (*mantrī jaratkuṭṭanī*).[49] In Daṇḍin's *Daśakumāracarita*[50] prostitute Kāmamañjarī's mother talks of *gaṇikāmāturādhikāra*. Even if the younger daughters were the earning stars of the family it was the old bawd/mother referred to as *kuṭṭanī* in the sources, who was the real authority and manager of the *veśyā* household. So crucial and indispensable was her role, that in her absence,[51] it is said, the house becomes a happy hunting ground for all kinds of rogues and penniless men who become difficult to dislodge, and the *veśyā* gets no peace by day or night. In *Dhūrta-viṭa Saṁvāda*[52] a *veśyā* protected by her mother is described as a river teeming with crocodiles from which it is best to stay away. It would not be wrong to conclude that it was the presence of the *kuṭṭanī* which prevented the *veśyā* from becoming an object of exchange between pimp and client. It was the *kuṭṭanī* who ensured wealth for the prostitutes. Thus, we find in the *Samayamātṛkā* that the bawd Kaṅkālī was adopted as mother by *veśyā* Kalāvatī. Sociological data from the colonial period would also support this analysis. Srinivsan,[53] referring to the *devadāsī* household, says:

> The person in charge in the *dāsī* establishment – the *taikkizhavi* (old mother) – was the senior-most female member . . . the strict discipline of this old lady over both the private and the professional lives of her relatives, her control over income, its pooling and expenditure, provided the fundamental source of unity for the *dāsī* household. The critical role that she thereby played in the status and prestige of an establishment was appreciable. . . . Most homes had photographs on the walls of previous such leading lights of the family, before whom daily worship was offered.

The authority of the mother figure within the *veśyā* household can be appreciated better if we analyse the standing and nature of the *kuṭṭanī's* relations with the different men in her life. Apart from clients (*bhujaṅga*) there were certain hangers-on and the *viṭa* was perhaps the most important of them. He was a cultured man in the prostitute's gathering. According to Bharata,[54] 'one who is skilled in pleasuring the prostitute (*veśyopacārakuśalo*), sweet (*madhuro*), courteous (*dakṣiṇa*), a poet (*kavi*), proficient in argumentation (*ūhā-pohkṣamo vāgmī*), and shrewd (*caturaśca*) is *vito bhaveta*'. In *Sarasvatīkaṇṭhābharaṇa*[55] Bhoja refers to the *viṭa* as accomplished (*guṇavāna*). In Rudraka's *Śṛṅgāratilaka*,[56] he is described as a master of one art (*ekavidyoviṭa*), while still others like Bhānudatta in the *Rasamañjarī*[57] described *viṭa* as the master of the science of erotics (*kāmatantrakalākovidaviṭa*). Although Kṣemendra in his satirical *Samayamātṛkā*[58] and *Deśopadeśa*[59] is dismissive of the *viṭa* (*kṣīṇāya guṇahīnāya sadoṣāya kalābhṛte, viṭāya kṛṣṇapakṣendukuṭilāya namo namaḥ*), this criticism has to be placed in its context. The time in which Kṣemendra was writing (the eleventh century) in Kashmir saw a shrinking of urban centres and the urban economy in many parts of the country. It is only to be expected that those institutions which drew their sustenance from a flourishing urban *nāgaraka* culture would show signs of degeneration as well.

Vātsyāyana[60] defines a *viṭa* as a man who has exhausted his wealth in enjoyment (*bhuktavibhavastu*), is endowed with good qualities (*guṇavāna*), is married, and is respected among *veśyā* and in *goṣṭhī*, and earns his livelihood thereby. In fact, Yaśodhara[61] explains this by stating that he draws his very sustenance from *veśyā* and *nāgaraka* (*vṛttimanyāmnichan veśyājana nāgarakajana chopajīvati*). It is thus clear that the *viṭa* was not a male centre of authority in the prostitute's universe. He was only an intimate and cultured hanger-on. He was an indispensable part of the cultured gatherings that higher-class prostitutes like *gaṇikā* continuously hosted. He also performed the functions of a trusted messenger between the hetaira and her clients,[62] and he sometimes acted as an escort.[63] He could be called upon to mediate between *veśyā* and their clients in quarrels relating to fees.[64] No doubt the *viṭa* performed a useful function for the *veśyā* household, but within the household itself it was the *kuṭṭanī* or mother who presided. Neither were the *viṭa* male challengers nor did they emerge as alternative centres of authority in the household.

There is a reference in the *Kuṭṭanīmatam*[65] to one *Śūlapāla* (keeper of prostitutes) who looked after the arrangements of the theatrical performances given by *veśyā* belonging to his establishment. A verse refers to him not allowing a *veśyā* on stage for she was in her monthly period. An eleventh-century inscription from Rajasthan[66] also refers to the *Śūlapāla* accompanying courtesans to give music and dance performances on religious and festive occasions. However, these descriptions do not give the impression that the *Śūlapāla* was in a position of control. He was more the male escort of the establishment (in a serving capacity) who went with the courtesans whenever they stepped outside.

The *ḍiṇḍika*, who were represented as low and vulgar characters in Śyāmalaka's *bhāṇa Pādatāḍitaka*, are another set of men associated with prostitutes. *Ḍiṇḍika* are here described as ugly like monkeys, who in their actions are devils (*piśāca*).[67] In Bhoja's *Śṛṅgāramañjarīkathā*,[68] *kuṭṭanī* Viṣamaśīlā is compared to a group of *ḍiṇḍika* who accumulate wealth by 'draining the purses of others'. It seems, says, Munshi,[69] that these *ḍiṇḍika* were pickpockets who stole money. To the class of *ḍiṇḍika* also belonged the *khala* or rogue. In Kṣemendra's *Deśopadeśa*,[70] as also in the *Kuṭṭanīmatam*,[71] he is described as a dishonest man without principles. It is thus obvious that while the more cultured *viṭa* were part and parcel of the *gaṇikā* household, scum like *ḍiṇḍika*, *khala*, and *dhūrta* (cheats) also surrounded them, particularly the lower level prostitutes like *rūpājīvā*.

This must have certainly contributed to the brutalization of the *veśyā's* environment.

In spite of the presence of these men around the *veśyā*, the *kuṭṭanī* never allowed them to get the better of her. Viṣamaśīlā, mother of *veśyā* Śṛṅgāramañjarī in *Śṛṅgāramañjarīkathā,*[72] states that she is never cheated by *viṭa;* she is requested by *dhūrta* to deceive others but is never troubled; she deceives others but is never herself deceived; she stupefies others but does not get stupefied herself. She is an 'expert in subduing paramours . . . she deceives even the clever, unsettles even the steady, makes a fool even of the wise, dances about even the *dhūrta,* makes the clever foolish, and renders weak even the daring.' In spite of the exaggerated nature of the description, in Viṣamaśīlā we get the picture of the power and strength of the *kuṭṭanī.* It was the *kuṭṭanī* who had the 'agency'; she was never at the command of the others, and could not be manipulated by the men who frequented her establishment. As Bhoja[73] says for Viṣamaśīlā, 'she has brought about the fall of many beast-like men into her various snares like *māyā'.*

It was precisely this power of the *kuṭṭanī* which made her a figure of dread and caricature in the male sources. In all the texts of our period, the *kuṭṭanī* such as Vikarālā of *Kuṭṭanīmatam,* Kaṅkālī of *Samayamātṛkā,* and Viṣamaśīlā of *Śṛṅgāramañjarīkathā* are described in identical terms: hideous, cruel, and unscrupulous. Their very names, Yamajihvā, Vikarālā, Bhujaṅgavāgurā, and Makaradaṁṣṭrā, invoke fear and dread.

STRATEGIES OF THE VEŚAVĀSA

Given the reality of the prostitute's existence in the essentially hostile patriarchal social world with which it was inextricably linked,[74] there was a need to consolidate the position of the *veśyā* household. This was achieved through an intricate system which, seen from a male perspective, was based on falsehood, deception, and deceit. Dāmodaragupta says in *Kuṭṭanīmatam*[75] that the deceit of the *veśyā* is a slander current among people (*vañcakavṛtta veśyā ityāpavādo janeṣu yo rūḍa*). The prostitute function is derisively[76] called *Vaiśika Tantra* in overwhelmingly male sources. Yaśodhara[77] in his *Jayamaṅgalā* commentary refers to Śvetaketu's treatise on this subject.

This was condensed into seven chapters, the 'Vaiśika' of Pāñcālabhābhravya being one of them. Then at the request of the *gaṇikā* of Pāṭalīputra, one Dattaka undertook to write about the courtesans and their lives. It is indeed surprising that these women, who as a class were the only literate group of women in the society, needed male writers to record their lives. Bhoja[78] mentions Dattaka who made the secret knowledge about prostitutes known to others. Yaśodhara[79] also refers to Dattaka's efforts. Perhaps this organized male attempt to write on the secrets of prostitute lives was part of a concerted attempt to disseminate knowledge about prostitutes among men.

In order to study this 'hegemonic discourse' we need to adopt the strategy of 'reverse discourse'.[80] Prostitute strategy was self-affirming and empowering for the practitioners. In fact, if one views prostitute strategies as the way she organized and conceptualized the rules she invented, it may indicate a pattern of life-choices and values which would suggest an alternative female culture that both subverted and mocked the dominant patriarchal one.

Kṣemendra's *Samayamātṛkā*[81] begins with a salutation to Kāmadeva and goddess Kālī, an unusual combination in the classical sources of our period. But perhaps there is logic here—while Kāmadeva is the presiding deity of love, Kālī is the fearsome goddess who drinks blood. Kṣemendra in this work was aiming at warning men against the wiles or strategies of prostitutes[82] who used all kinds of methods, even false love, to bleed their paramours of their wealth. However, unintentionally Kṣemendra's satire on the prostitute's wiles ends in a documentary on the triumph of the *veśyā*. Kalāvatī's adopted mother, *kuṭṭanī* Kaṅkālī, with her skills[83] was able to secure the maximum gain for Kalāvatī.

The prostitutes' strategies subverted the values and norms of patriarchy, particularly parental authority. In Īśvaradatta's *Dhūrtaviṭasaṁvāda*[84] a young man given to keeping a prostitute's company tells the *viṭa* that fathers are a headache personified (*mūrtimānaśiraroga*) and he even expresses the wish that as Paraśurāma cleared the earth of all *kṣatriya* he would like to make the world free of all fathers. This statement[85] is virtually unique in the classical Sanskrit sources. The *veśyā*'s subversion of parental authority was also a topic of lament in Dāmodaragupta's *Kuṭṭanīmatam*.[86] Another interesting example which illustrates this analysis comes from the fourth tale of *Śṛṅgāramañjarīkathā*.[87] The clever courtesan, Devadattā, had an extraordinary capacity to strategize and get results. Through her clever ploys she was able to get her paramour Suradharman to yield the secret of his hidden treasure. Suradharman was in the habit of concealing secrets by saying that his 'mother' alone knew everything. After Devadattā was successful, she asked Suradharman, 'Ah, does your mother know or do I know?' Folding his hands Suradharman said 'Mother does not know anything, you know everything.' Devadattā then crisply replied, 'As I know everything, then out with you', and she kicked him out of her house.

Fritz Blackwell[88] notes that 'perhaps most dangerous thing about the prostitute is the fact that her *dharma* is not passive, built upon devotion to husband and family like the wife's; it is quite active, designed by its very nature to destroy the man, at least financially, and even his family if necessary.'[89] It was this dangerous and subversive potential of the prostitute strategy that made men warn their 'respectable' women against it. Yaśodhara[90] quoting Kātyāyana in his *Jayamaṅgalā* commentary talks of acts (*veśa*) which are fit for prostitutes (*veśyā*) but not for the women of the household (*kulayoṣitā*). Because of these acts the former are called *veśyā*. Obviously, men feared the self-affirming power of these strategies and were eager to ensure that they were not practised by their own women. The patriarchal authority within the *gṛha* must remain intact.

Prostitute strategies also militated against many other cherished values of patriarchy. For instance, the prostitute avoidance of pregnancy and childbirth was completely opposed to the patriarchal view. In Kṣemendra's *Samayamātṛkā*[91] the bawd expresses the view that giving birth (*prasava*) is a curse (*śrāpa*) for a woman's youth (*yauvana*) and beauty. But if she is condemnatory of one of the most cherished goals of patriarchy, it is because she sees this as something that completely circumscribes woman's personal growth. In fact, the bawd contrasts[92] the attractiveness of the *veśyā* who knows the art of dressing up and of enlivening a gathering with her smiling (*satatasmitāsu*) demeanour. The *kulavadhū*, on the other hand, are constantly pregnant (*nityaprasūti*), their youth (*yauvana*) destroyed (*hata*). They have no taste for the pleasures of cultured gatherings (*goṣṭhivilāsasarasakeli nirādareṣu*). Although this different socialization of the prostitutes did not radicalize their status in the wider society, it did provide a space and platform from which to mock the existing positions, roles, and ideologies of patriarchy.

If prostitutes were castigated for their wiles 'ordinary' women under patriarchy were not spared either. The entire range of patriarchal brahmanical literature has condemned women for being sinful, dishonest, heartless, and the root of all evils.[93] This campaign against *triyā caritra* or womanly character was used by the patriarchs to keep women psychologically subjugated. Prostitutes used opprobrium against them to their own advantage to create greater space for themselves: they had little incentive to obey the ethics of the dominant culture and invented their own standards and lived by their own directives to achieve greater economic and social independence for themselves.

VEŚYĀ AND THE *ARTHA PURUṢĀRTHA*

For prostitutes, in the hierarchy of *trivarga* (i.e. *dharma, artha, Kāma*) *artha* was the highest goal[94] and this was a goal that they shared with the king of the realm. In Daṇḍin's *Daśakumāracarita*[95] it is said that the *kuladharma* of the *veśyā* was to assiduously accumulate riches. In the *Mṛcchakaṭika*[96] there is a fairly detailed description of the courtesan Vasantasenā's household which was run on a lavish scale. Maitreya admired it but did not quite know whether to call it *gaṇikāgṛha* or *Kuberabhavana*. In the eyes of the contemporary observers, the prostitute's command over her own resources 'masculinized' her. As Cārudatta observes in *Mṛcchakaṭika,*[97] 'through (the absence of) money a man becomes a woman; and she who is a woman becomes a man also through (the possession of) money' (*arthataḥ puruṣo nārī yā nārī sā'rthataḥ pumān*). It was this recognition of the prostitute's status and ownership of wealth that resulted in the acknowledgement of this section of society as autonomous subjects for the purposes of taxation, discipline, and punishment. This acknowledgement was also recognition of the fact that prostitutes had 'agency'. Prostitutes in antiquity were virtually the only group of women who by themselves were dealing with the state without any male mediation. *Nammayasundarīkathā,*[98] a twelfth-century text, refers to the state receiving 25–30 per cent of the prostitute's income as tax. Since the state was benefited, it had a vested interest in perpetuating the matriarchal feature of the prostitute household.[99] The *Nārada Smṛti*[100] also states that the ornaments of the prostitute cannot be confiscated (since they are like the tools of the trade).

If the ownership of resources 'masculinized' the prostitute *vis-à-vis* the state and ensured her recognition as an autonomous subject, even within the household prostitutes were recognized as the bread-winners of the family. Thus, in the absence of the earning of the *veśyā* Kāmamañjarī, her entire family (*kuṭumba*), said her mother in *Daśakumārcarita,*[101] would be without support and sustenance. In Bhoja's *Śṛṅgāramañjarīkathā*[102] Makaradaṁṣṭrā says, 'You [the paramour] have killed my daughter, by whose favour will this family live now? How will I live? You have destroyed the head of the family.' Dominance of women (apart from the fact that sisters/daughters alone inherited) within the prostitute household was in a large measure due to the nature of its economic base. Household property was largely earned income acquired in the form of cash, goods, and more importantly jewellery, and it was through women that the prostitute household acquired these.

In the *Jayamaṅgalā* commentary, Yaśodhara[103] defined the prostitute as always bejewelled (*sadālaṁkṛtā*). In *Mṛcchakaṭika,* Vasantasenā is depicted as well-ornamented. In the same play Dhūtā the *pativratā* wife of Cārudatta, for her part proudly claims[104] that 'my husband alone is my ornament' (*āryaputra eva mamābharaṇa*). This statement is significant not because it tells us about the wife's loyalty to her husband, but because it draws attention to the wife's lack of economic rights. Even their *strīdhana* had to be shelled out to the husband (Dhūtā gives her own precious jewel necklace to her husband in need). Interestingly enough, since the play *Mṛcchakaṭika* aimed at depicting the transformation of *gaṇikā* Vasantasenā into a *kulavadhū,* we see the metamorphosis occurring with Vasantasenā giving up her ornaments (i.e. her pride in her ownership of wealth). In the play[105] her lover Cārudatta's son refuses to recognize her as 'mother', because his mother does not wear ornaments. Vasantasenā not only takes off her jewels, she also fills the toy clay cart of the little boy with them. In that moment of maternal generosity Vasanta-senā transgresses the *kula dharma* of *gaṇikā.* This act transforms her psychologically and symbolically, preparing for her entry into the patriarchal household as wife. The significance of this event in the play is evident from the fact that it gives the play its title *Mṛcchakaṭika* (the little clay cart).

In Dāmodaragupta's *Kuṭṭanīmatam*[106] *veśyā* is described as *ratiśilpajīvikā* (one who has made a craft of sex and as a form of livelihood). But in this process she, unlike the *kulavadhū,* managed to acquire control over her own *dharma* and *artha.* It is ironical that women whose socio-sexual status was not legitimate were more easily recognizable as economically independent actors. Both textual and epigraphic records attest to the status of a *veśyā* as independent owners of resources and this gives them the autonomy to make religious donations in their own capacity. An eighth-century epigraph of the Cālukyas of Bādāmī refers to a *veśyā* making donaṭions to a temple.[107] In Yaśodhara's commentary[108] we find a reference to the *veśyā* initiating similar donations.

THE CULTURED *GAṆIKĀ*

There is a tendency to view the prostitute merely as an erotic being. But there is more to her than a body on sale (*paṇyabhūtam śarīram*), as the *viṭa* alleges in the *Mṛcchakaṭika.*[109] The courtesan class among the prostitutes (*gaṇikā*), were more famous for their cultural accomplishments than for their erotic appeal. It was intellectual and artistic accomplishments (proficiency in the sixty-four arts) that made a courtesan (*gaṇikā*) out of a common prostitute. She became, says Yaśodhara in her commentary,[110] worthy of respect from even the king (*rājñapūjitā*). The connoisseurs showered praise on her (*guṇavādina saṁstutā kalākauśalamiti praśansitā*) and she even became a teacher and was idolized by those who wanted to learn from her (*prārthanīyā kalopadeśārthinā*). On the other hand a common *veśyā* like *rūpājīvā* was described by Yaśodhara[111] as one who was distinguished only by beauty (*Rūpasya pradhāna*) and not by her skills (*kalā*); obviously she was no more than an ordinary street-walker.

In antiquity prostitutes were those women who played an import-ant role as creators and sustainers of culture. This association of prostitutes with an educated, cultured dispensation was a long-standing one. Rājaśekhara in his *Kāvyamīmāṁsā*[112] explicitly states that *gaṇikā* are among those women who are proficient in *śāstra* and poetry. Describing *veśyā* Śṛṅgāramañjarī, Bhoja[113] says 'she is faultless in local dialects, civilized in speech, . . . bold in questioning and answering different kinds of riddles . . . unrivalled in composing stanzas, well-enlightened in essays and treatises, excellent in composing poetry; foremost in composing *gāthā*'. This fact is acknowledged by Bharata in his *Nāṭyaśāstra*[114] 'one excelling (*viśeṣayet*) in all the arts (*kalā*) is called a gallant (*vaiśika*). Or he is so called because of his dealings with the courtesans (*veśopacāre*)'. This association of cultured men with the courtesans is significant. He is *vaiśika* for he is cultured, but he is also a cultured one for he keeps the company of courtesans, who by implication were themselves the epitome of culture. Srinivasan's[115] sociological study of the *devadāsī* household in southern India reveals that *devadāsī* were permitted to read and write and pursue vocational skills traditionally denied to all other women in India. And what was most important was that their knowledge was not for private consumption but the public platform, a fact which gave them both money and prestige. As Devangana Desai[116] also notes, it was to give a public platform to the art of the *devadāsī* that structures such as dance halls (*nāṭyamaṇḍapa*) and music halls (*sabhāmaṇḍapa*) were added to temples in the early medieval period.

Unlike the *kulastrī* who had to have a low voice[117] or be altogether silent, the prostitute was articulate. In most works of poetics belonging to our period, in the delineation of the character of *sādhāraṇa strī* there is emphasis on her articulate tongue. *Daśarūpakam* of Dhanañjaya[118] describes her as a *gaṇikā* whose attributes are knowledge and accomplishments (*kalā*), chutzpah, and eloquence (*pragalbhatā*) and a crafty cleverness (*dhūrtatā*). Although in the sub-classification of the *aṣṭanāyikā* in the text on the poetics we get a *pragalbhā* type even among the *non-sāmānyā nāyikā,* the logic of her delineation is different. This *pragalbhā* is one who is at the full development of youth and is, therefore, no longer marked by the restraining force of bashfulness,[119] which is the inherent trait of girls of good families. Eloquence is not her inherent trait, which is that of the *gaṇikā*. This is evident from the fact that in literary works, the 'clever speech' of the courtesans had a proverbial status even if non-prostitutes were resorting to it. This was how the speech of princess Vegavatī was described in Buddhasvāmin's *Bṛhatkathāślokasaṁgraha.*[120] Sternbach[121] quotes a Sanskrit verse that illustrates this point. It says, 'In the presence of a sovereign, among scholars and on meeting with the courtesans even an eloquent man is embarrassed for fear intimidates his heart.'

Not only were prostitutes articulate as a rule, they were in many cases grouped among those women in the classical Sanskrit literature who were entitled to speak the 'masculine language', Sanskrit. In the classical drama courtesans are those rare female characters who made use of Sanskrit. In Śūdraka's *Mṛcchakaṭika, gaṇikā* Vasantasenā speaks in Sanskrit. Although in Act III of the play we find brāhmaṇa Maitreya making fun of women who read Sanskrit, in Act IV comes a specific reference to Vasantasenā speaking in Sanskrit (*saṁskṛtmāśritya*) with Maitreya. Thus, Bharata[122] underlines that 'for the pleasure of all kinds of people, and in connection with the practice of arts, the courtesans are to be assigned Sanskritic recitation which can be easily managed.'

Bhoja in *Sarasvatīkaṇṭhābharaṇa*[123] described a *gaṇikā* as *ubhaya catuḥśaṣṭikalāvida.* In *Śṛṅgāramañjarīkathā*[124] the *veśyā* Śṛṅgāramañjarī is described as distinguished in the sixty-four arts. In *Kuṭṭanīmatam*[125] we are told about a prostitute's proficiency in these (*catuḥśaṣṭikarmakuśalānām*). Yaśodhara in his *Jayamaṅgalā* commentary describes both groups of these arts. The first is the sixty-four *aṅgavidyā*;[126] while some among these were purely aesthetic arts like dance, singing, painting, others were meant for intellectual development; for instance, accomplishments[127] such as *Kāvyasamasyāpurāṇam* (completing a verse from a given single line), *pratimālā* (capping verses), *prahelikā* (riddles), *duroacakyoga* (expressing that which is difficult in words or sense), *pustakavācanam* (book reading), *malicchitvikalpa* (using synonyms of the *mlecchabhāṣā*), *deśabhāṣāvijñānam* (using *deśya* words to make known that which is unknown), *dharaṇamātṛkā* (remembering heard texts), *kāvyakṛpā* (composing poems), *abhidhānakoṣa* (knowledge of dictionaries), *chandojñānam* (knowing the metrical works), *kriyākalpa* (knowing poetics), and *vṛkṣa āyurveda* (arbori-horticulture). Expertise in this branch of *āyurveda* shows the *gaṇikā* to be healing women with knowledge of the medicinal properties of various roots and plants. In Daṇḍin's *Daśakumāracarita*[128] the *veśyā* Kāmamañjarī's mother lists the subjects in which she carefully trained her daughter from childhood and refers to writing and conversation (*lipijñānavacanakauśalā*) and to some extent in grammar, logic, and philosophy. It is thus apparent that there was an intellectual context to a prostitute's formal training. In Hemacandra's *Prabandhacintāmaṇī,* a twelfth-century text, a prostitute is described as 'a storehouse of intellect' and for whom the king considered 'a kingdom would be too small a present'.[129] Interestingly, in *Mṛccha-kaṭikam* Śūdraka while introducing himself[130] talks of the manifold skills in which he has proficiency. He knows the Vedas, mathematics and *kalāvaiśikī* which was a reference to the sixty-four *aṅga vidyā.* Thus, we see that even if others such as King Śūdraka himself refer to their being knowledgeable in that branch they also give it the appellation of *vaiśika.*

The second group of sixty-four arts in which prostitutes were trained—were the *samprayogikā,* which Vātsyāyana mentions in the second book of the *Kāmasūtra.* Prostitutes, by mastering it, gained proficiency in the science of erotics. In fact, it is ironical that women of such learning and accomplishment were given the appellation of *sāmānyā* or *sādhāraṇa strī.*

This confluence of knowledge, sexuality, and spirituality[131] in the personality of the prostitute in the historical period helps us recover the prostitute from the image of a mere 'sexual body'. We have seen that courtesans functioned outside the restrictions which patriarchy imposed on other women (wives and daughters). The prostitutes could function within those public spaces which were ordinarily preserved for males—teaching, conversing and also having freer sexual interaction. It was the power of this well-rounded personality of the prostitute which was acknowledged even in a rabidly anti-prostitute text like Kṣemendra's *Samayamātṛkā*[132] which states that courtesans ravish men just as the sweet speech of poets ravishes people. 'They are attractive creatures, possess excellent qualities, are carefully anointed, are exciting and well-disposed, give men through their arts the highest pleasure and satisfaction, and offer ever new enjoyment'. The attraction of prostitutes for the paramour was thus much more than sexual; this was the attraction of her personality in which her education played an important role. Bawd

Viṣamaśīlā advises *veśyā* Śṛṅgāramañjarī[133] thus: 'Always be careful in propitiating the minds of others; for it is possible to please a person only if his mind has been attracted, and only he whose mind has been propitiated dedicates his wealth and his life.'

THE *VEŚYĀ's KĀMA PURUṢĀRTHA*

The prostitute sexuality is a problematized area of scholarly investigation. The terms that stand for prostitute[134] are *asatī, kulaṭā, svairiṇī* (all these meaning promiscuous women), *abhisārikā* (women on a rendezvous), *dhṛṣṭā* (impudent one), *lañjikā* (adulteress), *līlāvatī* (flirtatious woman), *didhiṣu* (twice married), etc. Patriarchal ideology was intolerant of any form of female sexuality in which their autonomy of desire and behaviour was asserted and maintained. All such women under patriarchy were categorized as prostitutes. The *Manusmṛti*[135] and commentator Medhātithi forbid Brāhmaṇas to accept food from *gaṇa* and *gaṇikā*. This homology had a certain logic. Historically, the *gaṇa* form of state formation was associated with women whose sexuality was not constrained by patriarchal norms.[136] The formation of a brahmanical, monarchical state not only marginalized the *gaṇa* but its 'free women' too, who ended up as stigmatized *śūdra*[137] on the obverse side of the brahmanical social set up. The *gaṇikā* (women of *gaṇa*, by now prostitutes) were presented in brahmanical-dominated sources as defiled and impure. In *Kuṭṭanīmatam*[138] it is said that for a prostitute the consideration of *varṇa* (colour) is only for cosmetic purposes (*prasādhana*) and *varṇa* is not a consideration for sexual intercourse (*ratiprasaṅgeṣu*). In other words, the 'caste' of the paramour was of no consequence. Prostitutes were thus women who were not only sexually promiscuous but whose sexuality could not be harnessed towards procreation in the correct *varṇa* order. For patriarchy, the non-marital, non-reproductive and libidinous female body was dangerous. As against this deviant, dangerous 'whore', there was the virtuous woman or *satī* whose sexuality was a reproductive one and eschewed any active sexual desire or pleasure. Moreover, for many radical feminists, prostitute sexuality cannot be understood as free or liberated. Scholars have argued[139] that prostitution supports the 'objectification' of women's sexuality and it is linked to violence against them. Here the prostitute body is seen as an 'abused' body. The sources of our study amply demonstrate violence against prostitutes. In *Mṛcchakaṭika, gaṇikā* Vasantasenā was strangled by the king's brother-in-law for repulsing his overtures. On regaining consciousness she perceived her state as one that befits the profession of a prostitute (*yatsadṛśam veśabhāvasya*).[140] In the eleventh tale of Bhoja's *Śṛṅgāramañjarīkathā, veśyā* Malayasundarī's paramour Pratāpasiṁha physically abused her, and instead of being punished by the king he got away scot-free,[141] and it was the *veśyā* who became an object of ridicule. Prostitutes were also vulnerable[142] because of their movable wealth such as ornaments. *Samayamātṛkā*[143] refers to prostitutes (*paṇyāṅganā*) being vulnerable in every city to those who covet their jewels (*bhūṣaṇalubdhe*). Although women in general could be at the receiving end of male violence, prostitutes were particularly vulnerable because they were the only women who were visible in the public sphere. Moreover, while men in the private sphere could dominate women's sexuality, the prostitute's sexuality was only accessible on purchase in the public sphere.

If in the patriarchal discourse the deviant prostitute sexuality is not 'normal', for radical feminists it is a 'dominated' sexuality and it is therefore to be categorized as negative. Pateman[144] argues that prostitute sexuality is a public recognition of men as sexual masters; it puts submission on sale as a commodity in the market. Prostitution, she states, is an inherently gendered practice in which women are constructed as the sexual servants of men and the buying of sexual service is defined as a benefit for men. Luce Irigaray[145] also sees prostitution as sex which is not one's own and is constructed according to the desire of the other. A prostitute is, in Irigaray's words, merely an 'obliging prop' for the enactment of men's fantasies. Thus, Irigaray links the prostitute body to male-defined female sexuality. For Mackinnon[146] since heterosexuality institutionalized male dominance and female submission, there can be no scope for prostitute 'agency' in the commerce. But Mackinnon in her totalizing theory[147] tends to ignore the existence of the multiplicity of desires some of which do not conform to the requirements of the masculinist system. Liberal feminists like Gayle Rubin and Carol S. Vance,[148] however, argue against treating any kind of sexual practice as either 'bad' or 'abnormal'. Heterosexual coitus itself cannot be taken as a mark of women's sexual subordination for even their own sexual choices are often exercised. Both Rubin and Vance have examined the issue of 'pleasure' and 'agency' in the sex trade.

A careful analysis of the literary sources of our period would reinforce the liberal feminist view regarding prostitute sexuality. If one juxtaposes the socialization of the *kulavadhū* (a household woman) against the *vāravadhū* (a prostitute), the latter appears far removed from 'domination'. The notion of shame (*lajjā*) is an important element in controlling female sexuality under patriarchy. Here the female body is controlled and regulated both at the level of the individual and the social body. In fact, patriarchy rests on the foundation of the controlled female body. Along with purity and pollution, honour and shame are two of the most prominent cultural ideologies of brahmanical patriarchy, and have played an important role in controlling women's behaviour and the spaces that they can occupy, as also the limits of their socio-sexual relations. In the *bāhyā* and the *abhyāntarā* (a woman of the inner apartment) classification of the *nāyikā* we see the operation of the *purdah* system. Sociologically speaking[149] *purdah* delimits the spheres that women can legitimately occupy. *Kuṭṭanīmatam*[150] tells us that the veil (*vadanāvṛttijālikā*) was what distinguished respectable (*āryā*) women from ordinary (*anāryā*) ones. The latter were usually prostitutes. In *Samayamātṛkā,*[151] Kṣemendra refers to a mischievous courtesan who passed herself off as the daughter of a high-ranking royal officer by half-covering her face. In *Dhūrtaviṭasaṁvāda,*[152] a *kulavadhū's* veil is tellingly referred to as *lajjā-paṭa* (what covers the shame). A woman of a good family not only had to have a veil (*avaguṇṭhana*) on her face but was also required, says *Kuṭṭanīmatam,*[153] to have humility, a low voice and slow movements. The *bāhyā* on the other hand was without the veil. In *Mṛcchakaṭika,* Vasantasenā was without a veil till the king's announcement declared her to be the bride (*vadhū*) of Cārudatta, and immediately[154] upon this announcement Śārvilaka veiled her. The system of the veil also affected the way the sexuality of women was perceived. In the *Nāṭyaśāstra*[155] it is said that when the courtesan goes out to meet her lover, she decorates her body with various ornaments, and displays much passion and joy. The *abhyāntarā nāyikā,*[156] on the other hand, walked the street covering her face with a veil, timidly with her limbs contracted, and very often turned her face away and looked back. According to the *Nāṭyaśāstra*,[157] a *bāhyā nāyikā* could be depicted displaying her love: 'She expresses her passion by casting side-long glances (*kaṭākṣa*), touching her ornaments, itching ears, scratching the ground with her toes, revealing the breasts and the navel, cleaning the nails and gathering her hair'. In a high-born lady (*kulāṅganā*), however, the signs of love are to be depicted differently:[158] 'She looks continuously with laughter in her eyes, conceals her smile, speaks slowly (*mandavākyā*) and with a downcast face (*adhomukhī*), gives a reply with a smile, conceals her sweat and appearance, with throbbing lips, and trembling limbs.' Not only was a prostitute allowed greater freedom of expression of her sentiments, she was also entitled to greater freedom as far as her bodily gestures were concerned. Bharata notes in the *Nāṭyaśāstra*[159] that high-class women could not be shown using cosmetics (unguents and collyrium), painting the body, coyly handling their breasts and combing their hair. They also could not be shown dressed poorly (*nāpāvṛtā*) or wearing only one piece of cloth (*ekavastrā*). They could not use colours for their lips. This was done to distinguish them from women of inferior types who, with a view to exposing their charms, dressed scantily and took pleasure in using cosmetics.

The entire notion of 'shame' acquired a totally different meaning for the prostitute. In the *Kuṭṭanīmatam*[160] we are told that 'for a *veśyā* covering the lower part (*jaghanāvaraṇa*) is not out of "shame" but to arouse desire in others'. Prostitutes were also quite open in discussing their sexual experiences with all types of clients. In a comic verse[161] a *veśyā* tells others that when she closed her eyes in the ecstasy of pleasure her inexperienced paramour ran away, thinking her to be dead.

The above data would lend itself to the interpretation, that as compared to the circumscribed sexuality of the women in patriarchy, the prostitute enjoyed greater freedom of sexual expression. We get an interesting example in *Bṛhatkathāślokasaṁgraha*[162] of *Madanamañcukā* who was the daughter of a *veśyā*. She took the vow of constancy and was transformed into into an ideal *pativratā;* she guarded any access to her body like a Sītā.

Much is said about a prostitute's sexuality being slavishly commanded by the man, who as client, pays for it. But if one contrasts the location of the man's wife in the inner apartment (*antaḥpura*) and that of the *veśyā's* life outside, we observe a binary spatial structure where the former is completely closed and its occupants owe complete fidelity to the husband. The husband-wife tie was one which did not necessarily depend on the existence of an erotic relationship in order to constitute itself. The sexual relations between the two were carried on the basis of a statutory relationship that empowered the husband to 'demand' from his wife all services including sexual ones. The *pativratā* ideology ensured their compliance. Within the confines of the *antaḥpura,* the marital partners were also hierarchically placed. While *kulavadhū* were thus relegated to a private sphere and their status was in being *asūryaspṛśyā,* the *gaṇikā* who were significantly enough called *prakāśanārī,*[163] were women *par excellence* of the public sphere. Vasantasenā is appreciatively described as *nagarasya-bhūṣaṇam* and *nagaraśrī* in *Mṛcchakaṭika.*[164] In *Daśakumāracarita,*[165] *veśyā* Kāmamañjarī was similarly described as an ornament of the city of Campā. These *gaṇikā* and their paramours met in common and open spaces like brothels, gardens, or the temple of Kāmadeva. All these were spatially open areas in which people moved about freely. Freedom of space also dictated the freedom of choice. One could not in such a case exercise statutory authority. A *gaṇikā* was free to accept or reject any proposition. Vasantasenā exercised this prerogative quite tellingly when she rejected the king's brother-in-law for the impoverished Cārudatta. In order to secure her consent no *pativratā* ideology could come to the rescue. Her favours (which many were in a position to refuse) had to be secured by persuasion and very often this persuasion took the form of gifts that could outshine those offered by the rivals.

The prostitute's autonomy introduced an element of male anxiety in the relationship, a precariousness that was most often used by the *veśyā* to milk her clients. Luce Irigaray[166] sees the prostitute as a 'speaking subject' who actively intervenes in the male exchange economy (which had the exchange of women at its foundation). A prostitute took herself to the market and named her price, and in so doing she disrupted the male exchange economy (since she was breaking the silent exchange of women and was thereby no longer a passive participant in the exchange). Although it is true that a prostitute negotiated sexuality only as a commercial exchange inside the male exchange economy, she did negotiate it. Should the prostitutes then be seen as an empowered lot (her sexuality being used as a bargaining chip), who had the power to set the terms of her sexuality and demand substantial payment for her time and skills?

In the sources of our period the sexual life of the prostitute—the unlimited freedom and the unbounded pleasure of intercourse with any man they like—is often portrayed in a positive light. Kṣemendra in *Kalāvilāsa*[167] says that because of this independence prostitutes are envied by some women who think, 'fortunate are courtesans (*veśyā dhanyeti*) who enjoy life without restrictions with many young men' (*bahuvidhataruṇanirgala saṁbhoga sukhārthabhoginī*).

Prostitutes are described as proficient in providing sexual pleasures (*kalākelikuśalā*) and this quality of theirs became proverbial.[168] We find many aphorisms which state that a good wife is one who behaves in bed like a *veśyā* (*śayane tu veśyā*). This notion does attribute a degree of agency to the *veśyā*. In fact, the free sexual behaviour or sexual experience of the prostitutes is seen as giving greater pleasure than consorting with wives. This is expressed very pithily in Īśvaradatta's *Dhūrtaviṭasaṁvāda*[169] where a young man tells a *viṭa* that he is about to be married. The *viṭa* expresses surprise that the young man wants to leave *veśyā mahāpatha* for *kulavadhū kumārgeṇa*. He asks how pleasure can be had from consorting with *kulavadhū* who are blind to sexual pleasures (*jātyandham surateṣu*), who talk inaudibly (*antaramukhabhāṣiṇī*), who are so shy that they have never seen their own lower part (*jaghana*), and are no better than a yoked animal (*strirūpabadhampaṣu*)? The prostitute sexuality is thus not so much a 'deviant' sexuality; rather, she has to be seen as an 'erotic teacher'.

Far from being an 'obliging prop' for the enactment of male fantasies we find from our sources that prostitutes were taking pleasure in their sexual encounters. In *Bṛhatkathāślokasaṁgraha*[170] we are told that *veśyā* Gaṅgādattā openly desires and asks for access to the body of the hero Sannudāsa. In fact, the sexual encounter between Gaṅgādattā and Sannudāsa[171] is described as a mutual exchange of bodies (*śarīram*) on equal terms. In *Kuṭṭanīmatam*,[172] we see a *veśyā* performing *puruṣāyita* or *viparītarata* form of coitus where the woman rides the man. Yaśodhara in his *Jayamaṅgalā* commentary[173] refers to many patrons (*viṭa*) uniting with one *veśyā* and this is referred to as *goṣṭhiparigraha*. It is important to note that one woman uniting with many men is not considered acceptable by Vātsyāyana and his commentator Yaśodhara.[174] In Book Two of the *Kāmasūtra*[175] where Vātsyāyana described various sexual practices he attributes orgies, to women's kingdoms (*grāmanārīviṣaye* and *strīrājya*); and Vāhīka[176] Yaśodhara[177] refers to the men who partner women in these orgies as those who live like kept women.

The above descriptions would put a question mark on the notion of prostitute sexuality as completely male dominated, i.e. the view that prostitution caters to and reinforces the idea of male desire and where macho desires are given primacy. One could argue that a feature of the paramour's sexual activity with the prostitute is the opportunity it would provide to men to escape conventional hetero-sexual roles (*goṣṭhiparigrahā* and *puruṣāyita* are examples of this) which place emphasis on masculine prowess and domination. In fact, *veśavāsa* or the prostitute quarters were those liminal places where socially-dominant sexual relations and socially-acceptable sexual practices could be transgressed. Prostitute quarters became privileged spaces for experimentation with censured sexual behaviour.

Irigaray sees prostitute sexuality as 'phallic' sexuality, but prostitutes could at times assert sexual autonomy. In the sources of our period we get one indirect reference to prostitute linkage with lesbian love. The *Mitākṣarā* commentary on *Yājñavalkyasmṛti*,[178] quotes the *Skandapurāṇa* as saying that prostitutes constitute a separate caste springing from the *apsarā* Pañcacūḍā. In the *Anuśāsana Parva* of the *Mahābhārata*[179] it is the self-same Pañcacūḍā *apsarā* who talks of sapphic love among women.

THE *VEŚYĀ's PREMA*

Although most writers on poetics talk in terms of the feigned love of the prostitute Rudrabhaṭṭa in *Śṛṅgāratilaka,* who like his predecessors (Bharata and Vātsyāyana) accepted *sāmānyā* as one of the *nāyikā,* makes an important observation: though some consider her (*sāmānyā*) interested only in money and not in love, he is of the view that she too as a woman has her love without which hers will become a case of the semblance of sentiment (*rasābhāsa*).[180] Viśvanātha in his *Sāhityadarpaṇa*[181] also attributes occasional real love to a *veśyā* (*kvapi satyānurāgiṇī*).

In spite of these exceptional views, a prostitute's love is depicted in the sources as a false one. *Kuṭṭanīmatam*[182] states, 'Prostitutes are adroit in yielding their bodies (*sarvāṅgārpaṇadakṣā*) but not their hearts (*asamarpitahṛdaya*).' It is said for *veśyā* Śṛṅgāramañjarī[183] that 'she pleases others though not in love herself, and comes in contact with lovelorn though not attached herself'. The prostitute's love, the sources argue, is rooted in mercenary considerations. As *Kuṭṭanīmatam*[184] notes, 'The wealth of the paramour is the barometer on which the prostitute's (*vārastrī*) attachment (*rāga*), love (*prema*), and sexual desire (*madanaruja*) can be measured. All these sentiments are friends of wealth which increase when wealth increases and decrease with the decrease of wealth.'

Insofar as a prostitute herself uses her love as a strategy of material gain, the expression of this sentiment is circumscribed. *Veśyā* codes also circumscribe it. In *Kuṭṭanīmatam*, when *veśyā* Harlatā feels genuine love for Sundarsena, she is cautioned against it by her friends. It is said[185] that for a prostitute (*paṇyanārī*) a love that originates in a sense of empathy (*sadbhāvājanurakti*) is not good. The *veśyā* is advised to shower her love[186] only after ascertaining the wealth of the suitor, for her beauty is a means to an end. A *veśyā*[187] who is attracted only towards handsomeness (*abhirāma*) of the paramour and neglects the factor of gain (*vividhalābhanirpekṣa*) becomes a laughing stock among the clever courtesans. In *Bṛhatkathāślokasaṁgraha*[188] a prostitute bent on constancy (*satīvratam*) is described as a bad woman (*durācāreva*). In *Mṛcchakaṭika*,[189] the *viṭa* describes Vasantasenā's rejection of paramours like Śakāra as *veśavāsaviruddha* which was dependent on young men. He advises Vasantasenā to wait upon all equally (*veśyā'si sarvam bhaja*).[190] In another such verse referred to in Rājaśekhara's *Kāvyamīmāṁsā*,[191] an old bawd tells her daughter who was bent on constancy to her lover that 'for us marriage means to love boys in childhood, young men in youth and old men in advanced age. On which road you want to travel, O daughter? For in our family no one has ever been abused of being a *satī* (*satīlāñchana*)'. In Bhoja's *Śṛṅgāramañjarīkathā*,[192] another bawd tells her daughter that 'the secret of the profession of harlotry is that one's own self should always be protected from love as from a tiger'.

Veśyā Rāgamañjarī in Daṇḍin's *Daśakumāracarita*[193] declares that she is *guṇaśulkā* and not *dhanaśulkā*, or attracted to the merit and not the wealth of the paramour; further, her sexual favours (*bhogyayauvanam*) will be granted only to the one who marries her (*pāṇigrahaṇa*). This insistence by Rāgamañjarī is seen by her mother as acting against *svakuladharma,* i.e. *veśyā* codes, and as a desire on the part of Rāgamañjarī to enact the role of a household woman (*kulastrīvṛta*). The certitude of the bawd that 'love' was a sentiment fit for household women needs to be problematized. Can one say that *kulastrī* were more 'free to love'? If the *veśyā* love was circumscribed by the *veśavāsa* code, the *kulavadhū's* love was circumscribed by the patriarchal *pativrata* ideology. A wife was not required so much to love as to show devotion to her husband. It needed the penetrating eye of the old bawd Viṣamaśīlā in Bhoja's *Śṛṅgāramañjarīkathā*[194] to expose this myth of love for women. The bawd tells her daughter that love is threefold—once born on hearing, once on sight, and the third on union. All three, says Viṣamaśīlā, 'should be abandoned from a distance, for by these even family women are made objects of contempt'. We thus see that love as an autonomous emotion was something which women could not or dared not experience under patriarchy. The prostitute commodified her love for material gain, and the *kulastrī* erased hers or bartered it to accommodate herself in the patriarchal household.

But even if a prostitute used her love as a strategy she alone was in a position to choose to display this emotion fearlessly. Vasantasenā shows such affection for Cārudatta in *Mṛcchakaṭika.*[195] She knew that Cārudatta was poor (*daridra*), yet she was in love with his virtues (*guṇanirjitādāsī*). It is significant that in the play Vasantasenā did not see her involvement with Cārudatta in the light of a prostitute-client relationship at any point of time. In the play when Vasantasenā's maid Madanikā asked her who it was that had to be served (by Vasantasenā), Vasantasenā replied that she wanted to enjoy, sport, and not serve (*rantumichāmi na sevituṁ*).[196] Yet again when Vasantasenā prepares[197] to pay a visit to Cārudatta of her own accord she uses the terms sporting and enjoying (*cārudattamabhirantuṁ gacchāvaḥ*) to describe her tryst as an *abhisārikā* who does not care even for the gathering clouds and incessant rain.[198] This tie of genuine love between *gaṇikā* Vasantasenā and Cārudatta is also recognized by Vasantasenā's mother. When called upon to give testimony in the court and asked about the whereabouts of her daughter, that lady replied that her daughter was enjoying the pleasures of youth with her friend (*mitra*) Cārudatta (*tatra me dārikā yauvanasukhānubhavati*).[199]

In the classical Sanskrit sources of our period, prostitues were one of the *nāyikā* types referred to as the *bāhyā* or *sādhāraṇastrī*. They were also the central figures in the entire business of *kāma*. It was their conscious commodification of *kāma* which enabled them to gain autonomy over both *artha* and *dharma,* the other two ends of human life. Nonetheless, the *veśavāsa* or prostitute quarter cannot be treated as a space of complete equality. It had its own hierarchy. A *gaṇikā* was the presiding diva of these quarters in a way a *rūpājīvā* could not be. The lesser status of the latter also made her more dependent on the generosity of her male clients. A close scrutiny of the textual evidence allows us to jettison the prostitute-as-victim image and to see prostitutes as 'social agents' with relative autonomy within the confines of the patriarchal system.

NOTES

1. Ludwick Sternbach, 1942, 1945.
2. *Jayamaṅgalā,* 6.6.50.
3. *Samayamātṛkā,* 8.103.
4. Ludwick Sternbach, 1953: 63.
5. Leah Otis, 1987: 2–3.
6. *Nāṭyaśāstra,* 24.149.
7. In *Mṛcchakaṭika*, the *viṭa* tells *veśyā* Vasantasenā (Act 1.31) she is as common as the creeper that grows beside the road (*mārgajāta lateva*).
8. *Nāṭyaśāstra,* 24.151–3.
9. *Daśarūpakam,* ch 2, pp. 149–50.
10. V.R. Raghavan, 1951: 27–8.
11. *Kuṭṭanīmatam,* verse 789.
12. Cārudatta often addresses her as beloved (*priya*), and not by appellations which describe her physical allure.
13. *Mṛcchakaṭika*, Act IX, p. 328.
14. Ibid., Act V.36.
15. Sukumari Bhattacharji, 1999: 196–228.
16. Simone de Beauvoir, 1988: 266
17. Ibid.: 585.
18. Veena Oldenburg, 1991: 23–61.
19. Shannon Bell, 1994: 11.
20. Oldenburg, 1991: 23.
21. Jess Walls, 1982: 6–7.

22. de Beauvoir, 1988: 581.
23. *Kuṭṭanīmatam*, verse 146.
24. *Mṛcchakaṭika*, Act IV.28.
25. Amrit Srinivasan (1988: 187) in her sociological survey of the *devadāsī* household, points out that men in these households stayed as appendages of either their sister or mother, only on sufferance.
26. *Mṛcchakaṭika*, Act IV.29.
27. A. Srinivasan (1988: 180) points out that in the *devadāsī* household the young woman did not owe her paramour either work or children.
28. *Manubhāṣya*, 5.88.
29. A. Srinivasan, 1988: 186.
30. *Devadāsī* in the sources of our period are essentially treated as *veśyā* or courtesans of god (B.P. Mazumdar, 1960: 371–2), and it is their sexual service which is emphasized. As Parasher and Naik (1986: 63–91) have shown in their study of Karnataka inscriptions dating from 700 to 1200, there was a blurring of the *devadāsī/veśyā* divide, if at all one existed in the first place. This is also apparent from the story of *veśyā* Rupiṇikā in the *Kathāsaritsāgara* (vol. I: 139), 'who went at the time of worship to the temple to perform her duty'.
31. Oldenburg, 1991: 40–1.
32. Henrietta Moore, 1988: 42.
33. *Mṛcchakaṭika*, Act IV, pp. 166, 168.
34. *Kathāsaritsāgara*, vol. V, p. 16.
35. Even the non-brahmanical texts are no exception. In the Buddhist sources, in spite of the greater prominence of the *gaṇikā*, prostitution is regarded as *nīcakamma* and the brothel a *nīcaghara* (A.K. Tyagi, 1994: 146).
36. *Manubhāṣya*, 4.85.
37. *Mṛcchakaṭika*, Act III.7.
38. *Bṛhatkathāślokasaṁgraha*, 11.86.
39. *Mṛcchakaṭika*, Act IV.24.
40. Ibid., Act X, p. 402.
41. *Bṛhatkathāślokasaṁgraha*, 12.83, 13.1–2.
42. *Śṛṅgāramañjarīkathā*, p. 78.
43. *Śṛṅgārahāṭa*, p. 41.
44. In the sixth tale of *Śṛṅgāramañjarīkathā* we find a *kulastrī—lāvaṇya-sundarī*—taking to the life of a *veśyā* of her own accord in order to make money to free her imprisoned husband. And when her objective of getting 100 elephants is realized, she leaves the life of a *veśyā* to once again become the wife of her husband. This is the only instance in our sources of two crossovers by a woman at her own initiative over the *kulastrī-vārastrī* divide.
45. *Jayamaṅgalā*, 7.1.22–3.
46. Not only were *veśyā* living in their own household variously described as *gaṇikākuṭumba, veśyāgṛha* (Sternbach, 1945: 135–8), in most cases they

were in separate areas of the town. We get a reference to *veśyāvīthi* (*Śṛṅgārahāṭa*, p. 32) in our sources. *Mānasollāsa* refers to *veśyā* houses on the outskirts of the town (cited in Sukumari Bhattacharji, 1999: 215).

47. Sternbach, 1953: 64.
48. *Jayamaṅgalā*, 6.2.3–4, 8; 6.2.60–1.
49. Sternbach, 1953: 17.
50. *Daśakumāracarita*, pp. 132–4.
51. *Samayamātṛkā*, 1.40–9.
52. *Śṛṅgārahāṭa*, p. 100.
53. A. Srinivasan, 1988: 188.
54. *Nāṭyaśāstra*, 35.77–8.
55. Cited in *Śṛṅgāramañjarīkathā*, p. 52.
56. Ibid.
57. Ibid.
58. *Samayamātṛkā*, 8.18, 24, 25.
59. Cited in *Śṛṅgāramañjarīkathā*, p. 52.
60. *Kāmasūtra*, 1.4.32.
61. *Jayamaṅgalā*, 1.4.32.
62. *Kuṭṭanīmatam*, pp. 339–40.
63. *Mṛcchakaṭika*, Act V, p. 190.
64. *Kuṭṭanīmatam*, verse 342, *Śṛṅgārahāṭa*, p. 158.
65. Ibid., verses 68, 796.
66. Ajay Mitra Shastri, 1975: 119.
67. *Śṛṅgārahāṭa*, p. 184, 196.
68. *Śṛṅgāramañjarīkathā*, p. 53.
69. Ibid.
70. Ibid.
71. *Kuṭṭanīmatam*, verse 114.
72. *Śṛṅgāramañjarīkathā*, pp. 20–1.
73. Ibid., p. 23.
74. In *Mṛcchakaṭika* (Act 1.31) the *viṭa* tells Vasantasenā that the courtesan quarter is dependent on young men for help (*taruṇajanasahāya*).
75. *Kuṭṭanīmatam*, verse 485.
76. Kṣemendra in *Kalāvilāsa* satirizes the prostitute strategies as their practice of sixty-four arts (cited in Sternbach, 1953: 45–7).
77. *Jayamaṅgalā*, 1.1.9–11.
78. *Śṛṅgāramañjarīkathā*, pp. 47–8.
79. *Jayamaṅgalā*, 6.3.44.
80. Bell, 1994: 14.
81. *Samayamātṛkā*, 1.1–2.
82. Ibid.: 1.3, 8.128.
83. Ibid.: 8.127.
84. *Śṛṅgārahāṭa*, pp. 71–3.

85. Ibid., p. 71.
86. *Kuṭṭanīmatam,* verses 411–24.
87. *Śṛṅgāramañjarīkathā,* p. 40.
88. Fritz Blackwell, 1977: 39.
89. Ibid.
90. *Jayamaṅgalā,* 6.3.45.
91. *Samayamātṛkā,* 8.101.
92. Ibid.: 8.93–4.
93. Sternbach, 1953: 74–5.
94. *Jayamaṅgalā,* 6.6.5.
95. *Daśakumāracarita,* p. 174.
96. *Mṛcchakaṭika,* Act IV, p. 170.
97. Ibid., Act III.27.
98. Sukumari Bhattacharjee, 1999: 203.
99. Thus, we are told in the *Arthaśāstra* (2.27.2–3) that a courtesan's establishment could not be inherited by her son. On her death or retirement her daughter or sister alone could take her place. The *Arthaśāstra* (2.27.11) also says that a prostitute cannot give her ornaments (the main form in which prostitutes owned wealth), to anyone but her mother.
100. *Nārada Smṛti,* 28.10.
101. *Daśakumāracarita,* p. 137.
102. *Śṛṅgāramañjarīkathā,* p. 40.
103. *Jayamaṅgalā,* 6.1.7.
104. *Mṛcchakaṭika,* Act VI, p. 216.
105. Ibid., Act VI, p. 218.
106. *Kuṭṭanīmatam,* verse 637.
107. Cited in L.K. Tripathi, 1988: 339.
108. *Jayamaṅgalā,* 6.6.22.
109. *Mṛcchakaṭika,* Act 1.31.
110. *Jayamaṅgalā,* 1.3.17–18.
111. Ibid., 6.5.29.
112. *Kāvyamīmāṁsā,* ch. 10, p. 138.
113. *Śṛṅgāramañjarīkathā,* p. 15.
114. *Nāṭyaśāstra*: 25.1.
115. Amrit Srinivasan, 1988: 190.
116. Devangana Desai, 1975: 155.
117. *Kuṭṭanīmatam,* verse 848.
118. *Daśarūpakam,* ch. 2, p. 148.
119. V.R. Raghavan, 1951: 22.
120. *Bṛhatkathāślokasaṁgraha,* 15.46.
121. Ludwick Sternbach, 1945: 16.
122. *Nāṭyaśāstra,* 18.41.
123. Cited in *Śṛṅgāramañjarīkathā,* pp. 93–4.

124. Ibid., p. 15.
125. *Kuṭṭanīmatam*, verse 499.
126. *Jayamaṅgalā*, 1.3.17–18.
127. E. Venkatasubbiah and E. Muller, 1914: 351–67.
128. *Daśakumāracarita*, pp. 132–3.
129. Cited in *KSS*, vol. III, p. 207, fn. 2.
130. *Mṛcchakaṭika*, Act 1, p. 8.
131. As *devadāsī*, prostitutes were particularly auspicious. It is important to remember that in ancient India they were the only class of women who were as near to the deities in the temples as the male priest. Parasher and Naik (1986: 76) in the context of the early medieval temples of Karnataka point out that an integral and necessary aspect of any ritual to be performed daily in the temples, was that pertaining to the *raṅgabhoga* (pleasure of entertainment) and *aṅgabhoga* (physical enjoyment) of the deity. This was performed by the *pātrās* and *śulās* (i.e. *devadāsī*), respectively.
132. *Samayamātṛkā*, epilogue 1.
133. *Śṛṅgāramañjarīkathā*, p. 23.
134. Ludwick Sternbach, 1944–5.
135. *Manusmṛti*, 4.209.
136. Shalini Shah, 1998: 3.
137. This is the term used for prostitutes in *Kuṭṭanīmatam*, verses 440, 797.
138. *Kuṭṭanīmatam*, verse 310.
139. S. Jackson and S. Scott, 1996: 342.
140. *Mṛcchakaṭika*, Act VIII, p. 302.
141. While the *Arthaśāstra* (2.27.14–7; 4.13.38–9), and also the *Nārada Smṛti* (6.19), do provide for state action against those who rape, disfigure, or kill a prostitute, the punishment is never very heavy (it is mainly in the form of fines). On the other hand, if a prostitute killed a client, the *Arthaśāstra* (2.27.22) states that she was to be awarded the death sentence either by burning or being drowned alive.
142. *Mṛcchakaṭika*, Act I, p. 62.
143. *Samayamātṛkā*, 8.35.
144. Cited in Christine Overall, 1992: 722.
145. Cited in Shannon Bell, 1994: 74, 88.
146. Catherine MacKinnon, 1982: 515–44.
147. Shannon Bell, 1994: 80.
148. Carol S. Vance, 1984.
149. Hanna Papanek and Gail Minault, 1982.
150. *Kuṭṭanīmatam*, verse 895.
151. *Samayamātṛkā*, 2.54.
152. *Śṛṅgārahāṭa*, p. 74.
153. *Kuṭṭanīmatam*, verse 848.
154. *Mṛcchakaṭika*, Act X, p. 402.

155. *Nāṭyaśāstra*, 24.223.
156. Ibid.: 24.224.
157. Ibid.: 24.160–2.
158. Ibid.: 24.163–4.
159. Ibid.: 24.236–8.
160. *Kuṭṭanīmatam*, verse 306.
161. Ibid., verse 399.
162. *Bṛhatkathāślokasaṁgraha*, 14.113.
163. *Mṛcchakaṭika*, Act III.7.
164. Ibid., Act VIII.23; VIII.39.
165. *Daśakumāracarita*, p. 130.
166. Cited in Shannon Bell, 1994: 89–91.
167. Sternbach, 1953: 65.
168. Ibid.: 12.
169. *Śṛṅgārahāta*, p. 74.
170. *Bṛhatkathāślokasaṁgraha*, 18. 63–6.
171. Ibid.: 18.73–5.
172. *Kuṭṭanīmatam*, verses 389, 575.
173. *Jayamaṅgalā*, 6.6.44; 2.6.48.
174. In none of the narrative or *kāvya* texts is this mentioned.
175. *Kāmasūtra*, 2.6.45.
176. These are the marginal areas of brahmanical patriarchy where 'normal' practices are suspended. Although sometimes (*Jayamaṅgalā*, 2.6.38, 48) the royal women of *prācya* land indulge in this practice, it is done only clandestinely (*pracchadayanti*).
177. *Jayamaṅgalā*, 2.6.45.
178. Manjushree, 1990: 52.
179. Shalini Shah, 1995: 56.
180. R. Raghavan, 1951: 20.
181. *Sāhityadarpaṇa*, ch. 3, p. 167.
182. *Kuṭṭanīmatam*, verse 313.
183. *Śṛṅgāramañjarīkathā*, p. 15.
184. *Kuṭṭanīmatam*, verse 303.
185. Ibid., verse 277.
186. Ibid., verse 278.
187. Ibid., verse 279.
188. *Bṛhatkathāślokasaṁgraha*, 18.103.
189. *Mṛcchakaṭika*, Act 1.31.
190. Ibid., Act 1.32.
191. *Kāvyamīmāṁsā*, ch. 6, p. 71.
192. *Śṛṅgāramañjarīkathā*, p. 25.
193. *Daśakumāracarita*, p. 174.
194. *Śṛṅgāramañjarīkathā*, p. 88.

195. *Mṛcchakaṭika,* Act VI, p. 218.
196. Ibid., Act II, p. 68.
197. Ibid., Act IV, p. 174.
198. Ibid., Act IV.33.
199. Ibid., Act IV.33.

4

Prema and *Śṛṅgāra*

In this chapter we will be analysing the 'love tradition' which, we shall argue, is essentially a feminine tradition, as against the 'erotic tradition' that is inherently masculine. *Prema* or love, in contradistinction to *śṛṅgāra*[1] or eroticism, deals with reciprocity and emotions in sexual relations (which may or may not be physical), as against the hegemonic masculinity of the erotic tradition that objectifies women and lacks empathy. We have seen that in the latter case a woman exists as a fetishized object of the male gaze, for exclusively male erotic stimulation. And in this process of being fetishized she ends up as disembodied parts—buttocks, breasts, thighs, waist, etc., she is not even a whole woman. The lyrical yet conventional descriptions of women's body parts in the *śṛṅgārī* poetry seem to operate like collective fetishes, culturally approved cues for the male individual to allow himself to indulge in erotic excitement without the risk of surrender or merger. One looks in vain for the features and lineaments of a living woman, but there are no individual women in Sanskrit erotic poetry, only types of women.

We notice in our sources that emotional reciprocity was relegated to the province of women, who were thought to be capable of both giving and receiving pleasure in the sexual act at the same time and in relation to the same individual. This is illustrated by Śīlā-bhaṭṭārikā's verse *yaḥ kaumāraharaḥ*[2] in which the poetess/*nāyikā* recalls a whole range of shared experiences with the *nāyaka*. The intimacy that is suggested is one that engages two personalities. This mutuality in love which we will impute to women as evident from the women's verses in classical Sanskrit poetry, as also to Bhavabhūti and Jayadeva, are at the heart of a unique dynamics of love. Instead of the conception of the erotic where man is seen as a pleasure chaser, we confront the woman's view of love with its emphasis on mutuality of pleasure. This pleasure is not aimed only at physical gratification, but is perceived as an emotional experience drawing upon life's connectedness. As Bhavabhūti points out in *Uttararāmacarita,*[3] 'Rāma loved Sītā naturally, a dearness which she increased by her own virtues. Similarly, Sītā loved Rāma more than life itself (*rāmaḥ sītāyāḥ prāṇebhyaḥ api priyaḥ abhavat*). Only their hearts knew their mutual affection (*hṛdayaṁ tvaveva jānāti prītiyogaṁ parasparam*)'. Within this love tradition, sex/sexuality is understood as a conscious and humanizing interaction between two equally valuable heterosexual participants, and never as an invasion or conquest of the one by the other.[4]

Is such a binary divide within the corpus of classical Sanskrit *kāvya* redundant? After all, while erotic desire does not imply love, it does provide a motive for love. From the point of view of gender, however, the distinction between love and erotic desire is crucial. Love is by definition free (although it would not exclude mutual commitment), but sexual/erotic desire has been historically a gendered construct. Love, as Bhavabhūti would say, cannot be extorted, it must be freely given—you love because you want to, not because you are forced or obliged to; and while love has a tendency to grow with time, erotic desire has a tendency to wither. This distinction comes through fairly clearly in the verses of the classical Sanskrit poetry as in Śīlābhaṭṭārikā's *yaḥ kaumāraharaḥ* and Vijjikā's *gate premābandhe.* The verses of these women celebrate love rather than the sexual urge, and even where the erotic urge is expressed it is another expression of love. The reason why we talk of masculine erotic *vis-à-vis* feminine love traditions is because in the Sanskrit *kāvya* literature the emotional trajectory was conceived differently for men and women. What was valorized for women was degraded for men, and vice versa. For instance, it stands out from Bharata's time onwards[5] that there are *uttama, madhyama,* and *adhama* types among both men and women. But the nature of that classification[6] is very interesting: thus, *uttama nāyaka* (in relation to *nāyikā*) is one who has a sweet disposition, is liberal, does not lose himself in love, and can give up the love when the woman slights him. *Madhyama nāyaka* (in relation to *nāyikā*) is one who without much enthusiasm tries to know and captivate the woman's heart but gives up the moment some misunderstanding crops up. *Adhama nāyaka* (in relation to *nāyikā*) is the low type who courts despite insults and goes on loving the lady even when her infidelity is known and friends try to dissuade him. In addition, there is reference to the *pravṛttaka* or *saṁpravṛttaka*, a degenerate type who is devoid of fear, anger, sense of shame and firmness, and is a mere plaything of women. As for the *uttama nāyikā* (in relation to *nāyaka*), she is one[7] who does not speak unpleasantly to the lover even if he has erred, does not exhibit prolonged anger; covers up the faults (of the lover), and is not fickle. She is sought after by virtue of her pedigree, beauty, and wealth, is adept in love, considerate, and has no jealousy or anger without due cause. *Madhyama nāyikā* (in relation to *nāyaka*) is one who herself seeks her lover and is also sought after by him. She is jealous and quick to anger, and naughty but easily pacified. The *adhama nāyikā* (in relation to *nāyaka*) is angry without reason and for long, and is severe and unfavourable.

Although earlier scholars have not necessarily used the terms *prema* or *śṛṅgāra* as binary opposites to analyse the huge corpus of classical Sanskrit texts, some of them appear to have instinctively felt this divide. Thus, S.K. De,[8] in his inimitable style, while commenting on the courtly Sanskrit plays states that 'The pretty sentiments depicted in these light-hearted plays hardly deserve such a warm-blooded term as *love*' (emphasis mine). Sukumari Bhattacharji[9] notes in her *History of Sanskrit Literature* that 'Real poetry of love is conspicuously lacking in Sanskrit literature. What passes for love poetry is only poetry of lust, where physical desires substitute emotional depths.' What Bhattacharji is referring to as 'love poetry' is actually this '*śṛṅgārī* poetry'. In more recent times, David Shulman[10] made the same observation when he categorized Harṣa's plays *Ratnāvalī* and *Priyadarśikā* as courtly drama of the erotic type, and adds that one hesitates at the romantic tag for them.

THE LOVE TRADITION

I suggest that the love or *prema* tradition in the classical Sanskrit literature is one marked by feminine sensibility; a sensibility that sets much in store by mutual reciprocity in sexual relations. It is a tradition where the emotional content in sexual relations is placed higher than physical gratification. Within this love tradition, I include all data from the narrative literature such as *Kathāsaritsāgara*, *Śukāsaptati* and *Bṛhatkathāślokasaṁgraha*, in which we find evidence of the celebration of female erotica that subverts the hegemonic masculine, tradition.

The Prema *of the Women Poets*

An important aspect of this work has been to try and recover women's voices within the classical Sanskrit literature, and this has not been an easy task. First, one is faced with the sheer paucity of work that can be safely attributed to women. There are only about 140 verses, preserved in the Sanskrit anthologies, and some are quoted in the treatises on rhetoric (*kāvyaśāstra*). The number of women who wrote these verses is no more than thirty-three.[11] This is a dismal scenario considering that one is taking many centuries of literary production into consideration.

The second major problem with the excavation of women's voices is the difficulty in determining authorship with any degree of certainty. For instance, the famous verse *yaḥ kaumāraharaḥ*[12] of Śīlābhaṭṭārikā is attributed to a male poet Kasyacita in Śrīdharadāsa's[13] anthology *Saduktikarṇāmṛta*, while Vidyākara[14] in *Subhāṣitaratnakoṣa* leaves it anonymous. Only Jalhaṇa[15] in *Sūktimuktāvalī* attributes it to Śīlābhaṭṭārikā. Another verse, *gate premābandhe*, attributed to Vijjikā in Vallabhadeva's[16] *Subhāṣitāvalī*, is said to be authored by Amaru in *Saduktikarṇāmṛta*[17] and is also anthologized in *Amaruśataka*.[18] Yet another verse, *kva prasthitāsi karabhoru*, attributed to Vikaṭanitambā and Govindasvāmī jointly in *Śārṅgadharapaddhati*,[19] is attributed to Amaru both in *Amaruśataka*[20] and in the *Subhāṣitāvalī*.[21] We thus see that not only is authorship neither final nor transparent, but, even more crucial, one cannot even be sure of the gender of these voices. This problem is not amenable to easy solutions. For the purpose of my analysis I have taken only those women's verses into consideration that are specifically attributed to them by J.B. Chaudhuri in his *Sanskrit Poetesses*, as also by the doyen of scholars of classical Sanskrit literature, V. Raghavan, in his important paper, 'Sanskrit and Prakrit Poetesses'.

Yet another vexatious issue is about identifying the literary genre of these verses. Since Sanskrit verses by women are not taken from any specific *kāvya*, but are part of a free floating body preserved in the anthologies and the text on poetics due to their literary merit, it is difficult to pinpoint their genre. If we treat them like other verses of the anthologies, as *śṛṅgārī* poetry of courtly origin, that does not explain why we should place them within the *prema* tradition at all. In fact, it would be better to see such verses (along with the poetry of Jayadeva and Bhavabhūti) as representing a crystallization of female *prema* sensibilities, as opposed to the masculine *śṛṅgārī* tradition.

Another hurdle is analysis of the content of these verses. Dasgupta and De[22] argue that these verses are 'not more than dainty trifles concerned with light erotic topics[23] in the conventional embroidery of romantic fancy. Almost all women poets are occupied with themes of love,[24] and even where verse is descriptive; there is often a romantic implication.' J.B. Chaudhuri[25] also notes that the verses of Sanskrit poetesses are 'rich with the subtle fragrance of an intense feminine heart and reflect its peculiar joys[26] and sorrows, strife and turmoil'. Such preoccupation with romantic verse reminds one of Byron,[27] who says in the first canto of *Don Juan*, 'Man's love is of man's life a thing apart; 'tis woman's whole existence'.

In this enterprise of analysing the nature of women's poetry another hurdle is how we should read these voices. Are they reflective of mere 'feminine consciousness' or can they be legitimately ascribed as 'female voices'? Borrowing Keohane, Rosaldo and Gelpi's[28] analysis, I use the term 'feminine' consciousness where a woman defines herself in the context of the male gaze, construct, and desire. 'Female' consciousness, on the other hand, implies consciousness about women as life-givers and life-sustainers. 'Feminist' consciousness' for its part is aware of the structural subordination of women. Keohane, Rosaldo and Gelpi also make it clear that at any given time more than one if not all three levels of consciousness, may co-exist. I suggest that the majority of the verses here discussed articulate female desire, and therefore can be accorded the status of female voices. However, these female voices do not come down to us in an unmediated form, completely unimpinged by the masculine world around them. Therefore, they can be retrieved only in the context of a myriad influences that react and re-react on them. After all, a response whether feminine, female, or feminist is in the ultimate analysis a response to the patriarchal/masculine 'other'.

It is an interesting fact of classical Sanskrit love poetry that while it is poetry on love and about love, it is not the poetry of a lover.[29] There is no love lyric in this sense in Sanskrit. The attitude and training of the Indian poet was such that the idea of expressing his own private feelings hardly ever occurred to him. In Sanskrit, love poems are universals in a typed situation, and not named characters in a particular circumstance. However, *yaḥ kaumāraharaḥ* of Śīlābhaṭṭārikā, which expresses the woman poet's longing for a lost intimacy, has a haunting personal quality to it that is rare in classical Sanskrit poetry. The poetess says,

> He who was the stealer of my virginity, is my husband (at present); those very same nights in the month of *caitra* (have arrived); the same breezes fragrant with the smell of the *mālatī* flower, are (blowing through) the *kadamba* tree; I am also the same old self. Still my heart is longing for stolen amorous sports (*caurya surata*) under the cave creepers on the bank of the river Revā.[30]

We see in this verse an imagery of night with fragrant breezes, the smell of flowers, and a soft creeper-laden river bank. This is an essentially sensuous setting close to the sights and smells of nature; a private world that is self-defined. The personalized quality of some of the women's verses was, perhaps, due to the fact that none of them was in search of a livelihood or was otherwise exposed to a public platform. Therefore, there was no imperative to please a patron. Women wrote, it would seem, for themselves.

The female love verses tend to probe the inner spaces of their mind. Given the fact that a woman does not have a private space of her own or even a private identity under patriarchy, and her own body is also not hers to possess,[31] a woman must look deeper into the privacy and secrecy of her mind, emotions, thoughts, and feelings to establish her privacy. This is a process which involves a great deal of 'self-consciousness' and, therefore, we could perhaps treat these 'love verses' as 'female voices'.

There are even stirrings of 'feminist consciousness' in some of the verses. Śīlābhaṭṭārikā boldly tries to question the male prerogative to desire even when they are old, while women are denied this right. Śīlā asks 'How unjustifiable and improper is the decree of fate, which makes men succumb to the sentiments of desire even when they are too old for them, especially when we see that the life of women is not limited to the contraction or fall of their heaving breasts?'[32]

There is little escaping the fact that the verses are essentially about heterosexual desire and display an ardent aspiration for male companionship. Nevertheless, they have a subversive quality about them. It is not a mere coincidence that in Jalhaṇa's *Sūktimuktāvalī*, out of 21 verses by seven women at least two verses are placed under *kulaṭāpaddhati*. In Vidyākara's *Subhāṣitaratnakoṣa*, four verses under *asatīvrājya* are authored by women (*kulaṭā* and *asatī* are both epithets for promiscuous women). In *Saduktikarṇāmṛta* too, under the sub-heading *asatī* at least three verses are by Vijjikā/Vidyā. Two of these women have interesting names: Vikaṭanitambā (one with huge hips) and Jaghanacapalā (one with an active lower part). What do these highly eroticized names or pseudonyms suggest? Jaghanacapalā has just one cryptic verse attributed to her, about the love of a (married?) woman called Jaghanacapalā for another (man?). She says 'on a bad rainy night, when dark clouds cover the sky and it is difficult to walk through the deserted city streets, and when the husband[33] is away in a foreign country, Jaghanacapalā feels immensely happy'.[34] Perhaps it was the blatant social illegitimacy of this sentiment which led male anthologists such as Vidyākara and Vallabhadeva to ascribe this verse to a sexually active woman.[35]

It is quite possible to argue that women were revelling in their own sensuousness and articulating their desires even if they were feminine ones of aspiring for male love. In the context of patriarchy with its ideology of circumscribing all expression of female sexuality, the very act of articulation rendered these love verses subversive. In these verses we notice a search for female erotica which would represent heterosexuality as both erotic and an area of contestation. If the heterosexual institution of patriarchy is to be understood as one where woman is only the object and not a subject who desires; if it has to be perceived as an institution where women have to respect the given social and ethical boundaries (of virginity and subsequently of satihood) as wife and daughter while men are free to take their pleasures elsewhere, then this particular meaning of the patriarchal heterosexuality is overturned by these women's voices. Their verses talk of illicit desires that are not always to be realized within marriage. Madhurāvarṇī[36] is forthright in articulating her desire:

My husband is like the moon in appearance, like a cuckoo in speech, like a pigeon in his kisses, like a swan in gait, like an elephant in his ardent love-making with his wife. Thus, in my husband there is not the slightest want of the good qualities commendable to young women, but if only (he had) not this one fault, namely, (that he) is married (to me).

Vijjikā refers to the transgression of a wife and mother and who tries to keep a tryst with a secret lover. She tells her neighbour (*prativeśinī*),

Do please keep an eye on my house, be it even for a short while. Oftentime the father of this child will not drink the tasteless water of the well. So, though alone, I am going quickly to the river, covered with *tamala*. Let the dense joints of reeds with hard sections scratch my body.[37]

We also get a fine verse on the love of a mature woman who is sure of her sexual desire and boldly tries to realize it. This verse of Sītā[38] describes a woman drinking with a man she desires as lover, and dropping a hint to him to that effect, she says

Do not be afraid O moon (the beloved desired), Rāhu is not in my liqueur (Rāhu here stands for the *nāyikā's* husband/guardian), Rohiṇī is in the sky (Rohiṇī stands for the beloved *nāyaka's* wife who is absent), O timid one! Why are you afraid? What is there to be surprised at this that the hearts of men become agitated oftentimes during their first union with experienced ladies? (*vidagdhavanitā navasaṅgameṣu*).

In this verse the equation of the timid *nāyikā* and the bold demanding *nāyaka* is reversed, overturning the object/subject hierarchy of the patriarchal heterosexual relationship.

Raghavan[39] quotes a verse by Vikaṭanitambā from the *Śārṅgadharapaddhati* which is a delineation of an *abhisārikā nāyikā*. In Sanskrit poetics, the *abhisārikā* is the only *nāyikā* among the primary *aṣṭanāyikā*[40] whose conception is not crucially dependent on her relation to the *nāyaka*. Her amorous mood is her own, the initiative in that tryst is also her own. The *abhisārikā nāyikā* captures the intensity of a woman in love making a secret (or not so secret in the case of *divābhisārikā*) tryst with her beloved. In Vikaṭanitambā's verse the *abhisārikā* is asked 'Young lady, tell me, are you not afraid to go alone?' She replies, 'Well, there is aid for me; Cupid with his feathered arrows'. What is remarkable about these verses, classified in nearly all the anthologies under the sub-heading *asatī* and *kulaṭā*, is that anthologists do so in spite of the convention that the cheated (*khaṇḍita*) or abandoned (*vipralabdha*) *nāyaka* does not exist in classical Sanskrit literature. It is noteworthy that Bhoja in his text on poetics, *Śṛṅgāraprakāśa,* while dealing with *saṁketa* (arranging an assignation) and *abhisāra* (the tryst) relies heavily on illustrations from Prakrit literature. Thus, out of twenty-five circumstances of *saṁketa* elaborated by Bhoja,[41] twenty-four have two illustrations each that are in Prakrit. As for *abhisaraṇa*, *Śṛṅgāraprakāśa* goes on to give details of the several stages a lady undergoes while hurrying to her tryst with her lover.[42] From separation and intention to go and meet him, up to her return, hiding the signs of her guilt, Bhoja[43] delineates several stages and for each stage, he gives at least two examples. Except for two, all examples are in Prakrit. The fact that the portrayal of *saṁketa* and *abhisāra* is heavily dependent on Prakrit poetry suggests the possibility that as subject matter, they entered Sanskrit literature from Prakrit.

It could be that Sanskrit women poets wrote about the *abhisārikā nāyikā* and about love in general, because Prakrit had long been the domain of women. Srinivasan[44] has convincingly demonstrated the presence of female authorship in a big way within Prakrit poetry. Jayavallabha, in his Prakrit anthology *Vajjālaggam*, notes[45] that Prakrit poetry that is charming, characterized by sentiments of love and full of sweet sounds, is dear to young women (*juvaiee jana-vallabha*). No wonder that even women writing in Sanskrit informed their poetry with Prakrit sensibilities.[46] Avantisundarī wrote in Sanskrit and in Prakrit and three verses of the latter have been preserved.[47]

It is a truism of the theory of literary criticism that the social milieu of litterateurs must be closely looked into to understand their work. Mammaṭa,[48] in his *Kāvyaprakāśa*, points out that 'one can know from the *kāvya* the manners and customs of the age' (*kāvyam vyavahāravide*). It is within the context of their patriarchal polygynous (many poetesses were aristocratic ladies, where this social practice was rampant), family milieu that many of the poetic outpourings of the women writers will have to be understood. The writers had a great deal to say on the fickleness of man's love. Man was like a bee, fluttered from one to the other, while women were trapped in the domestic space. Vijjikā[49] expresses the pathos of a neglected woman's situation:

When the ties of love have come to be rent asundered (*gate premābandhe*), when the heart's high esteem has disappeared, when friendly relations (between us) have ceased, when he passes before me like an (ordinary) individual; I do not know the reason why, my dear friend! My heart is not being rent to a hundred pieces thinking about those very same past days, spent in that way (that is happily, before estrangement).

Śīlābhaṭṭārikā's verses[50] convey the subtle sarcasm of a *khaṇḍitā nāyikā* who expects to be cheated by her beloved even as she sends a messenger (*dūtī)* to him 'You are a young woman, he too is a fickle young man. The quarters are black with darkness . . . the place appointed for the meeting is a deserted one.'

The reason for the *khaṇḍitā nāyikā*'s uniqueness in classical Sanskrit literature was that in a patriarchal polygynous setting the code of love did not demand strict fidelity from the husband. The *nāyaka*'s infidelity did not lower the nobility (*udāratā*) of his personality. On the other hand, if the *nāyikā* was unfaithful, she would cease to be noble and Sanskrit poetics[51] cannot permit the emotional concerns of the *nāyaka* over the loss of what had already lost its value. Bhānudatta, in his poetic text *Rasamañjarī* of *c*. 1300 CE, specifically states that there cannot be a *khaṇḍita* or a *vipralabdha nāyaka*, because if the *nāyaka* were to discover on the person of the *nāyikā* evidence of an adulterous sexual encounter, it would create a situation of *rasābhāsa*.[52] It is thus obvious that the social possibility of encountering a cheated *nāyaka* was so remote that it was actually laughable[53] to imagine it.

The weeping *virahaṇī* is also ubiquitous in classical Sanskrit poetry and we need to be sensitive to the socio-cultural constructions that gave rise to these literary conventions. O'Flaherty[54] says that the *virahaṇī*'*s* suffering has to be seen in its patrilocal and patriarchal setting. This woman is 'penned up at home while man has outside diversions; female *viraha* is thus a hierarchical and agnatic fact as well as a psychological reality'. Since 'woman can do nothing but miss'[55] *viraha* comes across as a primarily feminine weakness or destiny. The figure of the *virahaṇī* is in a social sense based on the lack of agency vested in a woman to overcome or end her separation from her lover/husband.[56] Commenting on the social reality of *viraha* for the woman Lee Siegel[57] says that the woman was abandoned in her most fragile and vulnerable condition—the open and supple state which she had cultivated in order to please her man. The traditional goal of a woman's life was to serve and comfort the man and to be accessible. Having become the creeper that needed the support of the manly tree, the woman could only cry copiously and wish to be reunited with her man. Thus says Mārulā:

Concealing before your elders (your) grief due to your separation (from your beloved one), why are you O my lovely girl!, checking the flood of tears overflowing your eyes? The edge of your bed, wetted night after night by tears and dried in the sun (the next morning) indicates your sad plight.[58]

Morikā[59] also draws a word picture of a *virahaṇī* who waits endlessly for the termination of the period of separation. She says:

The (lovelorn) girl, with her cheeks bathed with tears flowing in torrents, makes marks (on the floor representing days she had spent in solitude) apprehensive lest there be no termination of the period (of separation), does not count them (*likhati na gaṇayati rekhāṁ*).

Many women's verses are delineations of the *māninī nāyikā,* often a figure of neglect. Yet these verses do not seem to dwell on lovers'/ husbands' shortcomings or even the injustice of the social milieu which shaped their neglect. As J.B. Chaudhuri[60] points out, 'Even at the time of the greatest suffering, the whole blame is put on women themselves and never on men'. In a verse of Vikaṭanitambā, a *māninī nāyikā* is being told that her lover's indifference is her own fault:

Without considering the consequences of love, ignoring your friends, why have you without any cause become angry with your sincere love. You have brought (upon yourself) with your own hands these charcoals, the flames of which are burning glowingly in the fire of separation. So now, stop crying in the wilderness.[61]

A verse by Bhāvādevī[62] expresses the tragic dimension of the husband–wife relationship which started as a mutually loving relationship, but ended as a hierarchical one where the husband became the lord and master of his wife (*kalatraṁ*).[63] This verse does not end in indignant anger against an insensitive husband. Instead, the wife bemoans her own iron heart (*prāṇānāṁ kuliśa kaṭhinānāṁ*) which endures in spite of the suffering. In another verse Bhāvādevī continues in the same vein. It is the wife who needs to blame herself even for the deeds of a faithless husband. The *nāyikā* states:

Why are you falling at my feet? Stop! Husbands are certainly independent. For a while you enjoyed elsewhere, what blame can attach to you for that? It is the husbands who are the very life-breaths of their wives. Hence (as) I am still alive in spite of my separation from you, it is I who have committed sin, it is I who should beg your pardon.[64]

A verse by Mārulā too describes a *māninī nāyikā's* futile pride. It records a dialogue between her and the *nāyaka*

How is it you are so thin?
Well, my body is so by nature.
Why is your body soiled?
By attending to cooking in my elder's house!
Do you remember me?
No, no! So saying she began to tremble, fell on my chest, and cried.[65]

The *māninī nāyikā* of these verses are not bitter figures commenting on the heartlessness of men or launching tirades against social mores that leave men autonomous but condemn women to a social web in which all they can do is to romanticise about the powerful males to whom they can come close through emotional and physical ties. In a verse by an anonymous poetess,[66] a wife beseeches her husband who has gone away to return. What is interesting in this verse are the epithets used for the husband: a god who is *svādhīna* (independent), *kṣamāsindhu* (ocean of forgiveness), *sādhvīśaraṇa* (refuge of the faithful wife), and *karuṇābhājanavibho* (the merciful lord). It is thus obvious that female voices do not come down to us in an unmediated form. We have perforce to locate them within their patriarchal structuring.

Love verses, even those on love-making (*saṁbhoga*), have to be placed within the wider context of the feminine love/*prema* tradition which, we have seen, is marked by mutuality. Intimacy is primarily emotional and reciprocal.[67] This fact is well-illustrated by Śīlā-bhaṭṭārikā's *yaḥ kaumāraharaḥ* and Vijjikā's *gate premābandhe*. There are other verses in a similar mould. What the women desire most is emotional gratification. Thus Morikā underlines the fact that both men and women (metaphorically referred to as moon and night) need each other for fulfilment. She says,

O sinless one! You (her) dearest are worthy of her; as she (your) dearest is of you. Indeed the moon does not shine without the night and night too does not shine without the moon.[68]

Vikaṭanitambā says,

As he came to bed the knot fell open by itself, the dress held only somehow to my hips by the strands of the loosened girdle. So much I know, my dear; but when within his arms, I cannot remember who he was or who I was; or what we did or how?[69]

A verse by Vijjikā etches the memory of ecstasy. A friend tells another,

Bravo to you, who remember all the sweet love chat you had with your beloved at the time of intercourse. O friend, when my beloved decided to lay his hand on the knot of my lower garment I swear from that time itself I do not retain the memory of anything that happened afterwards.[70]

In these verses on love in union (*saṁbhoga*) we do not notice any Sapphic love passion; nevertheless, the nature of this love is different from the voyeuristic male *śṛṅgārī* poetry, where the woman is only an inert, fetishized object for the male gaze. These verses are about an experience that is an expression of feelings between people that creates bonds. As Vijjikā so pithily puts it in one of her verses,

Erotic fulfilment lies in mere interlocking of eyes of men and women. If a man desires physical union even after being the target of a woman's love glances, the woman is at fault, for, after reaching below the buttocks (*nitamba*) even animals realize the sexual goal (*ratiphala*).[71]

Noteworthy in this unique verse is that the *nāyikā* is claiming the 'gaze' for herself. She wants to look with the erotic passion that holds her man. The subject position of women's gaze is, however, as a rule virtually non-existent in classical Sanskrit poetry.

THE SENTIMENTALITY OF BHAVABHŪTI

The love tradition of the classical Sanskrit *kāvya* would remain incomplete without reference to Bhavabhūti. He conceives love as a heart-felt emotion, a deep empathy, and thus addresses himself to the 'inner meaning and experience of loving'.[72] At no place in his plays *Uttararāmacarita* or *Mālatī-Mādhava* does Bhavabhūti expend his energy like the rest of *śṛṅgārī* poets in delineating the charms of the *nāyikā*. Admitting of his powerful desire for Mālatī, Mādhava eschews any reference to her physical charms. He says,

Some internal affection, which is past exact determination, which baffles all power of expression, which again was never before experienced by me, and which is impenetrable owing to the great infatuation (*mahāmohagahano*) growing in strength on account of the total destruction of discrimination, stupifies and affects me simultaneously.[73]

Mādhava does not talk in terms of his seduction by Mālatī's physical form. The emphasis rather is on feelings. Mādhava says, 'I was thus subdued by this disclosure of the feelings which could be inferred as proceeding from love of her (*sneharasa*) who was bewitching to the heart in every way.'[74] Bhavabhūti dwells on the philosophical plane and the spiritual aspect of love, so that the physical aspect of love is something which is downplayed.

If for Bhavabhūti love is worthy of being treated as an expression of a highly spiritual truth, it is because he is among those rare litterateurs of classical Sanskrit who gave pre-eminence to *karuṇa-rasa* over the *śṛṅgārarasa.* [75] Rejecting as he did the primacy of *śṛṅgārarasa,* Bhavabhūti could not but view love as a spiritual communion. He describes love as a 'state when two become one, in joy as in sorrow. When you find rest together and feelings never age but deepen and ripen as you move through the layers of time. That rare state of human fulfilment one finds only once in life.'[76]

Bhavabhūti did not view woman as an instrument for inciting male erotic fancy, rather he saw her as the recipient of man's affection which was both passionate and warm. Reminiscencing about time spent with Sītā in the forest, Rāma says in the *Uttararāmacarita,*[77] 'lying close to each other as we talked together softly, secretly, cheek closely pressed to cheek, our arms were buried in their tight embrace and the night was gone without our knowing the hours as they passed.' The mutual affection in such a love relationship was powerful enough for the *nāyaka* and *nāyikā* to claim to know each other perfectly. Thus Sītā says about Rāma, 'I know his heart and he also knows mine.'[78] And upon separation from Sītā, Rāma bemoans, 'Where is it, that immense delight rooted in perfect trust? Where is that mutual love (*vā anyonya prema*), the profound curiosity about one another, the union of hearts in joy as in sorrow (*sukhe vā dukhe vā hṛdayayoḥ tat aikyaṁ*)?'[79]

The ideal love relation which Bhavabhūti envisaged was monogamous, even connubial. Kāmāndakī notes in the play *Mālatī-*

Mādhava[80] that 'the husband to women and the lawful wife to man are the dearest objects, friends, all relatives put together, all things that the heart covets, a treasure and life itself, let this be mutually known.' So love intrigues (as in Śrī Harṣa's plays) and the subterfuges in an *antaḥpura* setting employed by a polygynous *nāyaka* do not find place in Bhavabhuti's plays. In fact, Bhavabhūti's *nāyaka* sets much in store by the singularity of his devotion to the *nāyikā*. Rāma says, while offering his arm as a pillow to Sītā in *Uttararāmacarita,*[81] 'Ever since the time of my marriage, whether in the house or in the forest in childhood and after that in youth, this arm of Rāma has been your pillow lulling you to sleep and not resorted to by any other woman.' Bhavabhūti further makes Rāma describe his wife[82] as 'prosperity of my house, collyrium pencil of ambrosia to the eyes and her touch like a balm of sandalwood on the body'. Thus, for Rāma the very act of desertion of such a wife was like the end of life. He says, in *Uttararāmacarita,*[83] 'The purpose of Rāma's life is at an end today. The earth is now a sterile withered wilderness, worldly life is without interest, full of worry is the body. I have no refuge left.' The sorrow of Rāma upon separation from his wife was not just mental but physically debilitating. In the play[84] he is depicted as exceedingly wasted (*parikṣīṇo*). Another unique feature of Bhavabhuti's *nāyaka* is that he cries unashamedly at the loss of his beloved. Lakṣamaṇa says[85] Rāma's state would make the stones weep. Thus Bhavabhūti transcended the norms set in the text on poetics[86] in the portraying of the *dhīrodātta nāyaka* (who is not given to the display of emotion) like Rāma. In Bhavabhūti's hands, the *nāyaka* Rāma comes closest to the figure of the *virahaṇī nāyikā*. In the depiction of his sorrow, Rāma is feminized by Bhavabhūti.

While at one level Bhavabhūti raised love to philosophical and spiritual heights eschewing all references to the erotic, at another level he could not discount the procreative angle. For him, love is perfected through children. He says,[87] the child is 'the most powerful link between parents. An offspring is really the one knot of the hearts of the parents, since in it is centred their affection.'

Bhavabhuti's view of women and even more importantly man's love for woman was a totally new presentation, a major departure from the vast corpus of classical Sanskrit literature. Bhavabhūti's *nāyaka* reserved his romantic love for a single woman, his *svīyā*.

Although a later litterateur, Rājaśekhara, was fond of seeing himself as an incarnation[88] of Bhavabhūti, we see no similarity in the treatment of love in Rājaśekhara's writings. Although his play *Viddhaśālabhañjikā* had a romantic setting, Rājaśekhara was preoccupied with the idea of physical love and its satiation. Unlike Bhavabhūti there is no celebration of a heartfelt sentiment that is also monogamous. In fact, in *Viddhaśālabhañjikā* in one stroke *nāyaka* Vidhyādharamalla marries two women. The play has nothing to say about the two women's feelings and Vidhyādharamalla can only lust after the attractive feminine form. In the very beginning of the play, Vidhyādharamalla 'falls in love' (if at all this phrase can be used here) with Kuvalayāmālā who he happens to eye just after her having bathed in the Narmadā. The King's Vidūṣaka calls him *mahilā lampaṭa jāta*.[89] As for Mṛgāṅkāvali, the other *nāyikā* of *Viddhaśālabhañjikā*, she is pretty eyes, breasts, waist and buttocks, a bundle of feminine charms (*lāvaṇya paṇyaṁ vapuḥ*).[90]

JAYADEVA'S RADICAL NOTION OF LOVE

Apart from Bhavabhūti, another mainstream author of classical Sanskrit literature whom I have placed in the love tradition as against erotic tradition, is Jayadeva and his *Gītagovinda*. Many scholars from Pischel and Renou to Suniti Kumar Chatterjee have argued for a folk Apabhraṁśa origin for Jayadeva's *Gītagovinda*. D.D. Kosambi[91] even suggests that the *Gītagovinda* was drafted in a popular idiom before being translated into Sanskrit for the court, and therefore it could and did appeal to people outside the court as well. After all, Jayadeva joined the Senā court of Bengal at a late date. He also wrote vernacular poems in musical mode and some of these compositions have survived as in the *Guru Granthsāhib*. B.S. Miller,[92] Kunal Chakrabarty,[93] and others point out that the meters of the *Gītagovinda* songs and the mode of their articulation clearly resemble the meters of medieval poetry in the vernacular language known as Apabhraṁśa. The predominant metrical patterns of Jayadeva's *kāvya* correspond with the basic rhythmic design of non-Sanskrit medieval poetry. Jayadeva perhaps adopted the meters of the vernacular poetry in order to create a medium within the conventional poetic Sanskrit.

Another reason for tracing the *Gītagovinda* to folk origins is the presence of Rādhā as a *nāyikā*. C. Mackenzie Brown[94] points out that the name Rādhā appears in popular folklore and Prakrit poetry as early as the sixth century,[95] long before its mention in the Puranic literature. It would seem that this celebration of the Rādhā–Kṛṣṇa love relation in popular folklore was the source of Jayadeva's *Gītagovinda*. Two other Sanskrit works[96] which similarly applied Prakrit and Apabhraṁśa meters to Sanskrit were Somadevasūri's *Yaśastilakacampū*[97] and Kṣemendra's *Daśāvatāracarita.*[98] It is notable that reference to Rādhā in the specific context of her adultery occurs in both these works. Perhaps it would not be far-fetched to surmise that Rādhā's relationship with Kṛṣṇa is adulterous, the love of a mature woman for an adolescent, but one that was mutually passionate and equal, and picked up from the non-Sanskrit Prakrit–Apabhraṁśa poetry and made into an extraordinary Sanskrit *kāvya* by the poetic genius of Jayadeva. In the *Gītagovinda,* Rādhā epitomizes a less constrained sexual behaviour and a certain power of the woman over her lover, a note on which the *Gītagovinda kāvya* ends.

Hein[99] points out that Rādhā of our earliest knowledge was established in the cultural life of very humble people. For centuries mention of Rādhā is found only in Prakrit poetry,[100] Apabhraṁśa works, and the writings of the Jainas. The closest external associations of Rādhā's cult are with the low-class Śaiva movement. Rādhā belonged to the religions of the lower and middle classes of simple people. She appeared for the first time in the mainstream of Sanskrit literature in the *Gītagovinda.* Hein notes that from then on the erotic love which had formerly delighted only the lower classes became the possession of a substantial cross-section of society.

Given this scholarly opinion on the folk-Apabhraṁśa background of the *Gītagovinda kāvya*, will it be legitimate to ask, as Lee Siegel does,[101] whether its notion of love was different from the courtly erotic love of the predominant Sanskrit *kāvya* literature, 'which is an art, cultivated and mannered emotion rather than something more spontaneous, natural and fundamental'. I would argue that its content of the *Gītagovinda* and the treatment of the Rādhā–Kṛṣṇa relationship transcended the usual *nāyaka-nāyikā* relationship in Sanskrit *śṛṅgārī* poetry.

Jayadeva's text is unique in the sense that it overturns many of patriarchy's cherished norms. It valorizes woman's adultery. Benoy Kumar Sarkar[102] calls Rādhā a revolutionist, for she had transgressed the conventional morality of her surroundings. In *Gītagovinda,* Rādhā–Kṛṣṇa's adulterous union is actually apotheosized.[103] In one verse[104] the place of their love-making is referred to as *nikuñjamanmathamahātīrthe* (Love God's bower that is a pilgrim spot). In *Gītagovinda*[105] the epithet for Rādhā is *gopavadhū* (wife of *gopa*) as against *gopī* (which means milkmaid), which is an important indication of her married status.[106] In fact, *Gītagovinda*[107] also describes Vṛndāvana (site of Rādhā–Kṛṣṇa dalliance) as a place where adulterous love relations exist.[108] In social terms if a man illicitly loves a woman who is not his wife he does not threaten patriarchal structures since his actions can be accommodated. But for a woman, adulterous love involves an infringement of the order of patriarchy. Woman's adultery would constitute a break from worldly relations and a substantial bid for autonomy. It is the social regimentation of the patriarchal family which gives illicit female love its special daring. Rādhā not only harboured an illicit love for Kṛṣṇa but she was also an older woman who dared to love adolescent Kṛṣṇa. In the very opening verse of *Gītagovinda*[109] we are told that an older Rādhā is asked by Nanda (Kṛṣṇa's foster-father) to be Kṛṣṇa's escort, and she establishes an erotic relationship with him.

Gītagovinda also jettisoned the erotic *śṛṅgārī* poetry's ideal of a heroic lover, for whom no woman is exceptional and who simply desires a variety of amatory alliances, into a romantic lover whose passion and intensity matches that of Rādhā for him. The erotic quest of Rādhā and Mādhava is mutual. The deep emotional sentiment and reciprocity of their love is evident from a verse where it is said,[110] 'Mādhava still waits for you in love's most sacred thicket, where you perfected love together (*ratipaterāsāditāḥ siddhaya*).' If Rādhā seeks Kṛṣṇa, he too seeks her. He says, 'you are my ornament my life, my jewel in the sea of existence. Be yielding to me forever, my heart fervently pleads!'[111] Not only does Kṛṣṇa yearn for Rādhā, he even begs her forgiveness[112]—'forgive me now! I won't do this to you again. Give me a vision, beautiful Rādhā!'[113] He understands Radha's anger and curses himself for his mistake[114]—'She saw me surrounded in the crowd of women and went away. I was *too ashamed, too afraid* to stop her. Damn me! My wanton ways made her leave in anger' (emphasis added). Rādhā stands in Kṛṣṇa's mind as someone special who is desired in her uniqueness. When he thinks of Rādhā Kṛṣṇa says,[115] 'Even when the sensuous objects are gone my mind holds on to her in a trance. How the wound of her desertion deepens!' And as his attachment grows, which underlines the emotional content of his love, he discovers that he would rather serve[116] and adore Rādhā than vanquish and demand. Jayadeva tells us[117] that 'feeling for Rādhā bound his heart with a chain of memories buried in other-worldly lives . . . as he searched for Rādhā in vain, arrows of love pierced his weary mind and Mādhava repented as he suffered in a thicket on the Jumna river bank.' Kakkar and Ross[118] say that 'this transformative moment, from desires' sensations to love's adoration gives the story of Rādhā and Kṛṣṇa its singular impact'. Lee Siegel[119] notes that while Radha's longing is typical of the attitude of the *gopīs* of Vraja, it is Kṛṣṇa's attitude towards Rādhā in the *Gītagovinda* that is a completely new development—'Kṛṣṇa becomes more humanized person, subject to the pain of love which in prior literature he had inflicted but not himself felt.'

As a supplicant and adorer of Rādhā, Kṛṣṇa overturns the dominant status given to him. The Rādhā–Mādhava relationship in the *Gītagovinda* also jettisoned the status of Kṛṣṇa, the supreme godhead, in the *Bhāgavata Purāṇa*. Miller[120] points out that in the *Bhāgavata Purāṇa*, there is an allusion to the arrogant girl (*dṛptā*). If this is reference to Rādhā (who is never mentioned by name in the *Bhāgavata*), then it seems to be rejecting her relationship with Kṛṣṇa as an inappropriate model for the devotee. The possessive attitude manifested in her secret encounters with Kṛṣṇa is antithetical to the values presented in the *Bhāgavata*. Radha's attitude is specifically criticised for its perversity (*daurātmya*). It is not unlikely that the authors of the *Bhāgavata* knew a rival cult centring on Kṛṣṇa and his *gopī* consort and were critical of it. Ranajit Sarkar[121] says much the same thing. He feels that perhaps Rādhā was already the centre of the *rasa* in the popular pre-*Bhāgavata* legends which the Bhagavatas tried to suppress, foreseeing the danger of such an individualization. Thus, says Miller,[122] the Rādhā of *Gītagovinda* stands in relation to Kṛṣṇa as his consort; yet she is neither a wife nor a devoted rustic playmate, but an intense, solitary, and proud figure who is Kṛṣṇa's partner. In fact, in *Gītagovinda* Rādhā contrasts[123] her love for Kṛṣṇa with his affair with other *gopīs*, which is described as common love or *sādhāraṇa praṇaya*. In *Gītagovinda*, Rādhā and Mādhava have an 'exclusive love relation' which was a rejection of the *Bhāgavata* principle of devotion to lord Kṛṣṇa. It is Kṛṣṇa who turns into a devotee of Rādhā in the *Gītagovinda*. He declares himself her slave[124] and even attends to her toilet like a maid.[125] Rādhā in the climax of her union with Kṛṣṇa is significantly referred to as *svādhīnabhatṛkā*,[126] i.e. one whose lover is in her power. It is interesting to note that in this verse Rādhā is Caṇḍī, a goddess who is not any deity's consort in Indian theogony. She is portrayed placing her feet on Kṛṣṇa's head.

Unlike the usual *nāyikā* of the *śṛṅgārīkāvya*, in the *Gītagovinda* Rādhā has a remarkable agency *vis-à-vis* her desires (and not merely in *viparītarata* posture). She is active in the pursuit of that desire; in fact, Rādhā is an *abhisārikā nāyikā par excellence*. She says at one place,[127] *yad-anugamanaya niśi gahanam api śīlitam*, i.e. in search of whom, at night I have frequented the woods even though they are deep. Rādhā's subjectivity in her love relations with Kṛṣṇa flows from the fact that in Jayadeva's conception she is Kṛṣṇa's equal.[128] We see her losing the consciousness of the duality of existence and in that moment she thinks of herself as Kṛṣṇa. Even though love of Rādhā–Mādhava is heterosexual, Rādhā is not an instrument of pleasure or an object of Mādhava's erotic desire; she has subjectivity in this love making. Jayadeva[129] carefully notes the expression of Rādhā's pleasure and ecstasy in that physical contact.

Ranajit Guha[130] says that in the *śṛṅgāra* or erotic mode of worship there is no notion of equality between the devotee and the deity. Guha was here referring to the medieval Vaiṣṇava theology where we find a three fold division of erotic *bhakti*[131]—*samartha rati* or yearning for union with Kṛṣṇa for his gratification; *sādhāraṇa rati* or yearning for union with Kṛṣṇa for self-gratification; and *sāmañjasa rati* or union with Kṛṣṇa for mutual gratification. The medieval Vaiṣṇava theologists, particularly those of Bengal, saw Rādhā as a paragon of *samartha rati* and Kubjā as representative of *sādhāraṇa rati*.

Ranajit Guha[132] notes that within this system the function of *śṛṅgārarasa* was primarily to spiritualize and astheticize male dominance. The *gopīs* of Vṛndāvana as also Rādhā exist for Kṛṣṇa's pleasure. The initiative is his to seduce and dally with and to desert his female partners. It is a relation of love, says Guha, which is an authentic instance of the primacy assumed by the male in the sexual politics of a patriarchal society. This implied, among other things, the passivity of the female. It is difficult to accept this thesis in the case of Jayadeva's *Gītagovinda*. The Rādhā of *Gītagovinda* longs for Kṛṣṇa for self-gratification. If at all Jayadeva was precursor of the erotic *bhakti* mode, he placed the Rādhā–Mādhava relation in the *sāmañjasa rati* category rather than *samartha rati*. Not only does Rādhā of *Gītagovinda* actively seek and experience erotic pleasure with Kṛṣṇa, she is also jealous (characteristic of an individual rather than a submissive devotee) when she is not Mādhava's favourite or when she imagines another woman being sexually pleased (*ramitā*) by Kṛṣṇa. An intensely proud Radha[133] accuses Kṛṣṇa of harassing and murdering women, referring to his childhood bent in killing Pūtanā. She accuses Kṛṣṇa for his infidelity[134] and tells him not to tell her lies—*yāhi Mādhava yāhi keśava mavada kaitavavadaṁ*.

It was a lack of hegemonic masculinity which found expression in Jayadeva's *Gītagovinda*. For his part Bankim Chandra Chatterjee noted:

> from the beginning to the end [the *Gītagovinda*] does not contain a single expression of manly feelings, of womanly feelings there is a great deal or a single elevated sentiment. The poet has not a single new truth to teach. Generally speaking, it is the poets (religious or profane) who teach us the great moral truths which render man's life a blessing to his kind; but Jayadeva is a poet of another stamp. I do not deny his high poetical merits in a certain sense, exquisite imagery, tender feelings, unrivalled power of expression but that does not make him less the poet of an effeminate and sensual race.[135]

For Bankim, sensuousness was equated with womanly feelings and being effeminate. We notice that the masculine ascetic ideology (with its misogynist tendency of equating women with passion and profanity) rears its head here, albeit this time under the guise of a new national culture which needed to assert its masculinity (epitomized in Bankim's *Ānandamaṭha* where a male *sanyāsī* who had renounced *gṛhasthāśrama* fought for the country's independence) in the context of colonial domination.

SUBVERSIVE LOVE

Within the rich corpus of Sanskrit texts we find an entire genre of narrative literature that can be characterized as women's tales. We do not mean to propose that these tales were authored by women, but they centred on them and thus reflected women as gazing subjects, rather than as gazed upon objects.[136] Narrative literature like *Śukāsaptati*, *Bṛhatkathāślokasaṁgraha* and *Kathāsaritsāgara* contain many tales of the treacherous female animated exclusively by her sexual passion. These stories of adulterous love in which women are insatiable and deceitful, in spite of their negative and condemnatory characterization, do manage to convey a different dimension of the relations between the sexes.[137] In most of such tales the woman, with exquisite quickness of wit or cunning, is able to triumph over her husband as well as her paramour. What is interesting about these love tales is not adultery *per se*, but an active subversion of what is considered appropriate female behaviour. In daring to love and to assert their individual erotic freedom the women refused to submit to their cultural fate as objects of male desire. The various epithets used for these women in *Śukāsaptati,* such as *bāhyaśayinī,*[138] *naralampaṭā,*[139] *paranarapriyā,*[140] *svairiṇī,*[141] *puṁścalī,*[142] and *kulaṭā*[143] convey the subversion of the dominant patriarchal social mores by them. Thus one may conclude that by their actions these women acquired a subjective status. Ramanujan[144] sees women-centred tales and references to promiscuous behaviour by women as having a definite function. By means of such stories women may be partly reconciled to the reality of their lives in patriarchy, where sexuality is the most tabooed dimension of their existence. Just as 'good men dream what wicked men do', women's tales, feels Ramanujan, are the dreams of good women. They put forward an alternate set of values and attitudes, theories of action other than the official ones.

Śukāsaptati contains seventy stories of adulterous women. It is a storehouse of folk tales that apparently were current in society and expressed a defiance against social morality. They were celebratory of sentiments of emotional intensity. However, for the male anthologist of these tales, the purpose of the entire collection was not to celebrate female erotica but to sound a warning to such women. As *Śuka* the narrator states[145] at the outset, what the lady of the house

Prabhāvatī is about to embark on (i.e. a secret adulterous love affair) is a difficult (*duṣkara*) and condemnable (*nindita*) act for the wife of a household (*kulastrī*). It would seem that tales of female deviance were collected to convey the patriarchal message of respect for the *satī* morality. But whatever the objective, the flavour of the tales is really a celebration of the ingenuity of women who asserted their freedom and were able to realize their desires to a large extent. While most wives in these tales were ingenious in availing of opportunity for secret affairs, some like Rukmiṇī, wife of Rāhā Rājaputra,[146] actually pledged to have an adulterous relation in full view of her husband.

Bold women who were prepared to subvert the familial and social authority of the husband are mentioned in many stories of Buddhasvāmin's *Bṛhatkathāślokasaṁgraha* and the *Kathāsaritsāgara.*[147] *Bṛhatkathāślokasaṁgraha* refers to an interesting conversation between an *abhisārikā*[148] and her paramour. The latter sarcastically tells her when she is late for an assignation that 'I was foolish enough to love you; it is like punching the sky and beating the chaff (to get grain). All this time I have been waiting impatiently, but your chaste (*pativratā*) ladyship won't come out of the home. If your young and handsome husband is so dear to you, why do you harass noble men (*kulaputra*) like us?' Hearing this, the bold woman (*pragalbhābhisārikā*) smiled and replied, 'Persons like you are really shameless; I have to keep my husband in good humour just for your sake. The unchaste (*kulaṭā*) do not sport (*ramante*) with their paramours without obtaining the confidence of their husbands (*bhartān viśvasya*). If however you wish to drink the honey without the obstacles of bees kill my husband who is always careless. If you are afraid of sin, obviously you do not love me.' *Bṛhatkathāślokasaṁgraha*[149] also contains a rare reference to women indulging in sexual orgies where spouse-swapping takes place. Here we notice that wives openly solicit the company of other men who are not their husbands and amuse themselves in their company.

While *Śukāsaptati* and *Bṛhatkathāślokasaṁgraha* furnish examples of adulterous women, *Kathāsaritsāgara* argues in favour of female adultery from another perspective, i.e. of legitimacy of woman's physical needs. In *Kathāsaritsāgara*[150] a Buddhist nun Yogakaraṇḍikā, narrating her previous life says that she was one of the two wives of a brāhmaṇa who frequently went to other countries on embassies by order of the king. Yogakaraṇḍikā says that while he was away from home, 'I lived with other men at my pleasure, and so did not cheat the elements of which I was composed and my senses of their lawful enjoyments. For considerate treatment of the elements and senses is held to be the highest duty.'

Not only does *Kathāsaritsāgara* justify adultery from a woman's point of view, it also furnishes us with examples where caste boundaries were transgressed. In fact, some of these stories tell us about upper-caste women in love with lower-caste youth: the *pratiloma* union which was so despised by the patriarchal brahmanical order. In *Kathāsaritsāgara*[151] we are told that a *cāṇḍāla* youth fell in love with a *kṣatrīya* princess whose life he had saved. She reciprocated his feelings and wanted him for a husband. *Kathāsaritsāgara*[152] goes on to give many more tales of such forbidden love, as for instance a fisherman having a relationship with a princess. In all these stories the threat of caste pollution does not prevent the genesis and fruition of desire (*kāma*). In some of these tales the social transgression represented by inter-*varṇa* union is glossed over by resorting to the motif of a former birth, or to the divine origin motif, but the fact remains that these tales are perhaps the record of actual social transgressions. Also, what is interesting in these stories is the women of higher caste/class status asserting their desire for men of lower social standing. These stories subvert the ideal of endogamy (an important means of the perpetuation of caste and gender subordination) and at the same time establish the social reality of *pratiloma* union.

Kathāsaritsāgara also refers to girls asserting the autonomy of their erotic desire against parental authority. There is the story of Uṣā and Aniruddha,[153] and also of princess Kaliṅgasenā.[154] Princess Kaliṅgasenā chose to be united with young and handsome king Udayana of Vatsa rather than old king Prasenajit of Śrāvastī who had been chosen for her by her father. Kaliṅgasenā boldly took the initiative by visiting Udayana and sent a marriage proposal to him of her own accord.

Kathāsaritsāgara also tells us about girls who asserted their right to renounce marital ties if they so desired. It refers[155] to Svayaṁprabhā (i.e. one who is radiant by herself) who had taken a vow of virginity and lived as an ascetic. This text[156] mentions a princess Kanakarekhā who resolved to stay unmarried to please herself. Svayaṁprabhā had the strength to resist marriage and her sister Somaprabhā showed the same independence in her sapphic bonding with her friend princess Kaliṅgasenā who is tellingly referred to as *svayaṁvarā sakhī*.[157] There is, in addition, the tale of Malayavatī,[158] who is depicted as a man-hating princess (*puruṣa-dveṣiṇī*). The moment she saw a man she ordered her retinue of maids to kill him. In her palace she amused herself by marrying her female attendants to one another (*kanyakānyonyavivāhādi-vinodanaiḥ*). The story tells us that Malayavatī became sexually attracted (*smaravaśābhavat*) to a man who was disguised[159] as a woman (*strīrūpa*). In another veiled reference[160] to lesbian sentiments, *Kathāsaritsāgara*[161] tells us about princess Padmāvatī whose confidante and maid Manohārikā tells her, 'Even women who see you are so much in love with your beauty that they desire to become men; so what man would not be a suitor for your hand.'

The literary sources of our period specifically refer to two communities of women who are associated with sexual/erotic autonomy. These were the *rākṣasī* women and witches known as *māyāvinī/ḍākinī*. What is most striking about them is that their sexual autonomy is backed by the strong social status that they enjoyed. In his play *Mahāvīracaritam,* Bhavabhūti contrasts the women of the Āryan household like Kauśalyā, Sītā, etc., with those of the *rākṣasa* household. Dikshit[162] states that while *ārya* women were mild, modest, submissive, and devoid of individuality, *rākṣasa* women like Śūrpaṇakhā and Laṅkā, had the rare qualities of courage, shrewd understanding in political matters, energy, and active brains. The *rākṣasī* women of *dakṣiṇāpatha* in the play *Mahāvīracaritam*[163] lived a life of freedom as compared to the circumscribed life of the *ārya* women. They move about freely but are well educated and have access to the political and administrative sphere. Śūrpaṇakhā is a confidant of minister Mālyavāna of Laṅkā, who says to her,[164] 'You are particularly loved by your brother Rāvaṇa, my child, and you are capable (*kāryajña*) also. So, I am telling you my troubles with an open heart.' Given their freedom and assured social standing it is not surprising that Śūrpaṇakhā of *Mahāvīracaritam* has no shame in desiring (*vṛśasyanti*) the younger Rāma,[165] as she was enamoured of his good looks.[166]

The *māyāvinīs* were also associated with a degree of sexual freedom. In *Nala Campū*, dated to early tenth century,[167] while referring to the adulterous passion of Rādhā for Kṛṣṇa, Trivikrama Bhaṭṭa described Rādhā as *māyāvinī*. She 'committed a fault of giving up modesty, ignoring the virtuous elders, set her passion on the highest/other man: (*parāpuruṣe māyāvinī*)'. In the sixty-first tale of *Śukāsaptati*,[168] Tejukā, who is given to extra-marital sexual encounters, is referred to as *māyāvinī*. In a verse of *Āryāsaptaśatī* a village woman is advised by a female friend to take the straight path and not indulge in the *nāgara* lifestyle 'because the village head punishes women by calling them *ḍākinī* if they as much as even caste a sidelong glance' (*kaṭākṣa*).[169]

In *Kathāsaritsāgara*[170] *māyāvinī/guptayoginī* are promiscuous and encourage the promiscuous morality. In one tale,[171] Śāsiprabhā, wife of a brāhmaṇa, was said to be 'addicted to following her lusts' (*svecchācāriṇyajānataḥ*) and was also described as a witch who possessed magical powers (*śākinīsiddhisaṁvarā*). In *Kathāsaritsāgara*[172] too we encounter a queen, Kuvalayāvatī, who tells her husband that 'in my girlhood I became a member of the society of *ḍākinī*[173] (*ḍākinīmantrasidhayaḥ*), and in our meetings we devoured the bodies of many men'. Here the phrase devouring bodies (*nṛmāṁsaśnajā*) of men could mean engaging with them sexually rather than eating human flesh. It is thus apparent that *māyāvinīs* or witches were those women who, in male-dominated societies, were perceived as powerful, and were hence feared. The term *māyā* from which the term *māyāvinī* is derived meant in the *Ṛgveda* 'cunning' and 'mysterious will-power'.[174]

THE EROTIC TRADITION

What we refer to as the erotic or *śṛṅgārī* tradition in the classical Sanskrit literature of our period was essentially a masculine tradition that 'objectified women' for the male gaze. And these women were all young (*yuvatī*) and beautiful[175] (*sundarī*). In fact, as David Smith[176] says, not to be both is impossible and inconceivable in Sanskrit *kāvya*. For instance, in Ratnākara's *Haravijaya* a huge range of expressions applied as adjectives and adjectival compounds in the earlier *kāvya* were used in this text to provide nouns meaning women. There is slickness in this multiplicity and it has a demeaning function.[177] None of the women in the *kāvya Haravijaya* have names, whereas *gaṇas* representing men do. It is because women lacked individuality that their so-called names only tell us their shape, size, and colour. It is interesting to note that in Śrīdharadāsa's anthology,[178] *Sadukti-karṇāmṛta,* it is only in the description of working women (*grāmya nāyikā*) that the typical *strīvarṇana* or description of every part of female physiognomy is jettisoned. In the verses by poet Sāraṇa on rustic women it is not physical attributes but the energy of their busy life which is the focus.

The sexual politics of erotic/*śṛṅgārī* poetry in classical literature requires analysis because the genre helped create and sustain the various ideologies of desire which were not a natural force but a socially created phenomenon. If desire is a cultural fact then we need to investigate the relation of power sustained by the discourse of desire. We notice that most male-authored *śṛṅgārī* poetry assumes the cultural superiority of men. The woman is beloved, but denied a voice and subjectivity of her own. In fact, in this tradition the woman's desire lies in 'being desired'. The *śṛṅgārī kāvya* may function as a mirror in which women see themselves, but the image of women represented there is mediated by the male gaze. As Berger[179] says in the context of European art 'Men look at women. Women watch themselves being looked at.' What Adrienne Rich[180] says about her experience as a female reader of the male literature can be legitimately applied to the reading of much of *śṛṅgārī kāvya* as well. Rich says that 'there were all those poems about women written by men; it seemed to be a given that men wrote poems and women frequently inhabited them. These women were almost always beautiful but threatened with loss of beauty, the loss of youth—the fate worse than death.'

John Brough in his anthology *Poems from the Sanskrit,*[181] notes that in the treatment of love Sanskrit poets were frequently un-ashamedly frank about details of physical passion. However, he prefers not to use to term 'erotic' since this term seems to him to have acquired in English an undesirable overtone which he feels would be unjustified in the case of the Sanskrit verses. He says that with a very few exceptions, sexual love is treated by the poets 'with delicacy and good taste'. Vulgarity in any form was severely criticized in Sanskrit treatises on poetics. It is said, for example, that the poet should never use in poetry the verb *yabh* (copulation), or, as one writer delicately puts it, 'a poet should avoid the use of the word that begins with *ya*'.[182] I do not agree with Brough's rejection of the term 'erotic', or his label of 'good taste'. Like the male Sanskrit authors of the *śṛṅgārī* poetry, Brough is essentially reading this literature with a man's spectacles. He admits[183] that in Sanskrit anthologies the charms of women are 'listed in a determinedly systematic way'. For instance, in the *Paddhati* 53 on *strīvarṇana* in Jalhaṇa's *Sūktimuktāvalī*, every single body part of women from hair (*keśa*) to breast (*stana*), downhair (*romāvalī*), navel (*nābhi*), buttocks (*nitamba*), lower part (*jaghana*), to thighs (*uru*) and feet (*caraṇam*) is painstakingly described. In fact, the poet's imagination luxuriates in the rich complexity of a woman's body. In spite of this, Brough chooses to classify this objectification as not being in 'bad taste'. For Brough, avoidance of the word *yabh* means 'good taste', even if women's anatomy is systematically dissected and fetishized. It is true that Sanskrit erotic poetry is not always a *Kāmaśāstra* manual where copulating positions are described (although *viparītarata* coital posture is a favourite subject of the *śṛṅgārī* poets) but the *rasa*, if one may use the term irreverently, is the same as the description of the act of copulation.

Not only was the *śṛṅgārī* poetry erotic, it was erotic only for men, and the entire imagery was for men's enjoyment. Women, though instrumental in generating this delight, were rarely the subject of it.

Within feminism the objectification of women has quite a specific meaning. Through the process of representation women are reduced to the status of objects. Their status as object alienates women, denying them their individuality and humanity. In the classical Sanskrit *kāvya*, men are shown in control of the gaze and women are controlled by it. As Berger[184] says, 'To look is an act of choice. We never look at one thing; we are always looking at the relations between things and ourselves.' Thus, looking is always an act that involves a power relationship. And who looks and at what, highlights the dominant and dominated equation. Within the patriarchal masculine structure of this *kāvya* literature men look at women, and women watch themselves being looked at.[185] This determines not only most relations between men and women but also the relation of women to themselves. The surveyor of woman in herself is male. The surveyed female thus turns herself into an object and most particularly an object of vision or sight. Women, therefore, see themselves through men's eyes. The female body in the manner of *śṛṅgārī* poetry is delineated as a sight of adornment exclusively for male scopophillic pleasure. The poetess Padmāvatī[186] recreates in a word picture the charms of a beautiful woman of Gujarat (*Gurjarī sulalite*), dwelling on her tresses, nose, face, conch-like throat, and creeper-like arms which flank the hill-like breasts. The *lalanāvarṇana* by Gaurī[187] is again a *nakhaśikha varṇana* in the manner of the male *śṛṅgārī* poets. Vikaṭanitambā's description of female beauty is in similar vein.[188] She too talks of women's thighs that are trunks of plantain trees, arms that are lotus stalks, and breasts that are the broad temples of the elephant. Vikaṭanitambā also talks of the small waist of the *nāyikā* which she warns might break under the weight of the heavy breasts.

All these verses have to be placed squarely in the context of the male gaze. They are authored by women; even though we do not see any clitoral imagery, they refer to breasts, small waists, thighs, etc. In other words all those anatomical parts of women's body which have traditionally been in the masculine *śṛṅgārī* poetry, the fetishized object of male desire. It is the hegemony of male desire which colonizes the female body even when she is looking at it herself. We cannot detect in these verses on female beauty by women poets, any celebration of female sensuousness which does not have male pleasure as a point of reference.[189] On the other hand, it can be argued, as Betterton[190] does in another context, that woman's pleasure is bound up with a narcissistic identification with the image of the female body,[191] usually shown to be desirable but passive. After all, the women were writing within an overwhelmingly patriarchal culture in which, like their male counterparts, they too were socialized into acceptance of their bodies as desirable and accessible to men. So the explanation for the women's obsession with female beauty could be that it had to do with narcissism,[192] finding pleasure in reflection and identification with an image that is masculinely determined.

However from a gender perspective it will be more fruitful to ask whether it is only vanity that makes women constantly look at themselves. Or is there a more significant social explanation for their so-called narcissism? As Rosalind Coward[193] pithily comments, 'because desirability has been elevated to being the crucial reason for sexual relation, it sometimes appears to women that the whole possibility of being loved and comforted hangs on how their appearance will be received.' What Coward says finds an echo in ancient Indian culture. In the *Mahābhārata,*[194] it is said that beauty (*rūpa*) and youth (*yauvana*) along with the capacity to serve (*śūśruṣā*) are the most potent form of power for women. In a verse in *Amaruśataka*[195] the dilemma for women not endowed with beauty is expressed poignantly by a *nāyikā*: 'She truly hath beauty and worth, while we are ugly and worthless. But say, should everyone who is not like her have nothing but to die?' Furthermore in our period of study, to take examples from just one anthology, *Subhāṣita-ratnakoṣa,*[196] in many verses we notice that a lot of the phrases and words like *harati*, *prīṇati*, *cetohārin*, *antardhunoti* are linked with the power of women's beauty. Verbs like *vijayate* and *jayati* both meaning literally 'is victorious' are used regularly says, Ingalls,[197] to predicate beauty of women. Thus, given the social legitimacy of this cultural ideal in the patriarchy, it is no wonder that women were always anxious to represent themselves as feminine.[198]

In *This Sex Which is Not One*[199] Luce Irigaray states that the gaze is inherently masculine. She claims that the kind of look which separates the subject from the object of the gaze and projects desire on to that object is essentially masculine. Female eroticism is bound up more with touch than with sight, since women's pleasure is auto-erotic. This, Irigaray argues, means that women have a problematic relationship with the whole process of looking. They are bound within visual discourse to became objects (and hence relegated to passivity) and never subjects of their own desire.

It needs to be asked whether in the erotic *śṛṅgārī* tradition women have the power at all to look. Are not men alone the 'bearers of looks', and women the images, as Laura Mulvey would argue? Mulvey[200] is of the view that in a world ordered by sexual imbalance, pleasure in looking has been split between active male and passive female. The determining male gaze projects its fantasy on to the female figure, which is styled accordingly. Women are simultaneously looked at and displayed, with their appearance coded for strong, visual, and erotic impact so that they can be said to connote 'to-be-looked-at-ness'. Women displayed as sexual object of the male gaze is the leitmotif of erotic *śṛṅgārī* poetry.

An analysis of the verses in just one anthology *Subhāṣitaratnakoṣa* tends to reinforce the veracity of Mulvey's argument. In one verse[201] we get the term '*netraikapeyaṁvapuḥ,* i.e. a figure that forms the sole drink for the eyes. Here it is the adolescent girl who is an object of the gaze of the male. In yet another verse[202] occurs the term *netra-viśrāmapātraṁ tava mukha*, i.e. your face is the sole place where I rest my eyes. Here too a *yuvatī* is the object of the male gaze. Also in this anthology of Vidyākara occur *amṛtavartir,*[203] *sudhāsekaḥ,*[204] and *netrāñjanatāṁ.*[205] All refer to women's beauty which is like a balm or nectar to the male eye. In one very interesting verse[206] the poet writes about the scopophillic pleasure the *nāyaka* derives from gazing at the *nāyikā*. 'My eyes with difficulty pass her thighs, to wander long in the land about her hips; then at her waist, uneven with triple fold become quite powerless to move. But now at last, like the traveller's parched by thirst, they have climbed the mountains of her breasts and see at last what they had hoped their counterparts, her eyes that flow with tears.' Such voyeurism is also apparent in verses in Rājaśekhara's play, *Bālarāmāyaṇa.*[207] The context is Rāvaṇa gazing at Sītā who had appeared in the *swayaṁvara* hall. Rāvaṇa dwells on every physical feature of Sītā and in a moment of great desire wishes she would be undressed so that he could see how in comparison with the golden fairness of her body, even gold appears black in contrast. In the opening benedictory verse of *Ratnāvalī*[208] we are told that the god Śambhū looked at his new bride Girijā with his three hungry eyes (*saspṛhalocanatrayapatha*) and got her flustered.

These references strengthen the argument about the power of male gaze to objectify and eroticize the woman's body. In the classical Sanskrit *kāvya,* woman's beauty is overwhelmingly described in physical terms: all anthologies and *mahākāvya* contain a section on *strī/nāyikā varṇana,* where women's physical anatomy is described in detail. Women's vulva (*padminī, citriṇī, śaṅkhinī, hastinī*) is a subject of portrayal as also her age (*taruṇī, yuvatī*) and nationality (women of Lāṭa, Andhra, Kashmir, etc.). The rationale is to point out the variety. In contrast to women, masculine beauty is a matter of character, it is inherent and lies in man's capacity of heroism (*tejas*), nobility (*audārya*) tenacity (*dhairya*), and gravity (*gāmbhīrya*).[209] These qualities are inherent and inward and also autonomous; they do not have women *nāyikā* as point of reference. In the *Naiṣadhacarita,*[210] verses on king Nala's beauty refer to the radiance of his fame, his virtue, learning, and might.[211] In *Daśa-kumāracarita*[212] occur many *nakha-śikha* descriptions of women, but male physical beauty is summarily given: he was extraordinarily handsome (*ananyasādhāraṇa saundarya*), or was like the god Kāmadeva (*mūrtimanta manmathamiva*). In the same text[213] while talking of the good looks of Upahāravarman what is really stressed are his virtues, the fact that he was cultured, skilled, educated, and of good lineage (*śilpasīlavidyājñāna kauśalo yuvā mahākulīnaśca*). Similarly in Subandhu's *Vāsavadattā,* it is the virtues of prince Kandarpaketu that are underlined. In Kumāradāsa's *Jānakīharaṇa* we find long descriptions of Kauśalyā[214] and Sītā[215] but just three verses on Rāma's beauty.[216] One of these verses talks of Rāma's eyes, but there is nothing physical in that description, it is a metaphorical one emphasizing Rāma's knowledge and his vision. In Śrīdharadāsa's *Saduktikarṇāmṛta,* under *cātupravāha* there are many verses which describe the qualities of the king. Thus we read praises of his learning, his righteousness, and valour and just one verse about his beauty (*rūpaṁ*) which the male poet writes to flatter the king.[217] When *śobhā* or splendour is described as a quality in the context of man/*nāyaka* it does not mean physical grace but an inner brilliance which comes from adeptness in various arts, and also valour, energy, aversion to low acts, etc.[218] On the other hand, *Daśarūpakam*[219] describes women's *kānti* or radiance as the luster of love *manmathavāpitacchāyā*. Thus, feminine beauty had its origin and fulfilment in love. Love makes women beautiful and beauty makes them loved. John Berger[220] was not too far off the mark when he pointed out that according to usage and convention the social presence of a woman is different in kind from that of a man. While a man's presence is dependent upon the promise of power (which he embodies), his presence suggests what he is capable of doing to you or for you. If the promise is large and credible, his presence is striking; if it is small or incredible, he is found to have little presence. In contrast, the presence for a woman, says Berger,[221] is 'intrinsic to the physical person. So to be born a woman has been to be born within an allotted and confined space into the keeping of men.'

If women were simply eroticized and objectified, that in itself may not have been a bad thing, since objectification may be an in-herent component of both male and female eroticism. Sexual excitement, as Stoller[222] suggests, inevitably involves objectification or fetishization of the other because either she or he is the carrier and bearer of what elicits a response. But what is crucial for our argument here, is to remember that,[223] to begin with, men do not simply look, their gaze carries with it the power of action and pos-session that is lacking in the female gaze. Women receive and return the gaze but cannot act on it.

If the gaze were the vehicle of passion, the path by which desire entered the heart and the means by which it was maintained, women certainly were denied the right to be the subjects or initiators of that passion. Given this fact it is not surprising that the only time women fix their gazes on men and describe male physical beauty is in the context of either kings or gods,[224] as for instance in the hymns of Candrakāntā *bhikṣuṇī* on Avalokiteśvara[225] and the verse of Priyaṁvadā[226] about Kṛṣṇa[227] being adored by the lotus eyes of the women of Vraja. Tribhuvanasarasvatī[228] and Padmāvatī[229] describe the majestic beauty of a king. In Bāṇa's *Kādambarī*,[230] the women of Ujjayinī look at prince Candrapīḍa, and in *Jānakīharaṇa*[231] the women of Ayodhyā look at the prince Rāma.[232] But although these verses in *Kādambarī* and *Jānakīharaṇa* are ostensibly about the female gaze, they end up presenting women as a spectacle rather than reflect the power[233] of the female gaze. They eroticize and objectify the women who are gazing rather than the male figure being gazed at. Further-more, what is important about the verses of the female gaze on gods and kings is the fact that they depict the eulogistic gaze of a worshipful devotee or a subordinate;[234] such a gaze is not that of an equal, nor is any erotic relationship established between the two. We find two rare references to the female gaze which refer to the male physical beauty as an equal. In *Kādambarī*, Mahāśvetā gazes at Puṇḍarīka's beauty and the text describer's the erotic sensation Puṇḍarīka has on her. Mahāśvetā is so disturbed by this sensation that she reproaches herself severely thus: 'Oh! Alas what is this that I have now set on foot which is improper, and highly shameful and unworthy of a well born maiden.'[235] The other instance is Sītā referring to Rāma's physical beauty while looking at his picture, 'Here my lord is represented distinguished by the beauty of his body which is muscular, comely, soft, resplendent and dark like an expanding fresh blue lotus.'[236] Since here the gaze is of a wife who is looking at her husband, there is legitimacy to it, and we do not find a Mahāśvetā-like self-condemnation.

Much is said about the specifically[237] female gaze in the literary sources of our period. *Kaṭākṣa,* the female side-long glance, is essentially erotic: *kāma* or desire is said to dwell in it.[238] One verse of *Subhāṣitaratnakoṣa*[239] states, 'I sing the praise of lovely eyed women, who are victorious over three eyed Śiva; who by their glances (*kaṭākṣa*) resurrect that love which he consumed by his.' Gaurī,[240] in a reference to sidelong glances states, 'Your *kaṭākṣa*, this wonderful snake, puts to swoon even wise men, the moment it is seen.' However, these erotic sidelong glances do not objectify the male, they invite that male to whom they are directed, to objectify the woman. Thus in *Kathāsaritsāgara*[241] a *nāyikā* says about her meeting with a *nāyaka* that 'I looked with sidelong glances at him whose eyes were fixed on me.' In *Subhāṣitaratnakoṣa*[242] the male protagonist ends up eroticizing the body of the woman whose glances at first had stolen his heart. He says, 'The glances of your eyes, which stretch to your ear, darker than water lily, were enough to steal a heart; what need is there, with such ado pretending to bind your loosened braid, to show you armpit, camphor dusted and marked with lover's nail?' When women do look (even if it is in private) they do not look by right, but are shy and hesitant. In *Kathāsaritsāgara,* when princess Pātālī beholds prince Putraka in her apartment, there is a 'contest between shame and love' in her eyes; 'they are alternately fixed on his face and averted'.[243] In the same text[244] when Udayana and Vāsavadattā behold each other for the first time and his eyes are fixed on her, Vāsavadattā's eyes are averted in modesty. A similar sentiment about women's shy glance that is quickly averted is also expressed in many verses of Jalhaṇa's *Sūktimuktāvalī.*[245] In *Subhāṣitaratnakoṣa,*[246] a poet commenting on the female sidelong glances says, 'First steady with admiration, then swinging off in fear; bowed down a moment in shame (*vrīḍā*) then dilating with desire to see; withheld by natural good breeding (*sahajābhijātya*) but then released by love. In many a different way her eyes went to her lover.' In another verse from this anthology[247] we are told about an adolescent girl who restrains her coquettish glances out of 'natural shame and fear of elders'. We are also told[248] about a *nāyikā* who 'drops her glance' when seen by the *nāyaka*. However, we never find a reference to a man dropping his glance when a female looks at him.

In Jalhaṇa's anthology *Sūktimuktāvalī* there are verses under two heads, viz., *nāyikāvalokanam* and *nāyakāvalokanam*. In the former *paddhati* there are twenty-four verses and in all of them the *nāyikā's* body is the fetishized object of the male gaze; but in the latter *paddhati* there are only three verses. All the three are culled from a single Sanskrit *kāvya* called *Bhikṣāṭankāvya* of Utprekṣāvallabha. In these verses there is reference to women looking at a man who is god Śiva in disguise. One verse[249] says that a certain maiden who was forbidden by her mother to go out, reached the grilled window of the house to gaze at Śiva, her eyes when seen from the road resembled for a moment a fish that was caught in a net spread by fisherman. What is interesting in this verse is the statement that a maiden looked, in spite of having been forbidden by elders. Also, while the verse opens with a woman's gaze, it actually ends with her being gazed at in return. Thus woman's gaze, does not hold the subject position for long; the poet quickly moves instead to describing the eyes of the woman as an object of the gaze. In another verse[250] there is focus on woman's gaze that did not have familial sanction. 'Disregarding the strong objections raised by the *guru* (elders), a certain young lady started to go towards the *nāyaka*; but oh alas! There came an impediment to quick movement, in the form of the weight of her bosom which acted as another *guru* (weight/heaviness).' Thus, Jalhaṇa, even while selecting three verses on woman's gaze, actually takes care to emphasize the social illegitimacy of the woman's gaze. These allusions attest to Mulvey's[251] analysis that within a patriarchal culture woman can only exist as an image, never as the bearer of looks. Woman alone will be displayed for the gaze and enjoyment of men. The male figure cannot bear the burden of sexual objectification in the woman's gaze.

THE ROOTS OF THE *ŚṚṄGĀRĪ* CULTURE

Having talked in term of the objectification of women as the most distinguishing feature of the patriarchal male erotic culture, we need to analyse it more thoroughly within its familial and social context, for it is in this context that many cultural traits originate.

The patriarchal erotic culture is marked by a duplicitous attitude towards female sexuality. The 'lover of the night becomes the law giver in the morning.'[252] In this social scripting, female sexuality needs to be reined in, controlled and sublimated and where it isn't the woman will inevitably suffer. On the other hand women are forced to make sexual commitments to the male within approved patriarchal frames. In their role as the sex-partners they have to exist as the fetishized objects. The asymmetry of male and female sexual relations is evident from the fact that while woman is a *bhogyā*, a man is never similarly described as woman's *bhoga*. Woman in fact is a consumable commodity, like food. In *Yaśastilaka,*[253] conversing with King Yaśodhara his spy describes food by likening it to women: 'rice white and clear like the glances of beautiful woman . . . butter fragrant as the mouth of a beloved woman; curries charming as the graceful movements of dancing girls, well cooked dishes, savory like a beloved woman's lips, curds well shaped and hard like the breasts of a young woman. . . .' Thus like food, woman was also a consumable product which was needed both for whetting and satisfying the male's sexual appetite.

Within the patriarchal family girls were particularly guarded[254] against sexual transgression. Any overstepping of familial and social norms brought disgrace and loss of prestige to the entire clan,[255] and the family would sometimes go to great lengths to cloister adolescent girls and even keep them secluded in a house built underground. In Subandhu's *Vāsavadattā*,[256] King Śṛṅgāraśekhara's rule is particularly lauded for the fact that no one dared to ride the *kanyā* (i.e. have sex with her) in his kingdom. In Bāṇa's *Kādambarī*, Mahāśvetā's tragedy arises from the fact that she could not decide whether she should follow her heart and go to her lover Puṇḍarīka, or stay back within the parental four walls as befitted the maiden of her station. She tells her friend Taralikā of her predicament:

> My senses are perplexed on account of their inability to know what course to adopt. . . . If in the first place, like an ordinary maiden casting off shame, relinquishing firmness of mind, being immodest, not regarding the evil talk of the people, transgressing good behaviour . . . not minding his birth, accepting infamy, led blindfolded by passion, not permitted by my father and not allowed by my mother, if I were to approach him of my own accord and make him accept my hand, it would be a grave breach of duty and disrespect of the elders.[257]

Mahāśvetā's dilemma is faced by no man in our sources. It was man's privilege to sow his wild oats and woman's duty to guard her virtue. Mahāśvetā's friend Kādambarī similarly reproached herself for daring to love Candrapīḍa. She felt[258] that modesty, simplicity, nobility, high birth, steadiness, and family norms were all chiding her for her rashness in falling in love. She described this emotion as immodest and not a proper course of conduct (*gahirta*) for a well-born maiden (*kulakanyā*). One who indulged in it was promiscuous (*svairiṇī*) and immodest (*durvinīta*). Kādambarī, torn between her overwhelming love for Candrapīḍa and the knowledge that unrestrained behaviour was incorrect, wanted to give up her life and atone for her sin.[259]

It was equally important for girls not to be as averse to marriage (*pariṇaya parāṅgamukhī*) as was Subandhu's Vāsavadattā.[260] Princess Vāsavadattā's father was eager to avoid[261] the sin which would accrue from her passing youth (*yauvanātikrmaṇadoṣa*). In the marriage-oriented world of patriarchy it was crucially important for girls to make a heterosexual commitment[262] even before they experienced sex *per se*. Thus, in Vidyākara's *Subhāṣitaratnakoṣa* there are fifty verses[263] on the *vayasaṁdhi* (adolescent age), and except for a solitary verse[264] which is on a young boy (who is an object of a grown-up woman's tender gaze), all the others are about young girls entering adolescence and slowly awakening to hetero-sexual love.[265] This slow awakening is underlined in the sub-classification of the *nāyikā* as *mugdhā*, *madhyā*, and *pragalbhā*.[266] *Mugdhā* denotes the sexually innocent (*ratovāmā*) and *pragalbhā* stands for the erotically experienced (*samastaratakovidā*). The texts on poetics, however, display asymmetry in the portrayal of the *nāyaka*. A *nāyaka* could not be depicted as sexually inexperienced. As Bhānudatta[267] states categorically in his *Rasamañjarī*, such a situation would lead to *rasābhāsa*[268] of the *śṛṅgārarasa* (*anabhijño nāyako nāyakābhāsa eva*).

In the *vayasaṁdhi* verses the patriarchal ideology of sexuality admits to a passive female sexuality which was waiting for male contact. The male eye and male touch were the *summum bonnum* of that growing up. In a verse of *Saduktikarṇāmṛta*[269] it is stated, 'When the rainy day of the sweet talk of grown up women in regard to love-enjoyment was proceeding with competitive zeal, a young girl, thrilled by the account, with her breasts just sprouting, encircled them with her tremulous glance directed gently at her bosom.' But while the girl had to internalize the values of attachment, the men could simply take their pleasures. As poet Gobhaṭa states,[270] 'a sweetheart and a vine attract more when in bud and if a full grown bee should top the bud, are quite unequalled'.

In the patriarchal social world, wifehood was the most significant milestone of a woman's life. Throughout her girlhood she was groomed for this role. A woman bereft of husband was likened to a house with walls but no roof (*gṛhabhittiriva*).[271] As the husband was the roof he also extracted privileges. A wife's sexuality was harnessed towards procreation.[272] In order to be sure that the wife was bearing his own child, she had to be completely loyal (*satī*) to him. A verse in Jalhaṇa's anthology *Sūktimuktāvalī*[273] hails the wife or *kulavadhū* as one who is loyal to her husband, sweet speaking (*priyavādin*), works for the husband in the day and smells nicely and is ornamented by the night. The good wife was not expected to cross the threshold of the house. In *Mudrārākṣasa,* the wife of *amātya* Rākṣasa is a *grhajana,* a person who is at home.[274] In Dingnāga's play *Kundamālā* we find the term *antaravāsinī*, one who stays indoors, as a synonym for woman.[275] If due to unforeseen circumstances a wife was exposed to the outside world, her fidelity became a matter of suspicion. In the *Kundamālā*, Sītā says, 'Even I, Sītā, am suspected thus! Indeed, accursed is the life of a woman.'[276] In Śaktibhadra's *Āścaryacūḍāmaṇi* Sītā makes a self-deprecatory remark saying that women by nature are not trustworthy *(aviśvasnīya khalu strīsvabhāva).*[277] In the same play Rāma points an accusatory finger at Sītā and calls her *chalitapuṁścalī,* a promiscuous woman who has a cheating disposition. He accuses her of having kept assignations with *rākṣasa* even before she was kidnapped in the Daṇḍaka forest.[278]

Given the social illegitimacy[279] of the wife's sexual transgression, in the erotic *kāvya* poetry, the female adultery, her love for *Jāra, upapati* and *prativeśī* is always depicted as a love on the sly. It is a secret tryst, as a verse in Jalhaṇa's anthology under *kulaṭā paddhati* notes,[280] '. . . the breathing is done gently, in the heart, which is in gentle movements. The ornaments make no noise; speech and answers (of lovers) are done by means of sign. Where the smooth bed is the sandy earth, the lover's quarrels and conciliations is done in silence, where kissing is done noiselessly . . . our obeisance to such quiet lover's sport.' Since adultery is secret, the husband's awareness of it is never referred to in these verses. There is no cheated (*khaṇḍita*) *nāyaka* in this sense in Sanskrit literature.[281] In *Saduktikarṇāmṛta*[282] and in Māgha's *Śiśupālavadha*[283] occur verses on *gotraskhalanaṁ,* the *nāyaka* calling the *nāyikā* by the name of another woman. But there is no instance in which it is the other way round. In our sources very rarely are husband and wife mentioned together in the reference to an adulterous love affair, as in an amusing verse from *Subhāṣitaratnakoṣa.*[284] 'At night a husband and a wife, each favouring a separate lover, have separated in the meeting grove, only to meet together unaware in darkness, with hearts that melt in eagerness for bliss. Both consummate their purpose; but what can one suppose they do once they recognize each other?' In a rare example where husband has full knowledge of his wife's adultery, both happen to be from a lower class/caste but the wife's paramour belongs to the elite section of society. A verse from *Āryāsaptaśatī*[285] refers to a weaver (*tantuvāyasya*) taking pride in the beauty of his wife (*svavadhū*), which has made her an object of desire among the elite (*nāgarabhoga*). This gave him a status among his kin (*jñatipura*) and made it difficult for him to keep his feet on the ground (*nipatati padam na bhūmo*).[286] Although the texts on poetics treat *parakīyā* as one of the *nāyikā* types, they sub-divide it into two, *kanyā* and *paroḍhā* (married woman). *Daśarūpakam*[287] states categorically that *paroḍhā* cannot be made a *nāyikā* in depiciting a principal (*aṅgīrasa*) sentiment.

A wife's confidence born of the love and loyalty of her husband is something lacking in the classical Sanskrit *kāvya.* The elite patriarchal society which this literature mirrored was notorious for its pervasive polygyny. As Lee Siegel[288] notes, 'within the aristocratic leisured sensibilities of a polygynous society, promiscuity was a formalized masculine virtue'. The clever rake, motivated by a rapacious and refined appetite for a multiplicity of women, became a conventional figure in *kāvya.* In Harṣa's *Priyadarśikā*[289] men are likened to bees 'greatly covetous of fresh juice'. A verse in *Subhāṣitaratnakoṣa*[290] states: 'This is a measure-less ambrosia . . . when with a household of young wives; richly adorned, beautiful and eager, willing traders in the joys of sex, a man may spend his days in dalliance.' Yet another verse of this anthology[291] justifies men's need for associating with ever new women thus: 'Where one sleeps in one's own house with her, one's own (*svagṛhaṇī*) subservient to one's wishes, can this routine of household sex, this wretched thing, deserve the name of love?'

A *khaṇḍitā nāyikā* in Sanskrit poetry had recourse only to tears,[292] silence, or bitter reproach. Furthermore, cheated wives were told not to be too angry,[293] for otherwise the husband may abandon them.[294] The wife was also advised not to feel insulted or insecure by the presence of younger co-wives, because she had the honour of being the mother of the son whom the husband loves dearly.[295] No cheated wife is ever advised to pay the husband back in the same coin. Given this social reality, often a cheated wife would blame the fate (*vidhistu parāṅgamukha*) rather than the erring husband.[296] Thus, in sociological terms within the polygynous households it was woman's pride, her self-respect, which was the major casualty. As a *khaṇḍitā nāyikā* tells her beloved,[297] 'I feel very light in my body as you have helped to remove heaviness off my drooping spirits, my sense of self-worth (*mama gaurava*) is lost and I am made to look small.'

Another casualty of this elitist polygynous society was that women were the losers in the field of romantic[298] love. Most men treated sexual activity as a sensual gratification and women as playthings. A verse from *Amaruśataka*[299] states, 'under the pretense of playful fun he closes the eyes of one and then turning his neck a little kisses the other one'. In *Jānakīharaṇa*[300] we see Rāvaṇa lying in bed with wife Mandodarī while *apsarā* Tilottamā presses his feet and he massages Tilottamā's breasts with his toes.

Even patriarchal texts which demanded exacting moral rectitude from women some time show sensitivity to the woman's predicament within this setup. *Yaśastilaka*[301] describes the woman's marriage rite as: sale by her parents in the presence of the gods, the brāhmaṇa and the fire (*devadvijāgnisamakṣaṁ mātṛpitṛvikritasya*).' However, such a husband could only be the master of his wife's body, not of her heart. The lord of her heart was he who was the object of her undivided love and in whom she found joy and bliss born of confidence. The text asserts the reciprocity of love as an essential condition for conjugal harmony. The adulterous *nāyikā* Amṛtamatī states quite confidently that there is nothing in the world that men cannot do except rekindle love in a heart filled with disgust. For who indeed can unite two hearts that are two iron balls – one hot and the other cold? Śūdraka too asserts in *Mṛcchakaṭika*[302] that the only way to hold a woman is by her heart (*hṛdaye gṛhayate nārī*).

As men were masters of women all the time and in all spheres they naturally had to be woman's superior in the erotic sphere as well. In most of the *kāvya* literature the shyness of the *nāyikā* was a much admired and alluring trait. So much so that coyness on the part of the *nāyikā* became a strategy to attract men. Māgha in his *Śiśupālavadha*[303] says, 'Young women in spite of a fierce sexual desire were acting with restraint (*dhairya*). They were yielding their bodies and yet behaving as if they did not wish it. Although they had capacity for erotic sauciness they were behaving in a shy manner.' The heroines of the romantic tales also behave coyly. Kādambarī and Mahāśvetā both talk of their love for Candrapīḍa and Puṇḍarīka only to their friends and not to the beloved. In the *Naiṣadhacarita*,[304] Damayantī addresses her romantic feelings for Nala only to his portrait. Face to face with Nala, she is completely tounge tied.[305] In the *Amaruśataka,* most verses on *saṁbhoga śṛṅgāra* deal with man's pleasure. In one verse[306] the physical desire of the male is so overpowering that the woman is rendered an instrument in the realization of that desire: 'Her fair bosom was pressed low under the close embrace, and the skin bristled with happiness; the garment slipped off from her ample hips as the ardour of love rose to a pitch of intensity and she whispered weakly. . . . It is enough! I wonder if she was sleeping or was dead or sank into my heart or simply melted away.'

However, not all *kāvya* poetry on *saṁbhoga śṛṅgāra* discounts female desire. This is particularly marked in Bilhaṇa's *Caura-pañcāśikā*. Each of the fifty verses is a remembered[307] moment of passionate love voiced in the first person by the separated *nāyaka*, who uses memory to evoke his mistress' presence. In spite of the fact that it is an account of a past incident, what is characteristic of the bulk of these verses is the depiction of the *nāyikā's* sentiments in that passionate union. The lover recaptures the memory of her through her responses to the union. And it is this brilliant delineation of the absentee *nāyikā's* emotions which makes this *Pañcāśikā* so very evocative of the absent *nāyikā*. The *nāyikā* of Bilhaṇa's *Caurapañcāśikā* is a person in her own right. Her emotions are deeply felt and surreptitiously enjoyed. 'Even now, I remember her in love, her body weak with fatigue; swarms of curling hair falling on pale cheeks, trying to hide the secret of her guilt (*pracchannapāpa*).'[308] But even while her love was secretive, the *nāyikā* experienced great abandon. Verses[309] refer to her 'deep eyes, glittering pupils dancing wildly in love's vigil'. He states: 'I remember her holding the reins (*suratatāṇḍava sūtradhāriṁ*) in our wild dance of love. Moon lustre lighting her face, her body trembling with passion.'

Verses in the *kāvya* literature occasionally talk in terms of a woman having an initiating role in the *saṁbhoga* union. A verse from *Āryāsaptaśatī*[310] refers to the ultimate male fantasy of having a wife who fulfilled all the roles at the same time, including being the boss in the bed (*talpe prabhuriva*) and the teacher in the *Kāma-śāstra* (*gururiva manasijatantre*). In work she was like maid (*śramebhujiṣyeva*), Lakṣmī in the house, and amongst the elders she was shyness incarnate. It is difficult to believe that in confining patrilocal households wives could have had either leisure or initiative to fulfil the teacher's role to any great extent.

NOTES

1. Bharata states in his *Nāṭyaśāstra* (24.95–6) that *śṛṅgāra* is that which results in the union of men and women, generating sexual pleasure. It is auspicious when properly enjoyed with mutual courtesies. The whole world in general likes pleasure, and for that women are the source (*sukhamicchati sarvadā sukhasya hi strīyo mūlaṁ*)
2. Chaudhuri, 1941, verse 82.
3. *Uttararāmacarita*, Act VI.31–2.
4. Germaine Greer (cited in R.P. Sharma, 1995: 243) says 'sex must be rescued from the traffic between powerful and powerless, masterful and mastered, sexual and neutral to become a form of communication between potent, gentle, tender people.'
5. V. Raghavan, 1951: 15–16.
6. Ibid.: 31.
7. Ibid.: 15–16.
8. S.K. De, 1969: 61.
9. S. Bhattacharji, 1993: 161.
10. David Shulman, 2001: 60.

11. Chaudhuri, 1941: I.
12. Ibid., verse 82.
13. *Saduktikarṇāmṛta*, verse 533.
14. *SRK*, verse 815.
15. *SM*, verse 301.9.
16. *Subhāṣitāvalī*, verse 1141.
17. *Saduktikarṇāmṛta*, verse 1368.
18. *Amaruśataka*, verse 38.
19. Cited in Raghavacharlu, 1934–5: 142.
20. *Amaruśataka*, verse 68.
21. *Subhāṣitāvalī*, verse 1946.
22. Dasgupta and De, 1962: 416.
23. Dasgupta and De's analysis finds an echo in the writings of modern critics who are equally dismissive of women's poetic abilities. Critic Theodore Roethke (cited in Mills, 1965: 133–4) tends to see this as the aesthetic and moral shortcoming of feminine texts. Women's writing, he argues, lacks a range of subject matter. It is a spun-out embroidery of trivial themes, it is concerned only with the surfaces of life, and evades the real agonies of the spirit as well as existential truths.
24. At least forty verses talk about love in all its aspects and some of the poet wrote exclusively on it (Chaudhuri, 1941: l).
25. Chaudhuri, 1941: lxxxvi.
26. It is interesting to note that when women renounce life as householders, as in the case of Buddhist *therīs*, their voice has a completely different resonance. Unlike women writing Sanskrit poetry, they are preoccupied not with love but with existential issues such as marriage and the entrapment that the drudgery of the kitchen space represents (Tharu and Lalita, eds., 1995: 65). They are also shown as struggling with personal tragedies like the death of children a cataclysmic event which pushes them to renunciation (Roy, 2003: 86). The focus of each lyric in the *Therīgāthā* is an epiphanic experience in which the painful constrictions of secular life fall away and the torment of feeling subsides as the peace and freedom of *nirvāṇa* are attained (Tharu and Lalita, eds., 1995: 67). Obvious in the dissimilar responses of the *therīs* and the Sanskrit poetesses to life and living is that there is nothing unique about an 'intense feminine heart with its peculiar joys and sorrows'—which only longs for the beloved's love and where sorrow is caused only by his deception or abandonment.
27. Byron, 1945: 658.
28. Keohane, Rosaldo and Gelpi, 1982: ix–x.
29. S.K. De, 1969: 16.
30. Chaudhuri, 1941: verse 82.
31. Juliet Blair, cited in Ardener, 1981: 207.

32. Chaudhuri, 1941, verse 83.
33. If in this verse, 'husband' is interpreted as the husband of an unnamed (suggested) 'other' (rather than as the husband of Jaghanacapalā), who is away on a journey, a fact which makes Jaghanacapalā happy, then this interpretation could lend itself to the possibility that the narrator Jaghanacapalā was engaged in a lesbian love relationship with that unnamed woman. After all, the homoerotic angle is not entirely absent in classical Sanskrit literature. As Ruth Vanita (2001: 67–8) points out, a close relationship between female friends is one of the tropes of same-sex love.
34. Chaudhuri, 1941, verse 35.
35. Even editors in modern times are quite shocked by the frankness of the women's verses, J.B. Chaudhuri (1941: li) notes 'what strikes us here is that nowhere is a single word of condemnation uttered against this *perverted species of humanity*. On the contrary, the poetesses seem to revel ... in the theme of unchaste love' (emphasis mine). Dasgupta and De (1962: 416) also point out that 'perhaps these verses which give the impression that she [the writer] is more fully ardent and less self-controlled than man, would lead to a dubious generalisation.'
36. Chaudhuri, 1941, verse 42.
37. Ibid., verse 105.
38. Ibid., verse 84.
39. Raghavan, 1934–5: 56–7.
40. *Proṣitabhatṛkā* is a grass widow. *Vipralabdhā* is left by the *nāyaka* for another woman. *Khaṇḍitā* is one who has become aware of the *nāyaka*'s deception. *Vāsakasajjā* is one who awaits her lover. *Virahautkanṭhitā* is separated from her lover and anxiously awaits him. *Kalahantāritā* is the *nāyikā* feuding with the *nāyaka*, and *Svādhīnapatikā* has her *nāyaka* under her complete control.
41. *Śṛṅgāraprakāśa*, p. 51.
42. George L. Hart (1976: 47–8) points out that in Tamil poetry it is the man who goes out at night to visit his beloved, who being unmarried is guarded by her parents. In some poems, the heroine comes a little way to a rendezvous near her house, often in the rain. Hart says that in Tamil literature this theme is full of religious significance, showing a man and woman destined to be married meeting at a mysterious time and attaining a sacred state in their union. Hart (1999: 244) has shown that chastity (*karpu*) for woman was such a binding force that in the entire corpus of pre-modern Tamil literature, there is not a single instance of a wife who is unfaithful to her husband, though the latter strays often.
43. *Śṛṅgāraprakāśa*, p. 51.
44. Srinivasan, 1985: 25, 37.
45. Cited in Kulkarni, 1993: 154.

46. Interestingly, the Prakrit play *Karpūramañjarī* was written by the tenth-century litterateur Rājaśekhara (Act I) at the request of his highly accomplished Sanskrit-educated wife Avantisundarī, and in this play the poet introduces an elaborate discussion on love.
47. Chaudhuri, 1941: lxxiii.
48. *Kāvyaprakāśa*, ch. 1, p. 5.
49. Chaudhuri, 1941, verse 113.
50. Chaudhuri, 1941, verses 80, 81.
51. Mammaṭa in his *Kāvyaprakāśa* (ch. 5, p. 143) and Viśvanātha in his *Sāhityadarpaṇa* (ch. 3, pp. 272–3) consider it an example of *rasābhāsa*.
52. Satyavdeva Chaudhary, 1959: 176–7.
53. From the time of Bharata's *Nāṭyaśāstra* (6.47) it has been held that whenever the sentiment of *śṛṅgāra* is either imitated or misplaced it would result in *hāsyarasa* (laughter).
54. O'Flaherty, 1981: 122.
55. Ibid.
56. A man's *viraha* – like that of Rāma on separation from Sītā, Kṛṣṇa from Rādhā, of Aja on losing his wife Indumatī to death in the *Raghuvaṁśa*, of the Yakṣa in the *Meghadūta*, or of Duṣyanta in the *Abhijñanaśākuntalam* – is qualitatively different. These are either self-created or fate-created conditions, and do not arise out of social or familial dis-empowerment of the male *nāyaka*. In the classical Sanskrit literature we do not come across any *nāyaka* whose *viraha* is on account of his abandonment by the *nāyikā*.
57. Lee Siegel, 1983: 104.
58. Chaudhuri, 1941, verse 44.
59. Ibid., verse 46.
60. Ibid., li.
61. Ibid., verse 132.
62. Ibid., verse 3.
63. Emotional intimacy in a relationship is something that characterizes the verses of women writers of Prakrit poetry as well. Thus Mādhavī is far more strident in her tone than the beseeching Bhāvādevī. She tells her boorish husband, those who lay aside their lordship, and when their ladies are cross plead and entreat like servants, are souls dear to women. They are the lovers; the rest are only wretched masters (Raghavan, 1934–5: 73–4).
64. Chaudhuri, 1941, verse 4
65. Raghavan, 1934–5: 60–1.
66. Chaudhuri, 1941, verse 1.
67. Sternberg and Barnes, 1988: 5.
68. Chaudhuri, 1941, verse 47.
69. Ibid., verse 137.
70. Ibid., verse 116.

71. Ibid., verse 114.
72. David Shulman, 2000: 50.
73. *Mālatī-Mādhava*, Act I.30.
74. Ibid., Act I.29.
75. *Uttararāmacarita*, Act III.47.
76. Ibid., Act I.39.
77. Ibid., Act I.27.
78. Ibid., Act III, p. 215.
79. Ibid., Act VI.33.
80. *Mālatī-Mādhava*, Act VI.18.
81. *Uttararāmacarita*, Act I.37.
82. Ibid., Act I.38.
83. Ibid., Act I.46.
84. Ibid., Act III.1.
85. Ibid., Act I.28.
86. *Daśarūpakam*, ch. 2, p. 116.
87. *Uttararāmacarita*, Act III.17.
88. Rājaśekhara in his play *Bālabhārata* makes this claim, cited in R.P. Poddar (1974: 1).
89. *Viddhaśālabhañjikā*, Act I, p. 10.
90. Ibid., Act I.33.
91. D.D. Kosambi, 1977: 204.
92. B.S. Miller, 1977: 11.
93. Kunal Chakrabarty, 2001: 299.
94. Hawley and Wulff (eds.), 1984: 58.
95. In fact, in *Gāthāsattasaī* it occurs at an even earlier date.
96. Cited in Miller, 1977, 45–6, n. 14.
97. B.S. Miller, 1975: 662.
98. B.S. Miller, 1977: 33–4.
99. Hawley and Wulff (eds.), 1984: 121–2.
100. *Gāthāsattasaī* 1.89.
101. Lee Siegel, 1978: 36.
102. B.K. Sarkar, 1986: 42.
103. In the *śṛṅgārī* poetry on the other hand, the adulterous desires of women are placed under the heading of *asatī/kulaṭā* and they are usually descriptions of illicit love tryst on the sly.
104. *Gītagovinda*, 5.7.
105. Ibid., 2.18.
106. Significantly, Kṛṣṇa in contemporary literature is also presented as an adulterer *par excellence*. In *Puṣpabāṇavilāsa* (verse 1) Kṛṣṇa is referred to as *jārāgṛṇī* i.e. foremost among the paramours.
107. *Gītagovinda*, 7.1
108. It is interesting that in Bengal, Vaiṣṇava theology (as also in the Vallabha *sampradāya* later) there is a theological bias towards the *parakīyā* as against

the *svīyā nāyikā* for Kṛṣṇa *bhakti*. The adulterous nature of Rādhā's love for Kṛṣṇa is appropriate as a devotional metaphor. In fact, the superiority of illicit love is argued by the Sahajīā Vaiṣṇava theologians in some detail (Dimock, 1991: 16). Their main point is that illicit love is given freely and makes no claim and is therefore selfless. So Rādhā's love, adulterous though it may be, is characterized by *prema* as against mere *kāma* in a legal/married relationship. As David Kinsley (1987: 92) also notes, 'Rādhā loves Kṛṣṇa in spite of everything, not because she has an obligation to him.'

109. *Gītagovinda*, 1.1.
110. Ibid., 5.7.
111. Ibid., 10.4.
112. To seek forgiveness as in the case of *māninī nāyikā* by the *nāyaka* is no more than a poetic rule without emotional content. But consciousness of guilt for having hurt your beloved is something that rarely reveals itself in the classical Sanskrit literary works. Bhavabhūti's *Uttararāmacarita* is an exception in this regard, and Jayadeva's *Gītagovinda* to a lesser extent also echoes this consciousness.
113. *Gītagovinda*, 3.9.
114. Ibid., 3.3.
115. Ibid., 3.14.
116. Ibid., 11.2, 22; 12.3, 6.
117. Ibid., 3.1–2.
118. Kakkar and Ross, 1986: 79.
119. Lee Siegel, 1978: 93.
120. B.S. Miller, 1975: 670.
121. Ranajit Sarkar, 1974: 5.
122. B.S. Miller, 1975: 668.
123. *Gītagovinda*, 2.1.
124. Ibid., 12.6.
125. Ibid., 12.12–20.
126. Ibid., 12.11.
127. Ibid., 7.4.
128. Ibid., 6.5.
129. Ibid., 2.12–17.
130. Ranajit Guha, 1989: 258–9.
131. Cited in Siegel, 1978: 59–60.
132. Ranajit Guha, 1989: 258–9.
133. *Gītagovinda*, 8.8.
134. Ibid., 8.2.
135. Cited in Hawley and Wulff (eds.), 1984: 25.
136. A. Appadurai, F.J. Koram and M. Mills, 1991: 8.
137. Joyce Flueckiger (1989) in her revealing study of the folk tales of Lorik-Chanda in two different regions of the Indian sub-continent, Uttar Pradesh

and Chhattisgarh, has shown that there is a direct link between women's actual social status and female images in folklore. In Chhattisgarh where women have greater economic independence and a much higher social status as compared to Uttar Pradesh, the female character of the Lorik-Chanda epic are initiators of action and romance and use their ingenuity rather than chastity to solve problems.

138. *Śukāsaptati*, p. 91.
139. Ibid., p. 78.
140. Ibid., p. 70.
141. Ibid., p. 91.
142. Ibid., p. 141.
143. Ibid., p. 78.
144. K. Ramanujan, 1991: 53.
145. *Śukāsaptati*, p. 8.
146. Ibid., p. 239.
147. *KSS*, vol. I, pp. 48, 79; vol. III, pp. 15, 102; vol. IV, p. 165; vol. V, p. 85.
148. *Bṛhatkathāślokasaṁgraha*, 1.19–25.
149. Ibid., 15. 61–7.
150. *KSS*, vol. I, p. 159.
151. Ibid., vol. VIII, p. 113.
152. Ibid., vol. VIII, p. 115.
153. Ibid., vol. III, pp. 82–3.
154. Ibid., vol. III, p. 85.
155. Ibid., vol III, pp. 40–2.
156. Ibid., vol. II, p. 187.
157. Ibid., vol. III, pp. 27–8.
158. Ibid., vol IX, pp. 36–7.
159. Vanita and Kidwai (2001: 2) describe cross-dressing as one of the tropes in ancient Indian writing that refers to same-sex attachment.
160. An interesting verse in Jalhaṇa's *Sūktimuktāvalī* (188.77) refers obliquely to lesbian love. It states that 'when the female friends (*sakhī*) of the lotus-eyed one saw her heavy lower part (*jaghana*) while she was asleep, they all turned men in their heart *(Puṁāva manasa yuyu)*'.
161. *KSS*, vol. VIII, p. 167.
162. R.D. Dikshit, 1964: 198.
163. Ibid., p. 199.
164. *Mahāvīracaritam*, Act IV, p. 149.
165. Ibid., Act V, p. 200.
166. Ibid., Act IV, p. 177.
167. Cited in B.S. Miller, 1975: 662.
168. *Śukāsaptati*, p. 251.
169. *Āryāsaptaśatī*, verse 140.
170. *KSS*, vol. III, pp. 191, 193.

171. Ibid., vol. VI, p. 4.
172. Ibid., vol. II, pp. 104–5.
173. In Vajrayāna Buddhism (M. Shaw, 1994: 3) *ḍākinī* are female enlighteners who leap and fly unfettered by clothing, encircled by billowing hair; their bodies curved in sinuous dance poses, their eyes blazing with passion, ecstasy, and ferocious intensity.
174. Cited by Penzer, *KSS*, vol. VI, p. 34.
175. We find an entire anthology by Utprekṣāvallabha called *Sundarīśataka*, wherein ugly women were cruelly derided. In *Bṛhatkathāślokasaṁgraha* (4.86–7) there is a reference to an unattractive woman (*locanadurbhagā*) and a man, well-versed in reading the physical signs of women, foretold that she would be bereft of husband, son, and riches.
176. *Haravijaya*, p. 180.
177. Ibid., p. 181.
178. *Saduktikarṇāmṛta*, verses 2003, 2005.
179. John Berger, 1972: 47.
180. A. Rich, 1979: 39.
181. J. Brough, 1968: 39–41.
182. Ibid., 41.
183. Ibid., 18.
184. Berger, 1972: 8–9.
185. Ibid., 47.
186. Chaudhuri, 1941, verses 54–9.
187. Ibid., verses 23–30.
188. Ibid., verses 135–6.
189. For instance many verses in Govardhana's *Āryāsaptaśatī* (319, 338, 470, 507, 553, 627, and 693) refer to the lower portion or *jaghana* of the female body open to the male gaze. But a man's lower part is never similarly on display to the female gaze in women's verses.
190. Cited in H. Robinson (ed.), 1987: 255–6.
191. Molly Emma Aitken (1997: 91–3) in her interesting study on the depiction of the *nāyikā* in Kangra paintings points out that it is not a woman but her beauty that is venerated in them. Female beauty all but divorced from the woman herself becomes the mirage of an ideal realm glimpsed from the other side of a non-crossable frame.
192. Although Fuss (cited in M. Thapan, 1995: 49) talks in terms of the 'homospectatorial look', by which she means that women visually appreciate and consume eroticized images of the female body and identify with these images completely. In other words, the gaze is not necessarily the external gaze (of men) that has been internalized by women in their pursuit of an elusive femininity but could also be the product of their own erotic fantasies and impulses, and need not always by heterosexually determined.

193. R. Coward, 1984: 78.
194. *Mahābhārata*, 12.308.73.
195. Cited in Vidya Dehejia, 1997: 96.
196. *SRK*, verses 369, 306, 594, 566.
197. D.H. Ingalls, 1962: 100.
198. While security and success for woman under patriarchy is predicated on her beauty, when women renounce the world they give up this social and cultural requirement. The first step which they take in that direction is to reject the physical beauty that makes them desirable in male eyes. Buddhist *therī* Subhā goes to the extent of mutilating herself (Roy, 2003: 89) and the south Indian *bhaktin* Avvai and Karaikkal Ammaiyar desire to turn into old hags (Chakravarti, 1999: 302, 307). Yet, neither in the Sanskrit poetry nor in the voices of the *therīs* and south Indian *bhaktins* is there an alternative conception of the female form. The fetishization of the beautiful female form in the Sanskrit verses and the somatophobia of the *therīs* and two *bhaktins* play out the masculine cultural discourse in which the female body is seen either as an instrument of seduction or of entrapment, and thus, as an impediment on the path to salvation.
199. Cited in Hillary Robinson (ed.), 1987: 256.
200. L. Mulvey, 1989: 19.
201. *SRK*, verse 347.
202. Ibid., verse 410.
203. Ibid., verses 427, 431.
204. Ibid., verse 564.
205. Ibid., verse 488.
206. Ibid., verse 476.
207. *Bālarāmāyaṇa*, Act III, pp. 24–5.
208. *Ratnāvalī*, Act I.1.
209. Cited in S. Kulashrestha (ed.), 1997: 62–4.
210. *Naiṣadhacarita*, 1.1–10.
211. Even where a king suffers from physical disfigurement it need not diminish his masculinity. Hariṣeṇa (*CII*, vol. III, no. 1, line 18, p. 217) in his *praśasti* of Samudragupta describes his body as being beautified by hundreds of attractive scars (*śatāṅka śobhā*).
212. *Daśakumāracarita*, p. 86.
213. Ibid., pp. 223–4.
214. *Jānakīharaṇa*, 1.27–41.
215. Ibid., 7.7–17.
216. Ibid., 6.56–8.
217. In describing kings, the Sanskrit *kāvya* do lay emphasis on appearance, but what they convey is really power and grooming. There is no palpable description of beauty for erotic consumption.
218. *Daśarūpakam*, ch. 2, p. 129.
219. Ibid., ch. 2, p. 168.

220. John Berger, 1972: 45.
221. Ibid., 46.
222. Stoller, cited in Willam Simon, 1996: 149.
223. Snitow Ann et al. (eds.), 1983: 311.
224. J.B. Chaudhuri (1941: viii) in his introduction to *Sanskrit Poetesses* does not find the eroticism of *bhikkuṇī* Candrakāntā's adoring gaze in the least bit objectionable. In fact, he is most appreciative—'the *stotra* stands as a rare example of a simple homage of a devoted female heart, characterized by spontaneity of expression and sincerity of tone.'
225. Chaudhuri, 1941, verses 6–13.
226. Ibid., verse 74.
227. Akkā Mahādevī is the only South Indian *bhaktin* who walks naked and flaunts her body and sexuality. In fact, 'desire' and the body as an instrument to realize that desire are celebrated. Akkā Mahādevī sings aloud in ecstasy, 'O Śiva! When shall I crush you on my pitcher breasts? O Lord white as jasmine, when do I join you, stripped of body's shame and heart's modesty?' (Ramaswami, 1997: 191).
228. Chaudhuri, 1941, verse 86.
229. Ibid., verse 51.
230. *Kādambarī*, Kale edition, pp. 116–17.
231. *Jānakīharaṇa*, 9.52–60.
232. In *Jānakīharaṇa* (9.52) it is said that women ran to the window to look at Rāma without the permission of the elders, not because they were promiscuous (*asatī*) or foolish (*mūḍa*) but due to the graciousness of the family of Raghu.
233. In *Naiṣadhacarita* (1.27) there occurs a reference to Nala being watched at by celestial maidens 'eagerly drinking him in with eyes that never closed and is still manifested by them by their flickerless eyes'. But the significant thing here is that Nala is being looked at by celestial beings—the normal power relation that operates in the gaze is not of any consequence here.
234. As Daud Ali (2000: 175) notes, the *nāyikā* became in early-medieval India richly coded signs for the postures that humans as *bhakta* should have with their human and divine lords. An ideology of servitude was linked with erotic pleasure (that may have existed in the gaze) for women. It is not incidental that in the south Indian *bhakti* tradition Anḍāla in her poetic work *Nachchiyar Tirumozhi* expresses her feelings for Viṣṇu in explicitly erotic terms (Chakravarti, 1999: 309).
235. *Kādambarī*, Kale edition, pp. 192–3.
236. *Uttararāmacarita*, Act. I, p. 193.
237. In *Naiṣadhacarita* (6.22) there is reference to Nala's side-long glances (*kaṭākṣa*) but the use of the term *kaṭākṣa* here is very different from that of female side-long glances. Nala being in women's inner apartment without permission did not want to gape so he resorted to side-long looks.
238. *SRK*, verses 329, 331, 482.

239. Ibid., verse 395.
240. Chaudhuri, 1941, verse 27.
241. *KSS*, vol. VIII, p. 15.
242. *SRK*, verse 466.
243. *KSS*, vol. I, p. 23.
244. Ibid., vol. I, p. 135.
245. *SM*, verse 148.2, 149.8.
246. *SRK*, verse 490.
247. Ibid., verse 339.
248. Ibid., verse 469.
249. *SM*, 177.26.
250. Ibid., 177.25.
251. Laura Mulvey, 1989: 20.
252. Veena Das, cited in Ranajit Guha, 1989: 323.
253. K.K. Handiqui, 1949: 29.
254. Controlling women is a crucial element of what Carol Patman (1988) has described as 'fraternal patriarchy'.
255. *Daśakumārcarita*, pp. 116, 285.
256. *Vāsavadattā*, p. 103.
257. *Kādambarī*, Kale edition, p. 213.
258. Ibid., pp. 251–2.
259. Ibid., p. 295.
260. *Vāsavadattā*, p. 110.
261. Ibid., p. 211.
262. Ironically, within patriarchy while female sexuality was an arena of many taboos, but in the brahmanical discourse all of women's social life-cycle rites overtly dealt with her sexuality (Mandakranta Bose, 2000: 95).
263. In Śrīdharadāsa's *Saduktikarṇāmṛta* all verses under *vayasaṁdhi* refer to the adolescent female alone.
264. *SRK*, 353.
265. Ibid., verses 339, 344, 357, 366, 368 and 372.
266. *Daśarūpakam*, ch. 2, pp. 136–42.
    Sāhityadarpaṇa, ch. 3, pp. 157–60.
267. Satyadeva Chaudhari, 1959: 180.
268. In *Kuṭṭanīmatam* (verse 399) such a *nāyaka* evokes only laughter.
269. *Saduktikarṇāmṛta*, verse 479.
270. *SRK*, verse 377.
271. *Bṛhatkathāślokasaṁgraha*, 4.79–80.
272. Bilhaṇa in *Vikramāṅkadevacarita* (2.32) declares that a wife looks best when seen with a son smiling in her lap, and not by being her husband's beloved and decorated with fine jewels.
273. *SM*, 422.6.
274. Cited in R.D. Dikshit, 1964: 195.

275. *Kundamālā*, Act IV, p. 53.
276. Ibid., Act I, p. 5.
277. R.D. Dikshit, 1964: 278.
278. Ibid., 279.
279. In the *Daśakumāracarita* (p. 435) anarchy of the state is linked to promiscuous *(bhagnacarita)* sexuality of royal women of the kingdom. Further in the same text (pp. 232–3) the adultery of queen Kalpasundarī with Upahāravarman is justified by inventing a mythical tale where the two are said to be the cursed former inhabitants of the heaven who were destined for each other.
280. *SM*, 300.1.
281. In contrast, the Latin poet Ovid (1982: 73) takes a very different view on the wife's transgression and advises husbands not to stand on their marital rights as their wives' adultery would bring them presents and influential friends.
282. *Saduktikarṇāmṛta*, verses 686–90.
283. *Śiśupālavadha*, 7.45.
284. *SRK*, verse 617.
285. *Āryāsaptaśatī*, verse 312.
286. The wife's sexuality in low-caste households was of a different order from the upper castes. This is brought out in the explicitly adulterous potter women's songs as analysed by Ann G. Gold (1996: 30–72). Usha Nilsson (2000: 148) also refers to the barbers wives' songs in Avadhi, where a very different notion of women's sexual desire is presented.
287. *Daśarūpakam*, ch. 2, p. 147.
288. Lee Siegel, 1983: 60–1.
289. *Priyadarśikā*, Act III, p. 22.
290. *SRK*, verse 566.
291. Ibid., verse 823.
292. *Amaruśatakī*, verses 47, 50, 55, 75.
293. *Āryāsaptaśati*, verse 48.
294. Ibid., verses 2, 44.
295. Ibid., verses 52, 61.
296. *Amaruśataka*, verse 28.
297. Ibid., verse 30.
298. Anthony Giddens (1992: 2) does not see romantic love as reactionary: he sees it as an 'active and radical engagement' with the 'maleness' of society. He says (pp. 44–6) that romantic love presumes a degree of self-interrogation. How do I feel about the other? How does the other feel about me? The very process of answering of these questions leads to a self-exploratory drive. 'The quest' is a recovery or discovery of the 'self'. This quest thus has an 'active characteristic' and the woman's aspiration, even romantic, cannot be characterized as 'passive'.

299. *Amaruśataka*, verse 18.
300. *Jānakīharaṇa*, 10.86.
301. K.K. Handiqui, 1949: 51.
302. *Mṛcchakaṭika*, Act I.50
303. *Śiśupālavadha*, 10.68.
304. *Naiṣadhacarita*, 9.144–54.
305. Ibid., 9 141–2.
306. *Amaruśataka*, verse 35.
307. Along with gaze, memory that recaptures past pleasure is an important means of invoking erotic passion. In fact, one of the epithets for Kāmadeva is *smara*.
308. The legend says that she was a princess who embarked on a secret tryst in defiance of her family.
309. *Caurapañcāśikā*, verses 4, 5, 7.
310. *Āryāsaptaśatī*, verse 257.

5

Conclusion

A few decades ago it would not have been possible to undertake an analysis of the notion of *kāma* in the classical Sanskrit literature as a serious research topic, for there was an assumption within the academic world that sexuality was private and personal, and there was no history to talk about. At best, sexual practices were the focus of research by social anthropologists like Malinowski, who wrote his pioneering work *The Sexual Life of Savages: North-Western Melanesia* in the beginning of the twentieth century. The biological aspect of sexuality was also a subject of research by scholars such as Havelock Ellis, Alfred Kinsey, and Masters and Johnson.

However, it is now accepted, particularly with the publication of Foucault's three volumes on the *History of Sexuality*, that sexuality, although the most private of concerns, has through human history been a matter in the public domain. Sexuality cannot be abstracted from its surrounding social layers. The emphasis of this book has been precisely that. One of the important theoretical concerns of feminist theory has been not to look at women in isolation or in opposition to men, but to deconstruct the ubiquitous masculinism of the historical culture. For the historian with gender concerns it becomes imperative to make this area a legitimate subject of research. Earlier scholars were in the habit of arguing that there was a unity of interest between men and women in the area of sexuality. This was a faulty assumption, given the fact that sexuality represented above all a primary area of interaction between two groups of people—men and women who had differential access to social, economic, and political power. Thus historians who concern themselves with writing the history of sexuality without paying serious attention to the ways in which the power relationship between the sexes is played out are subsuming the interests of women within those of men. I have consciously tried to address this dichotomy and retrieve the women's position and point of view.

Shulasmith Firestone in her book *The Dialectic of Sex*, asserted that sexuality is a primary structure of social life and that the body itself is a material condition. In this study of the patriarchal sexual social world we have talked in terms of 'emphasized femininity' and 'hegemonic masculinity'. The hegemonic masculinity is constructed in relation to the dominance of men over women, denying the latter a subject status, i.e. one having agency, and the right to maintain autonomy of behaviour and desire. Such masculinity is also characterized by compliance with subordination, and is oriented to accommodating the interests and desires of men. Associated with emphasized femininity are the qualities of sociability, sexual passivity, the acceptance of domesticity, and motherhood. Lately some feminists like Gayle Rubin have challenged the assumption that feminism is, or should be, the privileged site of a theory of sexuality. Feminism is the theory of gender oppression; to automatically assume that this makes it the theory of sexual oppression is to fail to distinguish between gender, on the one hand, and erotic desire, on the other. However, in the context of our sources it is difficult to separate sexual erotic pleasure from its social, familial, and historical roots. An investigation of the sources shows repeatedly that an autonomy of erotic desire does not exist for most women.

In this book we have examined the classical Sanskrit literature on love and eroticism produced between the seventh and thirteenth centuries, from a feminist perspective. That is to say, we have rejected the received text–reader hierarchy in which the latter is the passive feminine recipient of authoritarian discourse. Instead, I have relentlessly posited my own viewpoint on the texts. This practice of reading against the grain has helped illumine the sexual status of women within these ancient literary texts. The early-medieval period in India was dominated by a feudal socio-economic and cultural ethos. The literature of this period was, therefore, also a 'class literature'. The feudal courts which were the main patrons ('hedonist patrons' as Kosambi calls them) of this literature (nearly all litterateurs of the period like Bāṇa, Mayūra, Rājaśekhara, Bilhaṇa, and Govardhanācārya were attached to feudal courts), also dictated the taste, which was towards the florid and erotic.

Since the philosophical ideas of a given culture are a significant medium through which sexual behaviour is represented, I also tuned in to the theory of desire in the various philosophies, be they *dharmaśāstrīya*, *kāmaśāstrīya*, Lokāyata, Tantra and ascetism. An analysis of these ideologies, then current, help illumine the discourse on sexuality. The *dharmaśāstra* provided the normative setting. This is not to say that aberrations were ignored as for instance, in the reference to forms of marriage, types of sons, *svairiṇī* women, etc. Nonetheless, the argument has been that shastric norms were essentially those of the patriarchal family, where sex was for procreation, and homosexuality was completely rejected. Furthermore, the *dharmaśāstra* tended to relegate the *kāma puruṣārtha* or sexual desire to a place entirely behind that of the *dharma*, which alone was considered the aim of human life. The ascetic ideology, which was a rabidly masculine offshoot of the *dharmaśāstrīya* concept of *sanyāsa*, tended to demean the notion of *kāma*. Women, as inciters *par excellence* of desire in men, were equally vilified. However, in the Lokāyata, and in tantric philosophy, the view of *kāma* was not as negative as in the *dharmaśāstra* and the ascetic discourses instead *kāma* was celebrated as the desirable instinct of humankind. It is also significant that in both these philosophies the female principle was valorized. I have also traced the cult of the god Kāmadeva, presiding deity of the erotic literature, and tried to show that as a divinity he occupied a more robust position in the Vedic literature—in the *Atharvaveda* he is referred to as *Īśāna* and *ugraḥ*—but was marginalized in the brahmanical texts, while in the erotic literature the treatment of him was frivolous. It is a surmise that the demeaning of Kāmadeva's status was linked with the more restricted or circumscribed space for woman within society, where the dominant norms were patriarchal and brahmanical.

In the discussion on the physiology of *kāma* I have analysed the cultural elaboration (i.e. the construction of masculinity and femininity) of physiological facts as detailed in the literary discourse of two types, ayurvedic texts (like *Aṣṭāṅgasaṁgraha, Mādhava-nidāna*) and *kāmaśāstra* texts (like *Ratirahasya, Nāgarasarvasvam, Jayamaṅgalā*). An evaluation of the ayurvedic treatises shows how these texts framed the question of sexual pleasure. For the Ayurvedists it was only men's sexual pleasure which was of interest.

Their advice on diet, time of the sexual act, and virilification therapy, all focus on men. Women, if at all they were considered by the medical writers, were discussed primarily in the context of their uterus. This notion of a women's body dominated only by the notion of a healthy or diseased uterus, had to do with the fact that women were valued as procreative instruments and little else. In the *kāma-śāstra* discourse too, like the ayurvedic one, it was the pleasure of men which was of concern. Women are ubiquitous in the *kāmaśāstra* given the essentially heterosexual conception of the sexual act, yet women are never the subject, only the object of male desire. It is the winning of women by men for an amiable sexual relation that is the purpose (*prayojana*) of the *kāmaśāstra* literature. Since the *kāmaśāstra* visualized men as the initiators and the centre of sexual relations, and in control of them, it was only natural that primacy was given to male desire. In the androcentric virile model of sexuality which the *kāmaśāstra* elaborated, woman's pleasure lay in being objectified; either she was the passive recipient of male desire, or her pleasure lay in being desired. Thus we find in the *kāmaśāstra* literature tips on the cosmetic treatment for achieving a body that was the chief object of the male gaze. Given the bias of the *kāmaśāstra* towards an androcentric virile model of the sexual act, it focused on man's voracious sexual appetite as the only formula in the success of the erotic relationship, thereby devaluing erotic reciprocity as the basis of sexual relations between partners.

In the classical Sanskrit literature, prostitutes are one of the *nāyikā* types referred to as the *bāhyā* or *sādhāraṇastrī*. They are also the central figures in the entire business of *kāma*. In my analysis of the institution of prostitution I have tried to go beyond the standard patriarchal view of a prostitute as the perfidious whore whose non-marital, non-procreative sexuality was considered dangerous. I also critique the feminist counter-discourse which, too, indulges in a negative construction of the prostitute body. Such views tend to see the prostitute as the victim of patriarchal oppression through the centuries. I have tried to argue that prostitutes can be seen as social agents, with relative autonomy within the confines of the male body politic. Interestingly, their autonomy as social agents was to a large extent based on the fact that they consciously commodified their *kāma* in order to gain autonomy over both *artha* and *dharma*, the other two ends of human life. I also reject the notion of the prostitute as an eroticized body available for male consumption. Rather, we must place the prostitutes in the general society particularly the *gaṇikā*, as cultural figures *par excellence*. I have also tried to deal with the whole tangled notion of prostitute sexuality. Should it be seen as an 'abnormal' (non-marital, non-procreative) or a 'dominated sexuality' (one that puts submission on sale as a commodity in the market)? Are prostitutes merely obliging props for the enactment of male erotic fantasies? Is it possible to talk in terms of 'pleasure and agency' in prostitution? An analysis of the sources, juxtaposing the *kulavadhū* against the *vāravadhū*, makes a case for the efficacy of the latter viewpoint in dealing with prostitute sexuality.

Last, in this monograph it is argued that it is valid to talk in terms of the love tradition *vis-à-vis* the erotic tradition in classical Sanskrit literature. While the former was a feminine tradition, the latter was inherently masculine. The basis for this binary division is provided by the fact that while the love tradition (in which we include the poetry of the female poets Bhavabhūti and Jayadeva) deals with reciprocity and emotion in sexual relations, the erotic tradition (comprising the entire range of male *śṛṅgārī* poetry) is marked by a hegemonic masculinity that objectifies women and is particularly lacking in emotions and sensitivity. Within this tradition woman is not an equal partner, she exists as a fetishized object for male erotic stimulation. For instance, *nakha-śikha varṇana* where the physical charms of women are listed in a determinedly systematic manner, is ubiquitous in both the prose and poetry of classical Sanskrit literature. Thus, every single body part of the woman from *keśa* to *jaghana* and *uru* are painstakingly described. In fact, it would not be an exaggeration to state that the writer's imagination luxuriates in the rich complexity of the woman's body. In order to analyse and illumine this understanding of the erotic tradition, I have employed the theories of 'looking' first used by John Berger in the context of European art, and Laura Mulvey in the context of cinema. Both have basically argued that within a masculine culture men alone have the privilege to look, and women are the images. In other words, women within this culture have only the status of objects and can never be subjects. The process of reducing women to the status of objects alienates women, denying them their individuality and humanity. In a society in which sexual imbalance prevails, the pleasure in looking has been split between the active male and the passive female. The determining male gaze projects its fantasy onto the female figure, which is styled accordingly. In the word picture of the masculine *śṛṅgārī* poetry, women are simultaneously looked at and displayed, with their appearance coded for strong erotic impact, so that they can be said to connote 'to-be-looked-at-ness'. Woman displayed for the erotic contemplation of the male gaze is the leitmotif of the erotic *śṛṅgārī* poetry.

Bibliography

I. SANSKRIT TEXTS WITH TRANSLATIONS

Amaruśataka, ed. and tr. C.R. Devadhar, Poona: Oriental Book Agency, 1959.

Arthaśāstra of Kautilya, ed. and tr. R.P. Kangle, Part II, Delhi: Motilal Banarsidass, rpt., 1992.

Āryāsaptaśatī of Govardhanācārya, ed. and tr. Ramakanta Tripathi, Varanasi: Chowkhamba, 1965.

Aṣṭādhyāyī of Pāṇini, ed. and tr. Sirishchandra Vasu, Delhi: Motilal Banarsidass, 1962.

Aṣṭāṅgasaṁgraha of Vāgbhaṭṭa, ed. and tr. K.R. Srikantha Murthy, vols. I, II, and III, Varanasi: Chowkhamba, 1995–97.

Atharvaveda, ed. and tr. William Dwight Whitney, 2 vols. Delhi: Motilal Banarsidass, 1962.

Bālarāmāyaṇa of Rājaśekhara ed. and tr. Gangasagar Rai, Varanasi: Chowkhamba, 1984.

Baudhāyana Dharmasūtra, ed. and tr. G. Buhler, Delhi: Motilal Banarsidass, 1986.

Bhagvad Gītā, Gita Press, Gorakhpur edition, rpt., 1980.

Bṛhatkathāślokasaṁgraha of Buddhasvāmin, ed. and tr. R.P. Poddar, Varanasi: Tara Printing Works, 1986.

Bṛhatsaṁhitā of Varāhamihira, ed. and tr. Ramkrishna M. Bhatt, 2 vols., Delhi: Motilal Banarsidass, 1982.

Caurapañcāśikā of Bilhaṇa, ed. and tr. B.S. Miller, Penguin, 1990, ed. and tr. Tadpatrikar, Poona: Oriental Book Agency, 1946.

Carakasaṁhitā ed. and tr. P.V. Sharma, 2 vols., Varanasi: Chowkhamba, 1981–5.

Daśakumāracarita of Daṇḍin, ed. and tr. Kedarnath Sharma, Varanasi: Chowkhamba, 1965.

Daśarūpakam of Dhanañjaya, ed. and tr. Shrinivasa Shastri, Meerut: Sahitya Bhandar, 1969.

Gāthāsattasaī of Hāla, ed. and tr. R.G. Basak, Calcutta: Asiatic Society, 1971.

Gītagovinda of Jayadeva, ed. and tr. B.S. Miller, Delhi: Oxford University Press, 1977.

Haravijaya of Ratnākara, *Haravijaya : An Introduction to the Sanskrit Court Epic* by David Smith, Delhi: Oxford University Press, 1985.

Harṣacarita of Bāṇabhaṭṭa, ed. and tr. Jagganatha Pathak, Varanasi: Chowkhamba, 1964.

Jānakīharaṇa of Kumāradāsa, ed. and tr. Brijmohan Vyasa, Allahabad: Mitraprakashan, 1967.

Jayamaṅgalā Commentary on *Kāmasūtra* by Yaśodhara, ed. and tr. Madhavacharya, 2 vols., Bombay: Khemraja Shrikrishna Prakashan, 1995.

Kādambarī of Bāṇabhaṭṭa, *Pūrvabhāga*, ed. and tr. M.R. Kale, 4th edn, Delhi: Motilal Banarsidass, 1968, *Pūrva* and *Uttarabhāga*, ed. and tr. Ramteja Shastri, Kashi: Pandit Pustakalaya, 1965.

Kāmasūtra of Vātsyāyana, ed. and tr. Madhavacarya, 2 vols., Bombay: Khemraja Shrikrishna Prakashan, 1995.

Karpūramañjarī of Rājaśekhara, ed. and tr. R.P. Poddar, Vaishali: Research Institute of Prakrit, 1974.

Kathākoṣa tr. C.H. Tawney, Delhi: Munshiram Manoharlal, 1975.

Kathāsaritsāgara of Somadeva, ed. Penzer, tr. C.H. Tawney, 10 vols., Delhi: Motilal Banarsidass, rpt., 1968; Sankrit text with Hindi tr. Kedarnath Sharma Saraswat, vols. 1 and 2, 1960–1; vol. 3 tr. Jatashankar Jha and Prafulla Chandra Ojha, 1973, Patna: Bihar Rashtrabhasha Parishad.

Kaumudīmahotsava, ed. and tr. S.R. Sastri, Bombay, 1952.

Kāvyādarśa of Daṇḍin, ed. and tr. Ramchandra Mishra, Varanasi: Chowkhamba, 1972.

Kāvyālaṁkārasūtra of Vāmana, ed. and tr. Bechana Jha, Varanasi: Chowkhamba, 1971.

Kāvyamīmāṁsā of Rājaśekhara, ed. and tr. Gangasagar Rai, Varanasi: Chowkhamba, 1964.

Kāvyaprakāśa of Mammaṭa, ed. and tr. Satyavrata Singh, Varanasi: Chowkhamba, 1955.

Kundamālā of Diṅnāga, ed. and tr. Jaichand and Bhimasena, Lahore: Atma Ram & Sons, 1937.

Kuṭṭanīmatam of Dāmodaragupta, ed. and tr. Atrideva Vidyalamkara, Varanasi: Indological Book House, 1961.

Mādhavanidāna of Mādhavakara, ed. and tr. Dinanatha Shastri, Meharchand Lakshmandass, Delhi, vols. I and II, 2nd rpt., 1950.

Mahābhārata of Vyāsa, Critical edition in 19 vols., Poona: BORI, 1933–66.

Mahāvīracaritam of Bhavabhūti, ed. and tr. Ramachandra Mishra, Varanasi: Chowkhamba, 1968.

Mālatī-Mādhava of Bhavabhūti, ed. and tr. M.R. Kale, 2nd edn., Bombay: Gopal Narayan & Co., 1928.

Manubhāṣya of Medhātithi, tr. Ganganatha Jha, vols. 1–5, Calcutta: Calcutta University, 1920–6.

Manusmṛti, tr. Wendy Doniger and Brian K. Smith, rpt., New York: Penguin, 1992.

Mayūraśataka of Mayūra, ed. and tr. G.P. Quackenbos, New York: Columbia University Press, 1917.

Mṛcchakaṭika of Śūdraka, ed. and tr. M.R. Kale, Bombay: Bookseller's Publishing Company, 1962.

Nāgarasarvasvam of Padmaśrī, tr. Babulal Shukla Shastri, Delhi: Eastern Book Linkers, 1994.

Naiṣadhacarita of Śrī Harṣa, tr. K.K. Handiqui, Poona, 1965.

Nāradasmṛti tr. J. Jolly, Varanasi: Bhartiya Publishing House, 1978.

Nāṭyaśāstra of Bharatamuni, ed. and tr. N. Punni, vols. 1–4, Delhi: Nag Publishers, 1998.

Prabodhacandrodaya of Krishna Mishra, ed. and tr. Ramachandra Mishra, Varanasi: Chowkhamba, 1955.

Priyadarśikā of Sri Harsa, ed. and tr. N.G. Suru, Poona, 1928.

Puṣpabāṇavilāsam, ed. Satkari Mukhopadhyaya, tr. Somnath Shastri, Varanasi: Chowkhamba, 1969.

Rājataraṅgiṇī of Kalhaṇa, ed. and tr. Ramteja Shastri, Kashi: Pandita Pustakalaya, 1960.

Rāmāyaṇa of Vālmīki, Gita Press Gorakhpur edition, 2 vols., rpt., 1988.

Ratirahasya of Kokkokā, ed. and tr. Ramananda Sharma, Varanasi: Chowkhamba, 1994.

Ratnāvalī of Śrī Harṣa, ed. and tr. C.R. Devadhar and N.G. Suru, Poona: Oriental Book House, 2nd edn., 1954.

Ṛgveda, tr. R.T.H. Griffith, 2 vols., Varanasi: Chowkhamba, rpt., 1963.

Saduktikarṇāmṛta of Śrīdharadāsa, ed. S.C Banerji, Calcutta: Firma KLM, 1965.

Sāhityadarpaṇa of Viśvanātha, ed. and tr. Satyavrata Singh, Varanasi: Chowkhamba, 1970.

Samayamātṛkā of Kṣemendra, ed. and tr. Ramashankar Tripathi, Varanasi: Chowkhamba, 1967.

Śatakatrayam of Bhartṛhari, tr. B.S. Miller, Columbia University Press, 1967.

Siṁhāsanadvātrinśikā ed. and tr. Franklin Edgerton, Cambridge: Harvard University Press, 1926.

Śiśupālavadha of Māgha, ed. and tr. Haragovinda Shastri, Varanasi: Chowkhamba, 1961.

Śiva Purāṇa, ed. J.L. Shastri, 4 vols., Delhi: Motilal Banarasidass, 1995.

Smṛticandrikā of Devannbhaṭṭa, ed. and tr. J.R. Gharpure, Bombay, vol. 1, 1946; vol. 2, 1948–50.

Śṛṅgārahāṭa: Caturbhāṇī, ed. and tr. Motichandra and V.S. Agrawala, Bombay: Hindi Grantha Ratnakar, 1960.

Śṛṅgāramañjarīkathā of Bhoja, ed. and tr. Kalpana Munshi, Singhi Jaina Series, No. 30, Bombay: Bharatiya Vidya Bhavan, 1959.

Śṛṅgāraprakāśa of Bhoja, tr. V.R. Raghavan, Madras: Vasanta Press, Theosophical Society, 1963.

Śṛṅgāravairāgyataraṅgiṇī of Somaprabha Sūri, Kāvyamālā Series, Bombay: Nirnay Sagar Press, V.124.

Subhāṣitaratnakoṣa of Vidyākara, ed. V.V. Gokhale and D.D. Kosambi, Harvard Oriental Series, No. 42, 1957, tr. D. Ingalls, Cambridge: Harvard University Press, 1965.

Subhāṣitāvalī of Vallabhadeva, ed. and tr. Ramachandra Malviya, Varanasi: Anand Bandhu Prakashak, 1974.

Śukāsaptati, ed. and tr. Ramakanta Tripathi, Varanasi: Chowkhamba, 1966.

Sūktimuktāvalī of Jalhaṇa, ed. E. Krishnamacharya, Baroda: Oriental Institute, 1938.

Suśrutasaṁhitā with commentary by Ḍalhaṇācārya, ed. Trikamji Acharya and Narayanram Acharya, Varanasi: Chowkhamba, 2003.

Taittirīyasaṁhitā, ed. and tr. A.B. Keith, 2 vols., Delhi: Motilal Banarsidass, 1967.

Uttararāmacarita of Bhavabhūti, ed. and tr. P.V. Kane and C.N. Joshi, Delhi: Motilal Banarasidass, 4th edn., 1962.

Vāsavadattā of Subandhu, ed. and tr. Shankardeva Shastri, Varanasi: Chowkhamba, 1967, tr. Louis H. Gray, Delhi: Motilal Banarsidass, 1962.

Veṇīsaṁhāra of Bhaṭṭanārāyaṇa, ed. and tr. Adityanarain Pandey, Varanasi: Chowkhamba, 3rd edn., 1959.

Vetālapañcaviṁśati ed. and tr. Damodar Jha, Varanasi: Chowkhamba, 1968.

Viddhaśālabhañjikā of Rājaśekhara, ed. and tr. Ramakanta Tripathi, Varanasi: Chowkhamba, 1965.

Vikramāṅkadevacarita of Bilhaṇa, ed. and tr. Visvanath Shastri Bharadwaj, Varanasi: BHU, vol. 1, 1958; vol. 2, 1962; vol. 3, 1964.

II. SECONDARY WORKS

Agrawala, V.S., *Kadambari eka Samskritika Adhyayana*, Varanasi: Chowkhamba, 1958.

———, *Harsacarita eka Samskritika Adhyayana*, Patna: Bihar Rashtrabhasha Purishad, 2nd edn., 1964.

Aitken, Molly Emma, 'Spectatorship and Femininity in Kangra-style Painting', in Vidya Dehejia (ed.), *Representing the Body*, Delhi: Kali For Women, 1997, pp. 82–101.

Albrecht, M.C., J.H. Barnett and M. Griff (eds.), *The Sociology of Art and Literature: A Reader*, London: Duckworth, 1982.

Ali, Daud, *Courtly Culture and Political Life in Early Medieval India*, Cambridge: Cambridge University Press, 2004.

———, 'Technologies of the Self: Courly Artifice and Monastic Discipline in Early India', *Journal of the Economic and Social History of the Orient*, vol. 41, no. 2, 1998, pp. 159–84.

———, 'From Nayika to Bhakta: A Genealogy of Female Subjectivity in Early Medieval India', in Julia Leslie and Mary McGee (eds.), *Invented Identities: The Interplay of Gender, Religion and Politics in India*, Delhi: Oxford University Press, 2000: 157–80.

Altekar, A.S., *Position of Women in Hindu Civilization*, Varanasi: BHU Press, 1938.

Anderson, Leona, *Vasantotsava: The Spring Festivals of India, Texts and Traditions*, New Delhi: D.K. Printworld, 1993.

Apte, V.S., *Sanskrit-Hindi Koṣa*, Delhi: Motilal Banarsidass, 1966.

Ardener, S. (ed.), *Women and Space: Ground Rules and Social Maps*, London: Croom-Helm, 1981.

———, *Defining Females: The Nature of Women in Society*, 2nd edn., Oxford: Berg, 1993.

Bailey, Gregory M., 'Bhartṛhari's Manipulation of the Feminine', *Indo-Iranian Journal*, vol. 39 no. 2, 1996, pp. 201–21.

Banerji, S.C. and R. Banerji, *The Castaway of Indian Society: History of Prostitution in India since Vedic Times*, Calcutta: Punthi Pustak, 1989.

Basham, A.L., 'The Practice of Medicine in Ancient and Medieval India', in C. Leslie (ed.), *Asian Medical Systems: A Comparative Study*, Berkeley: University of California Press, 1976, pp. 18–43.

———, *The Wonder That Was India*, Delhi: Rupa Publications, 8th rpt., 1988.

De Beauvoir, Simone, *The Second Sex*, London: Picador, 1988.

Bell, Shannon, *Reading, Writing and Rewriting the Prostitute Body*, Bloomington: Indiana University Press, 1994.

Berger, John, *Ways of Seeing*, Harmondsworth: Penguin Books, 1972.

Bhattacharji, Sukumari, *The Indian Theogony*, Cambridge: Cam-bridge University Press, 1970.

———, *History of Sanskrit Literature: Classical Age*, Hyderabad: Orient Longman, 1993.

———, 'Prostitution in Ancient India', in Kumkum Roy (ed.), *Women in Early Indian Societies*, Delhi: Manohar, 1999: 196–228.

Bhattacharyya, N.N., *History of Indian Erotic Literature*, Delhi: Munshiram Manoharlal, 1975.

———, *History of the Tantric Religion*, Delhi: Manohar, 1982.

——— (ed.), *Tantric Buddhism*, Delhi: Manohar, 1999.

———, 'Proprietary Rights of Women in Ancient India', in Kumkum Roy (ed.), *Women in Early Indian Societies*, Delhi: Manohar, 1999, pp. 113–22.

Bhishagratna, K.L., *Suśrutasaṁhitā*, English translation, vols. 1–3, Varanasi: Chowkhamba, 1963.

Blackwell, Fritz, 'Misogyny and Philogyny: The Bifurcation and Ambivalence of the Stereotypes of the Courtesans and the Mother in Literary Tradition', *Journal of South Asian Literature*, vol. 12, nos. 3–4, 1977, pp. 37–43.

Bloomfield, Maurice, 'On False Ascetics and Nuns in Hindu Fiction', *JAOS*, vol. XLIV, 1924, pp. 202–42.

Bonner, F. and L.G. Goodman, et al. (eds.), *Imagining Women*, Cambridge: Polity Press, 1992.

Bose, Mandakranta (ed.), *Faces of the Feminine: In Ancient, Medieval and Modern India*, Oxford: Oxford University Press, 2000.

Bowie, T. and C. Christenson (eds.), *Studies in Erotic Art*, New York: Basic Books, 1970.

Brough, John, *Poems From the Sanskrit*, Harmondsworth: Penguin, rpt., 1969.

Bullough, Vern, *History of Prostitution*, New York: University Books, 1964.

———, *The Subordinate Sex: A History of Attitudes Towards Women*, New York: Penguin, 1974.

Butler, Judith, *Gender Trouble, Feminism and the Subversion of Identity*, London: Routledge, 1990.

Byron, *The Poetical Works of Lord Byron*, London, Oxford University Press, 1945.

Caplan, Pat (ed.), *Cultural Construction of Sexuality*, New York: Tavistock, 1987.

Chakrabarti, Kunal, *Religious Process: The Puranas and the Making of a Regional Tradition*, Delhi: Oxford University Press, 2001.

Chakravarti, Candra, *Sex Life in Ancient India*, Calcutta: Firma KLM, 1963.

Chakravarti, Chintaharan, *Tantras: Studies on their Religion and Literature*, Calcutta: Punthi Pustak, rpt., 1972.

Chakravarti, Uma, 'Conceptualising Brahmanical Patriarchy in Early India: Gender, Caste, Class and State', *Economic and Political Weekly*, vol. 28, no. 14, 3 April 1993, pp. 579–85.

Chakravarti, Uma, 'The World of the Bhaktin in South Indian Tradition: The Body and Beyond', in Kumkum Roy (ed.), *Women in Early Indian Societies*, Delhi: Manohar, 1999, pp. 299–321.

Chatterji, Lola (ed.), *Woman, Image, Text: Feminist Readings of Literary Texts*, Delhi: Trianka, 1986.

Chattopadhyaya, A., 'Spring Festival and Festivals of Indra in the Kathāsaritsāgara', *Journal of the Oriental Institute*, vol. XVII, Part 2, 1967, pp. 137–41.

Chattopadhyaya, B.D., *The Making of Early Medieval India*, Delhi: Oxford University Press, 1994.

———, *Studying Early India: Texts, Archaeology and Historical Issues*, Delhi: Permanent Black, 2002.

Chattopadhyaya, D.P., *Lokāyata: A Study in Ancient Indian Materialism*, Delhi: People's Publishing House, 1959.

———, *Science and Society in Ancient India*, Calcutta: Research India Publications, 1977.

Chaudhari, Satyadeva, *Bharatiya Kavyanga*, Allahabad: Sahitya Bhavan, 1959.

Chaudhuri, J.B., *Sanskrit Poetesses: Contributions of Women to Sanskrit Literature*, vol. 2, pt. A, Calcutta: Self published, 1941.

Clementin-Ojha, 'Outside the Norms: Women Ascetics in Hindu Society', *Economic and Political Weekly*, vol. 23, no. 18, 30 April 1988, pp. 34–6.

Corpus Inscriptionum Indicarum, vol. III, pt. 1, 1981, rpt.; vol. IV, pt. 1, 1955, rpt; vol. IV, pt. 2, 1955, rpt., New Delhi: Archaeological Survey of India.

Coward, Rosalind, *Patriarchal Precedents: Sexuality and Social Relations*, London: Routledge and Kegan Paul, 1983.

———, *Female Desire: Women's Sexuality Today*, London: Paladin, 1984.

Das, R.M., *Women in Manu and his Seven Commentators*, Varanasi: Kanchan Publication, 1962.

Das, Rahul Peter, *The Origin of the Life of a Human Being: Conception and the Female According to Ancient Indian Medical and Sexological Literature*, Delhi: Motilal Banarsidass, 2003.

Das, Veena, 'Feminity and the Orientation to the Body', in Karuna, Chanana (ed.), *Socialisation, Education and Women*, Delhi: Orient Longman, 1988, pp. 193–207.

Dasgupta, P.K., *Jayadeva and Some of his Contemporaries*, Calcutta: Sanskrit Book Depot, 1982.

Dasgupta, S.N. and S.K. De, *A History of Sanskrit Literature: Classical Period*, 2nd edn., Calcutta: University of Calcutta, 1962.

De, S.K., *History of Sanskrit Poetics*, 2nd edn., Calcutta: Firma KLM, 1960.

———, *Early History of the Vaisnava Faith and Movement in Bengal*, 2nd edn., Calcutta: Firma KLM, 1961.

———, *Ancient Indian Erotics and Erotic Literature*, Calcutta: Firma KLM, 1959.

Dehejia, Harsha V. (ed.), *A Celebration of Love: The Romantic Heroine in the Indian Arts*, Delhi: Roli Books, 2004.

Dehejia, Vidya (ed.), *Royals, Patrons and Great Temple Art*, Bombay: Marg Publications, 1988.

———, *Representing the Body: Gender Issues in Indian Art*, Delhi: Kali for Women, 1997.

Desai, Devangana, *Erotic Sculptures of India: A Socio-Cultural Study*, Delhi: Tata McGraw Hill, 1975.

———, 'Social Dimensions of Art in Early India', Presidential address, *Indian History Congress*, Gorakhpur Session, 1989–90, pp. 21–56.

Desai, Vishakha (ed.), *Gods, Guardians and Lovers: Temple Sculptures From North India*, Ahmedabad: Mapin, 1993.

Deyell, John S., *Living without Silver: The Monetary History of Early-Medieval North India*, Delhi: Oxford University Press, 1990.

Dikshit, R.D., *Women in Sanskrit Drama*, Delhi: Meharchand Lachhman Dass, 1964.

Dimock, Edward, *The Place of the Hidden Moon*, Delhi: Motilal Banarsidass, 1991.

Douglas, Mary, *Purity and Danger: An Analysis of the Concepts of Pollution and Taboos*, London: Routledge, 1966.

Dover, K.J., 'Classical Greek Attitudes to Sexual Behaviour', *Arethusa*, vol. 6, no. 1, 1973, pp. 59–73.

Dubey, Leela, 'On the Construction of Gender: Hindu Girls in Patrilineal India', *Economic and Political Weekly*, vol. 23, no. 18, 30 April 1988, pp. 11–19.

Dumont, Louis, 'World Renunciation in Indian Religions', *Contributions to Indian Sociology*, vol. 4, no. 1, 1960, pp. 33–62.

Dwivedi, Vachaspati, *Kathasaritsagara eka Samskritika Adhyayana*, Patna, 1977.

Engels, Frederick, *The Origin of the Family, Private Property and the State*, 1 Moscow, 1948.

Epigraphia Indica, vol. IV, 1979, rpt.; vol. XVIII, 1983, rpt., New Delhi: Archaeological Survey of India.

Evans, Marry (ed.), *The Woman Question: Readings on the Subordination of Women*, Great Britain: Fontana Paperbacks, 1982.

Ferguson, Ann et al., 'The Feminist Sexuality Debates, *SIGNS: Journal of Women and Culture in Society*, vol. 10, no. 1, 1984, pp. 106–35.

Firestone, Shulamith, *The Dialectic of Sex*, New York: Morrow, 1970.

Flaceliere, R., *Love in Ancient Greece*, New York: Crown, 1962.

Flueckiger, Joyce, 'Caste and Regional Variance in an Oral Epic Tradition', in Stuart H. Blackburn et al. (eds.), *Oral Epics in India*, Berkeley: University of California Press, 1989, pp. 33–54.

Foucault, Michel, *The History of Sexuality*, vol. I, London: Allen Lane, 1979; vol. II, Penguin, 1987; vol. III, Penguin, 1990.

Gagnon, J.H. and W. Simon, *Sexual Conduct: The Social Sources of Human Sexuality*, London: Hutchinson, 1973.

Gamman, L. and M. Marshment (eds.), *The Female Gaze*, London: The Women's Press, 1988.

Ganesh, Kamla, 'Seclusion of Women and the Structures of Caste', in M. Krishnaraja and K. Chanana (eds.), *Gender and The Household Domain: Social and Cultural Dimensions*, Delhi: Sage, 1989, pp. 75–95.

Ghosh, Manomohan, *Contribution to the History of the Hindu Drama: Its Origin, Development and Diffusion*, Calcutta: Firma KLM, 1958.

Giddens, Anthony (ed.), *The Trnsformation of Initimacy: Sexuality, Love and Eroticism in Modern Societies*, Cambridge: Polity Press, 1992.

Gilbert, P. and S. Taylor (eds), *Fashioning The Feminine*, Sydney: Allen and Unwin, 1991.

Giri, Kalipada, *Concept of Poetry: An Indian Approach*, Calcutta: Sanskrit Pustak Bhandar, 1975.

Godelier, Maurice, 'The Origin of Male Domination', *New Left Review*, vol. 127, May–June 1981, pp. 3–17.

Godol, J.K., 'Doubled Vision of Feminist Theory', *Feminist Studies*, vol. 5, 1979, pp. 216–27.

Gold, Ann G., 'Sexuality, Fertility and Erotic Imagination', in G.G. Reheja and A.G. Gold (eds.) *Listen to the Heron's Words: Re-imaging Gender and Kinship in North India*, Delhi: Oxford University Press, 1996, pp. 30–72.

Grosz, Elizabeth, *Volatile Bodies: Towards a Corporeal Feminism*, Bloomington: Indiana University Press, 1994.

Guha, Ranajit, 'Dominance without Hegemony and its Historio-graphy', in R. Guha (ed.), *Subaltern Studies*, vol VI: *Writings on South Asian History and Society*, Delhi: Oxford University Press, 1989, pp. 210–30.

Gulati, Saroj, *Women and Society*, Delhi: Chanakya Publications, 1985.

Gulik Van, *Sexual Life in Ancient China*, Leiden: E.J. Brill, 1961.

Halperin, David, 'Is there a History of Sexuality?', *History and Theory*, vol. 28, 1989, pp. 257–74.

Halperin, D., J. Winkler, and F. Zeitlin (eds.), *Before Sexuality: The Construction of Erotic Experience in the Ancient Greek World*, Princeton: Princeton University Press, 1990.

Handiqui, K.K., *Yaśastilaka and Indian Culture*, Sholapur: Jivaraja Jaina Ganthamala, 1949.

Hara, Minoru, 'Tapasvini', *Annals of Bhandarkar Oriental Research Institute*, vols. LVIII-LIX, 1977–8, pp. 151–9.

Hart, George L., 'Ancient Tamil Literature: Its Scholarly Past and Future', in Burton Stein (ed.), *Essays on South India*, Delhi: Vikas, 1976, pp. 41–63.

———, 'Womanhood and the Sacred in Ancient Tamil Nadu', in Kumkum Roy (ed.), *Women in Early Indian Societies*, Delhi: Manohar, 1999, pp. 229–54.

Hawley, J.S. and D.M. Wulff (eds.), *The Divine Consort Rādhā and the Goddesses of India*, Delhi: Motilal Banarsidass, 1984.

Hermann, A.C. and A.J. Stewart (eds), *Theorizing Feminism: Parallel Trends in the Humanities and Social Sciences*, Boulder: Westview Press, 1994.

Horner, I.B., *Women under Primitive Buddhism*, Delhi: Motilal Banarsidass, rpt., 1975.

Ingalls, D.H.H., 'Words for Beauty in Classical Sanskrit Poetry', in *Indological Studies in Honor of W. Norman Brown*, New Haven: American Oriental Society, 1962, pp. 87–107.

Jackson, S. and S. Scott (eds.), *Feminism and Sexuality: A Reader*, Edinburgh: Edinburgh University Press, 1996.

Jaini, P.S., *Gender and Salvation*, Delhi: Munshiram Manoharlal, 1992.

Jaiswal, Suvira, 'Female Images in the Arthasastra of Kautilya', *Social Scientist*, vol. 29, nos. 3–4, 2001, pp. 51–9.

Jha, D.N., 'Social Change in Ancient India', *Economic and Political Weekly*, vol. XIV, no. 35, September 1979, pp. 1499–1500.

——— (ed.), *Feudal Social Formation in Early India*, Delhi: Chanakya Publications, 1987.

———, *The Feudal Order: State, Society and Ideology in Early Medieval India*, Delhi: Manohar, 2000.

Kakkar, Sudhir, *Intimate Relations: Exploring Indian Sexuality*, Harmondsworth: Penguin, 1990.

Kakkar, Sudhir and J.M. Ross, *Tales of Love, Sex and Danger*, Delhi: Oxford University Press, 1986.

Kane, P.V., *History of Sanskrit Poetics*, 3rd edn, Delhi: Motilal Banarsidass, 1961.

———, *History of Dharmaśāstras*, 2nd edn., vol. II, Poona: BORI, 1974.

Katre, S.L., 'Kṛṣṇa, Gopas, Gopīs and Rādhā', in H.L. Hariyappa and M.M. Patkar (eds.), *P.K. Gode Commemoration Volume*, Poona: Oriental Book Agency, 1960, pp. 83–92.

Keith, A.B., *A History of Sanskrit Literature*, Delhi: Oxford University Press, rpt., 1941.

———, *The Sanskrit Drama: Its Origin, Development, Theory and Practice*, Delhi: Oxford University Press, rpt., 1964.

Kelkar, Meena, 'Man-Woman Relationship in Indian Philosophy', *Indian Philosophical Quarterly*, vol. 26, no. 1, 1999, pp. 71–87.

Kelley, Jonathan, 'A Theory of Human Sexuality', *International Journal of Sociology of the Family*, vol. 16, 1986, 125–42.

Keohane, N.O., M.Z. Rosaldo and B.C. Gelpi (eds.), *Feminist Theory: A Criticism of Ideology*, Brighton: The Harvester Press, 1982.

Khandelwal, Meena, 'Sexual Fluids, Emotions, Morality: Notes on the Gendering of Brahmacharya', in Elisa Sobo and Sandra Bell (eds.), *Celibacy, Culture and Society: The Anthropology of Sexual Abstinence*, Madison: University of Wisconsin Press, 2001, pp. 157–79.

Khanna, Madhu, 'The Goddess-Women Equation in Śākta Tantras', in Mandakranta Bose (ed.), *Faces of the Feminine*, Oxford: Oxford University Press, 2000, pp. 109–23.

Kiefer, O., *Sexual Life in Ancient Rome*, London: Panther, 1969.

Kinsley, David, *Hindu Goddesses: Vision of the Divine Feminine in the Hindu Religious Tradition*, Delhi: Motilal Banarsidass, 1987.

Kosambi, D.D., 'Introduction' to the *Subhāṣitaratnakoṣa*, Cambridge: Harvard University Press, 1957, pp. xviii–cxix.

———, *The Culture and Civilization of Ancient India in Historical Outline*, Delhi: Vikas, 1977.

———, *Exasperating Essays*, Pune: People's Book House, rpt., 1986.

Krishnamchariar, M., *History of Classical Sanskrit Literature*, Delhi: Motilal Banarsidass, rpt., 1970.

Krishnamoorthy, K., *Essays in Sanskrit Literary Criticism*, Dharwar: Karnataka University, 1964.

Kulkarni, V.M., *Studies in Sanskrit Sahitya Shastra*, Delhi: Motilal Banarsidass, 1993.

Kulshrestha, Sushma (ed.), *Erotics in Sanskrit and English Literature: Kalidasa and Shakespeare*, Delhi: Eastern Book Linkers, 1997.

Lal Coveney and M. Jackson, et al. (eds.), *The Sexuality Papers: Male Sexuality and the Social Control of Women*, London: Hutchinson, 1984.

Leick, Gwendolyn, *Sex and Eroticism in Mesopotamian Literature*, London: Routledge, 1994.

Lerner, Gerda, *The Creation of Patriarchy*, New York: Oxford University Press, 1986.

Lewis, C.S., *The Allegory of Love: A Study in Medieval Tradition*, 2nd edn., London: Oxford University Press, 1958.

Licht, Hans (P. Brandt), *Sexual Life in Ancient Greece*, Calcutta: The Standard Literature Co. Ltd., 1952.

Lienhard, Siegfried, *A History of Classical Poetry: Sanskrit, Pali, Prakrit*, Wiesbaden: Harrassowitz, 1984.

MacKinnon, Catherine, 'Feminism, Marxism, Method and State: An Agenda for Theory', *SIGNS: Journal of Women and Culture in Society*, vol. 7, no. 3, 1982, pp. 515–44.

———, 'Sexuality', in A.C. Herrman and A.J. Stewart (eds.), *Theorising Feminism: Parallel Trends in the Humanities and Social Sciences*, Boulder: Westview Press, 1994, pp. 257–87.

Madan, T.N., *Non-Renunciation: Themes and Interpretations of Hindu Culture*, Delhi: Oxford University Press, 1987.

Malinowski, B.M., *The Sexual Life of Savages in North-Western Melanesia*, London: Routledge & Kegan Paul, 1957.

Manjushree, *The Position of Women in the Yajnavalkya Smrti*, Delhi: Prachi, 1990.

Masson, J.M., 'The Childhood of Kṛṣṇa: Some Psychoanalytic Observations', *JAOS*, vol. 94, no. 4, 1974, pp. 454–9.

———, 'The Psychology of the Ascetic', *Journal of Asian Studies*, vol. XXXV, no. 4, 1976, pp. 611–25.

Mazumdar, B.P., *Socio-Economic History of Northern India (1030-1194 AD)*, Calcutta: Firma KLM, 1960.

———, 'Merchants and Landed Aristocracy in the Feudal Economy of North India: 8th-12th Century', in B.P. Sahu (ed.), *Land System and Rural Society in Early India*, Delhi: Manohar, 1997, pp. 142–50.

McClure, Laura K. (ed.), *Sexuality and Gender in the Classical World*, Oxford: Blackwell, 2002.

McQuillon, M., *The Deconstruction Reader*, Edinburgh: Edinburgh University Press, 2000.

Merwin, W.S. and J.M. Masson, *Sanskrit Love Poetry*, New York: Columbia University Press, 1977.

Meyer, J.J., *Sexual Life in Ancient India*, 1st edn., Delhi: Motilal Banarsidass, 1971.

Miller, Barbara S., 'Rādhā: Consort of Kṛṣṇa's Vernal Passion', *JAOS*, vol. 95, no. 5, 1975, pp. 655–71.

Miller, B.S. and R. Eaton (eds.), *Power of Art: Patronage in Indian Culture*, Delhi: Oxford University Press, 1992.

Mills, Ralph (ed.), *On the Poet and His Craft: Selected Prose of Theodore Roethke*, Seattle, University of Washington Press, 1965.

Mishra, U.P., *Prachin Bharata Mein Nari 600-1200 Isvi*, Bhopal: Hindi Granth Akademy, 1987.

Mishra, Shivshekar, *Manasollasa eka Samskritika Adhyayana*, Varanasi: Chowkhamba, 1966.

Moi, Toril, *Sexual Textual Politics: Feminist Literary Theory*, London: Methuen, 1985.

Monier-Williams, M., *English-Sanskrit Dictionary*, Delhi: Munshiram Manoharlal, 2nd edn., 1985.

———, *Sanskrit-English Dictionary*, Delhi: Munshiram Manoharlal, this edn, 1994.

Moore, H.L., *Feminism and Anthropolgy*, Minneapolis: University of Minnesota Press, 1988.

Motichandra, *The World of Courtesans*, Delhi: Vikas, 1973.

Muller, Max, *A History of Ancient Sanskrit Literature*, Varanasi: Chowkhamba, rpt., 1968.

Mulvey, Laura, *Visual and Other Pleasures*, Bloomington: Indiana University Press, 1989.

Nandi, R.N., *Religious Institutions and Cults in the Deccan c. 600–1000 A.D.*, Delhi: Motilal Banarsidass, 1973.

———, 'Origin and Nature of Saivite Monasticism: The Case of Kalamukhas', in R.S. Sharma and V.N. Jha (eds.), *Indian Society: Historical Probings*, 2nd edn., Delhi: People's Publishing House, 1977, pp. 190–201.

———, *Social Roots of Religion in Ancient India*, Calcutta: K.P. Bagchi & Co., 1986.

Nead, Lynda, 'The Female Nude: Pornography, Art and Sexuality', *SIGNS: Journal of Women and Culture in Society*, vol. 15, no. 2, 1990, pp. 323–35.

———, 'Getting Down to Basics: Art, Obscenity and the Female Nude', in Isobel Armstrong (ed.), *New Feminist Discourses*, London: Routledge, 1992, pp. 199–221.

Nilsson, Usha, 'Grinding Millet But Singing of Sita: Power and Domination in Avadhi and Bhojpuri Women's Songs', in Paula Richman (ed.), *Questioning Ramayanas: A South Asian Tradition*, Delhi: Oxford University Press, 2000, pp. 137–58.

Nochlin, Linda, *Women, Art, Power and Other Essays*, London: Thames and Hudson, rpt., 1994.

Obeyesekere, Gananath, *Medusa's Hair*, Princeton: Princeton University Press, 1984.

O'Flaherty, *Asceticism and Eroticism in the Mythology of Siva*, Delhi: Oxford University Press, 1973.

———, *Sexual Metaphors and Animal Symbolism*, Delhi: Motilal Banarsidass, 1981.

Oldenburg, Veena Talwar, 'Lifestyle and Resistance: The Case of the Courtesans of Lucknow', in Douglas Haynes and Gyan Prakash (eds.)

Contesting Power: Resistance and Everyday Social Relations in South Asia, Delhi: Oxford University Press, 1991, pp. 23–61.

Olivelle, Patrick, 'Renouncer and Renunciation in the Dharmaśāstras', in Richard Lariviere (ed.), *Studies in Dharmaśāstras*, Calcutta: Firma KLM, 1984, pp. 81–151.

Orr, Leslie, *Donors, Devotees and Daughters of God*, Oxford: Oxford University Press, 2000.

Ortner, Sherry, 'The Virgin and the State', *Feminist Studies*, no. 4, 1978, pp. 19–36.

Otis, Leah, *Prostitution in Medieval Society: The History of an Urban Institution in Languedoc*, Chicago: Chicago University Press, 1987.

Overall, Christine, 'What's Wrong with Prostitution? Evaluating Sex Work', *SIGNS: Journal of Women and Culture in Society*, vol. 17, no. 4, 1992, pp. 705–24.

Ovid, *The Erotic Poems*, ed. and tr. by Peter Green, Harmondsworth: Penguin, 1982.

Padgug, Robert, 'Sexual Matters: On Conceptualising Sexuality in History', *Radical History Review*, Spring Summer, 1979, pp. 3–23.

Panikkar, K.M., 'Presidential Address to Indian History Congress, Calcutta', *Proceedings of IHC*, 18th Session, 1955, pp. 11–22.

Papanak, Hanna and Gail Minault, (eds.), *Separate Worlds: Studies of Purdah in South Asia*, Delhi: Chanakya, 1982.

Parasher, Aloka and Usha Naik, 'Temple Girls of Medieval Karnataka', *The Indian Economic and Social History Review*, vol. 23, no. 1, 1986, pp. 63–78.

Parrinder, Geoffrey, *Sexual Morality in the World's Religions*, Rockport: One World Publication, 1996.

Pateman, Carol, *The Sexual Contract*, Palo Alto: Stanford University Press, 1988.

Penzer, N.M., 'Sacred Prostitution', in *Kathāsaritsāgara*, vol. 1, 1968, pp. 231–69.

Poddar, R.P., *An Introduction to Karpūramañjarī*, Vaishali: Research Institute of Prakrit, 1974.

Pollock, Sheldon, 'The Sanskrit Cosmopolis 300–1300: Transculturation, Vernacularization and the Question of Ideology', in Jan E.M. Houben (ed.), *Ideology and Status of Sanskrit Language*, Leiden: E.J. Brill, 1996, pp. 197–247.

——— (ed.), *Literary Cultures in History: Reconstruction from South Asia*, Delhi: Oxford University Press, 2004.

———, *The Language of the Gods in the World of Men: Sanskrit, Culture and Power in Pre-Modern India*, Berkeley: University of California Press, 2006.

Pomeroy, Sarah, *Goddesses, Whores, Wives and Slaves: Women in Classical Antiquity*, New York: Schocken Books, 1995.

Porter, Roy and M. Teich (eds.), *Sexual Knowledge, Sexual Science: The History of Attitudes to Sexuality*, Cambridge: Cambridge University Press, 1994.

Radhakrishnan, S. (ed.), *History of Philosophy: Western and Eastern*, London: Allen & Unwin, 1953.

Raghavacharlu, K., 'Vikaṭanitambā', *Quarterly Journal of the Mythic Society*, Bangalore, vol. 25, nos. 1–3, 1934–5, 141–2.

Raghavan, V.R., 'Sanskrit and Prakrit Poetesses', in *Quarterly Journal of the Mythic Society*, Bangalore, vol. XXV, nos. 1–3, 1934–5, pp. 49–74.

———, *The Number of Rasas*, Madras: The Adyar Library, 1940.

———, *Śṛṅgāramañjari of Saint Akbarshah*, Hyderabad: Archaeological Dept, Govt. of Hyderabad, 1951.

———, *Sanskrit Literature*, Delhi: Publications Division, 1961.

———, *Festivals, Sports and Pastimes of India*, Ahmedabad: B.J. Institute of Learning & Research, 1979.

Ramanujan, A.K., 'Toward a Counter System: Women's Tales', in Arjun Appadurai, Frank J. Koram, Margaret A. Mills (eds.), *Gender, Genre and Power in South Asian Expressive Traditions*, Philadelphia: University of Pennsylvania Press, 1991, pp. 33–55.

Ramaswamy, Vijaya, *Walking Naked: Women, Society and Spirituality in South India*, Shimla: IIAS, 1997.

Rao, Vidya, 'Wives, Twaifs and Nayikas: Transcending Boundaries of Ideology', *Indian Journal of Social Work*, vol. 57, no. 1, 1996, pp. 39–67.

Reiss, Ira, 'A Sociological Journey into Sexuality', *Journal of Marriage and the Family*, vol. 48, 1986, pp. 233–42.

Reiter, R. (ed.), *Towards an Anthropology of Women*, New York: Monthly Review Press, 1975.

Rich, Adrienne, *On Lies, Secrets and Silences: Selected Prose, 1966-1978*, New York: Norton, 1979.

Rich, Adrienne, 'Compulsory Heterosexuality and Lesbian Exist-ence', *SIGNS: Journal of Women and Culture in Society*, vol. 5, no. 4, 1980, pp. 631–60.

Richardson, D. and V. Robinson (eds.), *Introducing Women's Studies: Feminist Theory and Practice*, London: MacMillan, 1993.

Robinson, Hilary (ed.), *Visibly Female: Feminism and Art: An Anthology*, London: Camden Press, 1987.

Rousselle, Aline, *Porneia: On Desire and the Body in Antiquity*, Oxford: Basil Blackwell, 1983.

Roy, Kumkum, 'The King's Household: Structure/Space in the Sastric Tradition', *Economic and Political Weekly*, vol. XVII, no. 43, 24–31 October 1992, pp. 55–60.

———, 'Defining the Household: Some Aspects of Prescription and Practice in Early India', *Social Scientist*, vol. XXII, nos. 1–2, 1994, pp. 3–17.

———, *The Emergence of Monarchy in North India: 8th-4th Centuries B.C.*, Delhi: Oxford University Press, 1994.

———, 'Unravelling the Kamasutra', *Indian Journal of Gender Studies*, vol. 3, no. 2, 1996, pp. 155–70.

———, 'Of Theras and Theris: Vision of Liberation in the Early Buddhist Tradition', in Vijaya Ramaswamy (ed.), *Researching Indian Women*, Delhi: Manohar, 2003: 75-95.

——— (ed.), *Women in Early Indian Societies*, Delhi: Manohar, 1999.

Rubin, Gayle, 'The Traffic in Women', in R. Reiter (ed.), *Towards an Anthropology of Women*, New York: Monthly Review Press, 1975, pp. 157–210.

———, 'Thinking Sex: Notes for a Radical Theory of the Politics of Sexuality', in Carol S. Vance (ed.), *Pleasure and Danger*, 1984, pp. 267–319.

Sangari, Kumkum and Sudesh Vaid (eds.), *Recasting Women*, New Brunswick: Rutgers University Press, 1990.

Sarkar, B.K., *Love in Hindu Literature*, Delhi: Award Publishing House, 1986.

Sarkar, Ranajit, *Gita Govinda: Towards a Total Understanding*, Groningen: Publikaties van Het Instituut voor Indische inculturin, 1974.

Sastri, Narasimha, *Studies in Sanskrit Literature*, Mysore: Sree Panchacharya Electric Press, 1936.

Scott, Joan, *Gender and the Politics of History*, New York: Columbia University Press, 1988.

Seaman, B. and G. Seaman, *Women and the Crisis in Sex Hormones*, Brighton: Harvester Press, 1978.

Serebryakov, I.D., 'Sketches of Ancient Indian Literature', *Indian Studies Past and Present*, vol. 13, no. 4, pp. 349–96, Calcutta, 1972.

Shah, Shalini, *The Making of Womanhood: Gender Relations in the Mahābhārata*, Delhi: Manohar, 1995.

———, 'Gender and Sexuality in Ancient Punjab: A Case Study of the Karṇa Parva in the Mahābhārata', in Aparna Basu and Anup Taneja (eds.), *Breaking Out of Invisibility: Women in Indian History*, Delhi: Indian Council of Historical Research, 2002, pp. 24–42.

———, 'In the Business of Kama: Prostitution in Classical Sanskrit Literature from the 7th to the 13th Centuries', *The Medieval History Journal*, vol. 5, no. 1, 2002, pp. 121–56.

———, 'Female Sexuality in the Kāmaśāstrīya Discourse: Circa 7th–13th Centuries AD', *Social Science Probings*, vol. 15, nos. 1–2, 2003, 131–53.

———, 'Representation of Female Sexuality in the Ayurvedic Discourse of the Early Medieval Period', *Studies in History*, vol. 22, no. 1, 2006, pp. 45–58.

———, 'Women and the Notion of Kāma in the Dharmaśāstrīya Discourse', *The Indian Historical Review*, vol. 33, no. 2, 2006(a), pp. 1–17.

———, Review of Harsha V. Dehejia (ed.), *A Celebration of Love*, in *Indian Historical Review*, vol. 33, no. 2, 2006(b), pp. 204–6.

———, Review of Rahul Peter Das, *The Origin of the Life of a Human Being* in *Wellcome History*, vol. 34, 2007, pp. 20–1.

———, 'Poetesses in Classical Sanskrit Literature: 7th–13th Centuries CE', *Indian Journal of Gender Studies*, vol. 15, no. 1, 2008, pp. 1–27.

———, 'Women in Early Medieval North India', in R.S. Sharma and K.M. Shrimali (eds.), *A Comprehensive History of India*, vol. IV, no. 2, Delhi: Manohar, 2008, 217–25.

———, 'Gender and Sexuality in Early Medieval Sanskrit Literature', in D.N. Jha and Eugenia Vanina (eds.), *Mind Over Matter: Essays on Mentalities in Medieval India*, Delhi: Tulika, 2009, 151–77.

Sharma, Arvind (ed.), *Women in World Religions*, New York: State University of New York Press, 1987.

Sharma, Brij Narain, *Social Life in North India AD 600-1000*, Delhi: Munshiram Manoharlal, 1966.

Sharma, Brijendranath, *Social and Cultural History of Northern India c. 1000–1200 AD*, Delhi: Abhinav Publications, 1972.

Sharma, Priyavat, *Vagbhatta Vivechana*, Varanasi: Chowkhamba, 1968.

Sharma, R.P., *Women in Hindu Literature*, Delhi: Gyan Publishing House, 1995.

Sharma, R.S., *Lights on Early Indian Society and Economy*, Bombay: Manikatalas, 1966.

———, 'Material Milieu of Tantricism' in R.S. Sharma and V.N. Jha (eds.), *Indian Society: Historical Probings*, Delhi: People's Publishing House, 1977, pp. 175–89.

———, *Indian Feudalism c. AD 300-1200*, 2nd edn., Delhi: MacMillan, 1980.

———, *Urban Decay in Early India: c. AD 400-1000*, Delhi: Munshiram Manoharlal, 1987.

———, *Early Medieval Indian Society: A Study in Feudalization*, Kolkata: Orient Longman, 2001.

Sharma, Tripat, *Women of Ancient India: From 320 AD to Circa 1200 AD*, New Delhi: ESS Publications, 1987.

Shastri, A.M., *Indian as Seen in the Kuttanimatam of Damodargupta*, Delhi: Motilal Banarsidass, 1975.

Shaw, Miranda, *Passionate Enlightenment*, Princeton: Princeton University Press, 1994.

Shekhar, I., *Sanskrit Drama: Its Origin and Decline*, Leiden: E.J. Brill, 1960.

Shrimali, K.M., 'Money, Market and Feudalism', in A.K. Bagchi (ed.), *Money and Credit in Indian History*, Delhi: Tulika, 2002, pp. 1–39.

Shrivastava, Sanjay (ed.), *Sexual Sites, Seminal Attitudes*, Delhi: Sage, 2004.

Shulman, David, 'Bhavabhūti on Cruelty and Compassion', in Paula Richman (ed.), *Questioning Rāmāyaṇa: A South Asian Tradition*, Delhi: Oxford University Press, 2000, 49–82.

———, 'Embracing the Subject: Harṣa's Play Within a Play', in David Shulman, *The Wisdom of Poets: Studies in Tamil, Telegu and Sanskrit*, Delhi: Oxford University Press, 2001, 150–82.

Siann, Gerda, *Gender, Sex and Sexuality*, London: Taylor & Francis Publishers, 1994.

Siegel, Lee, *Sacred and Profane Dimensions of Love in Indian Traditions As Exemplified in the Gitagovinda of Jayadeva*, Delhi: Oxford University Press, 1978.

———, *Fires of Love, Waters of Peace: Passion and Renunciation in Indian Culture*, Honolulu: University of Hawaii Press, 1983.

Simon, William, *Post Modern Sexualities*, New York: Routledge, 1996.

Sinha, S.N. and N.K. Basu, *The History of Marriage and Prostitution*, New Delhi: Khama Publishers, 1992.

Smith-Rosenberg, 'The New Woman and the New History', *Feminist Studies*, vol. 8, no. 1, 1982, pp. 185–98.

Snitow, Ann, Christine Thompson, and Sharon Thompson (eds.), *Power of Desire: The Politics of Sexuality*, New York: Monthly Review Press, 1983.

Snyder, June MacIntosh, 'Public Occasion and Private Passion in the Lyrics of Sappho of Lesbos', in Sarah B. Pomeroy (ed.), *Women's History and Ancient History*, Chapel Hill: University of North Carolina Press, 1991, pp. 1–19.

South Indian Inscriptions, vol. III, pt. 3, ed. and tr. H. Krishnasastri, 1920, Archaeological Survey of India.

Spearing, A.C., *The Medieval Poet as Voyeur: Looking and Listening in Medieval Love Narratives*, Cambridge: Cambridge University Press, 1993.

Spelman, Elizabeth, 'Women as Body: Ancient and Contemporary Views', *Feminist Studies*, vol. 8, no. 1, 1982, pp. 109–31.

Sponberg, Alan, 'Attitudes Towards Women and the Feminine in Early Buddhism', in Jose J.I. Cabezon (ed.), *Buddhism, Sexuality and Gender*, Delhi: Shri Satguru Publications, 1992, pp. 3–36.

Srinivasan, Amrit, 'Reforms or Conformity? Temple Prostitution and the Community in the Madras Presidency', in Bina Agrawala (ed.), *Structures of Patriarchy*, Delhi: Kali For Women, 1988, pp. 175–98.

Srinivasan, K.S., *The Ethos of Indian Literature: A Study of its Romantic Tradition*, Delhi: Chanakya, 1985.

Stallworthy (ed.), *The Penguin Book of Love Poetry*, Harmondsworth: Penguin, 1976.

Ste. Croix, *The Class Struggle in the Ancient Greek World*, Ithaca: Cornell University Press, 1981.

Sternbach, Ludwik, 'Veśyā: Synonyms and Aphorisms', *Bhartiya Vidya*, Bombay, vol. IV (pts. 1 & 2), 1942, pp. 104–14 and pp. 157–68; vol. V, 1945, pp. 115–48 and Supplement pp. 1–19.

———, *Gaṇikāvṛttasaṁgraha: Texts on Courtesans in Classical Sanskrit*, Hoshiarpur: Vishveshvarananda Institute Publication, 1953.

Sternbach, L., L. Nayyar, S. Bhaskaran and K.V. Sarma (eds.), *Mahasubhasitasamgraha*, vols. I–VI, 1974–87, Hoshiarpur: Vishveshvarananda Institute Publication.

Sternberg, R.J. and Barnes, M.L. (eds.), *The Psychology of Love*, New Haven: Yale University Press, 1988.

Sur, A.K., *Sex and Marriage in India*, Bombay: Allied Publishers, 1973.

Sutherland, Sally (ed.), *Bridging Worlds: Studies on Women in South Asia*, Delhi: Oxford University Press, 1992.

Thadani, Giti, *Sakhiyani: Lesbian Desire in Ancient and Modern India*, New York: Cassel, 1996.

Thapan, Meenakshi, 'Gender, Body and Everyday Life', *Social Scientist*, vol. 23, nos. 7–9, 1995, pp. 32–58.

Thapar, Romila, *A History of India*, Harmondsworth: Penguin, 1966, rpt., 1981.

———, 'Renunciation: The Making of a Counter Culture?', in Romila Thapar, *Ancient Indian Social History: Some Interpretations*, Delhi: Orient Longman, rpt., 1996.

Trigunayat, Govinda, *Hindi Ki Nirguna Kavyadhara Aur Uski Darshanik Pristhabhumi*, Kanpur: Sahitya Niketan, 1961.

Tripathi, L.K. (ed.), *Position and Status of Women in Ancient India*, vol. I, Varanasi: Banaras Hindu University, 1988.

Tyagi, A.K., *Women Workers in Ancient India*, Delhi: Radha Publications, 1994.

Upadhyaya, Vasudeva, *The Socio-Religious Conditions of North India: 700–1200 AD*, Varanasi: Chowkhamba, 1964.

Vance, Carol (ed.), *Pleasure and Danger: Exploring Female Sexuality*, London: R&KP, 1984.

Vanita, Ruth and Salim Kidwai (eds.), *Same Sex Love in India*, Delhi: Macmillan, 2001.

Varadachari, V., *A History of Samskrta Literature*, 2nd edn., Allahabad: Ram Narain Lal Publisher, 1960.

Venkatasubbiah, A. and E. Muller, 'The Kalas', *Journal of the Royal Asiatic Society*, 1914, pp. 351–67.

Vidyalamkara, Atrideva, *Ayurveda Ka Brhat Itihasa*, Uttar Pradesh Govt. Suchna Vibhaga, 1960.

Warder, A.K., *The Indian Kāvya Literature*, vols. I-V, 1972–88, Delhi: Motilal Banarsidass.

Weeks, J., *Sex, Politics and Society*, London: Longman, 1981.

Wells, Jess, *A Herstory of Prostitution in Western Europe*, Berkeley: University of California Press, 1982.

White, David Gordon, *The Alchemical Body: Siddha Traditions in Medieval India*, Chicago: University of Chicago Press, 1996.

Williams, Monier, *Sanskrit-English Dictionary*, Delhi: Munshiram Manoharlal, 1994.

Winternitz, Maurice, *History of Indian Literature*, vol. III, pt. 1, Delhi: Motilal Banarsidass, 1963.

Yadava, B.N.S., *Society and Culture in Northern India*, Allahabad: Central Book Depot, 1973.

Zysk, Kenneth, *Asceticism and Healing in Ancient India*, Delhi: Oxford University Press, 1991.

Index